THE SOUL OF METHODISM

---

*The Class Meeting in Early
New York City Methodism*

Rev. Dr. Philip F. Hardt

University Press of America
Lanham • New York • Oxford

Copyright © 2000 by
University Press of America,® Inc.
4720 Boston Way
Lanham, Maryland 20706

12 Hid's Copse Rd.
Cumnor Hill, Oxford OX2 9JJ

Library of Congress Cataloging-in-Publication Data

Hardt, Philip F.
The soul of Methodism ; the class meeting in early New York City
Methodism / Philip F. Hardt.
p.   cm.
Includes bibiographical references and index.
1.   Methodist Church—New York (N.Y.)—History. 2. New
York (N.Y.)—Church history. I. Title
BX8249.N5H37 2000   287'.67471—dc21   00—056807 CIP

ISBN 0-7618-1793-X (cloth: alk. ppr.)

⊚™ The paper used in this publication meets the minimum
requirements of American National Standard for Information
Sciences—Permanence of Paper for Printed Library Materials,
ANSI Z39.48—1984

To my parents,
Mary and Frederick Hardt

Contents

Foreword

One of this volume's special merits is the way in which it tells the class meeting story in loving and circumstantial detail. Using one city, New York, as a case study, Hardt details the unique community structure of early American Methodist congregations – networked in small groups, tap-rooted in the church, consciously dependent upon the means of grace, yet also free to develop appropriate patterns of spiritual discipline and service, and Christian prophecy in society. The records, scattered as they are, have been ransacked and winnowed. In addition to all the familiar references, Hardt has come up with primary source material that most never knew existed. From this treasure trove of data he has constructed a credible narrative of how the class meeting came to be so distinctive a feature of Methodism in early America, how and why they worked, and what factors led to their eventual decline. Combining rich detail with clear and vigorous argument, this is an important contribution to understanding Methodist revivalism in the early Republic.

Kenneth Rowe, Drew University

Preface

During its first one hundred years, New York City Methodism[1] underwent a complete "sect-to-church" process[2] and increasingly placed less priority on its chief "prudential means of grace" - the weekly class meeting.[3] Initially, this dissertation was intended to be a "local study" of the first one hundred years of the John Street Methodist Episcopal Church, the "mother church" of American Methodism. Indeed, Nathan O. Hatch, a noted American Religious History scholar, in a lecture at Yale Divinity School, lamented that despite Methodism's strong influence in the nineteenth century, "there are no arresting biographies, no compelling local studies, and no renditions of Methodist ideology."[4] Early research efforts, however, led to numerous primary source materials on the Methodist class meeting such as class lists, classbooks (for attendance), lists of class leaders, minutes of the weekly Board of (Class) Leaders meetings, and periodical articles. Thus, even in its earliest stages, it was apparent that the spiritual vitality and sect-like quality of New York City Methodism and, for that matter, the entire denomination were bound up closely with the Wesleyan class meeting, which was referred to by some nineteenth century Methodist writers as the "soul of Methodism." Consequently, the direction of this study shifted to examine the changes in New York City Methodism using the class meeting as a "lens" in which to view some of these changes. Moreover, recent studies on the decline in the mainline Protestant churches from the late 1960s on added a certain urgency and a sharper focus to the task. Some of these include, in chronological order, *Why Conservative Churches Are Growing* by nineteenth century Methodist writers as the "soul of Methodism." Consequently, the direction of this study shifted to examine the changes in New York City Methodism using the class meeting as a "lens" in which to view some of these changes. Moreover, recent studies on the decline in the mainline Protestant churches from the late 1960s on added a certain urgency and a sharper focus to the task. Some of these include, in chronological order, *Why Conservative Churches Are Growing* by Dean Kelley, *And Are We Yet Alive* by Bishop Richard Wilke, *The Churching of America, 1776-1990: Winners and Losers in Our Religious Economy* by Roger Finke and Rodney Stark, and *Reinventing American Protestantism* by Donald E. Miller.[5] Of course, much more has been written on this subject but these four provided an overall framework in which to examine a number of developments, both from the perspective of all the mainline Protestant churches and also from the uniquely Methodist perspective. In addition to the authors mentioned above, Ernst Troeltsch's classic designations of "sect" and "church" and Max Weber's process called the "routinization of charisma" will be used to characterize New York City Methodism in its early, middle, and later stages.[6] Finally, this study will attempt to provide some answers, at least on the local level of Manhattan, to the following questions: Why did Methodism grow dramatically from 1784 to 1850 and then enter a state of gradual decline from which it has never recovered? Why was the weekly class meeting so important to New York City Methodism and what were some of the factors that caused it to gradually die out by the mid-nineteenth century? How did "stationed pastors" affect the well-organized local lay ministries of local preacher, exhorter, and class leader? In what ways did New York City Methodism become identical to the other, long-established Protestant denominations?

Acknowledgments

I am deeply grateful to a number of persons who nurtured, encouraged, and provided marvelous resources for this study. First, I would like to mention Fr. Mark Massa, S.J., my dissertation mentor, who suggested the topic and constantly encouraged me throughout the process. Second, Kenneth Rowe, Charles Yrigoyen, Jocelyne Rubinetti, and other staff members of the Methodist Archives Center at Drew University gave me a gracious welcome and guided me to some incomparable resources on early New York City and American Methodism. Third, I wish to thank the staff of the Rare Books and Manuscripts Division of the New York Public Library for their help in examining the Methodist Episcopal Church records which are held there. In addition, Mr. Warren Platt, Selection Officer for Religion at the Research Libraries of the New York Public Library, provided additional guidance and, in the process, became a close friend. Next, I must acknowledge a tremendous debt to the Reverend James R. McGraw, pastor of the John Street United Methodist Church, who allowed me to examine the archives in the church library and, in addition, was my pastor for over two years, as well as a trusted friend. Moreover, two other persons, Tara Penry and Lawrence Winnie, helped by reading drafts of the chapters and making suggestions. Finally, I must express deep gratitude to my wife, Vineeta, whose technical skills, patience, and love have tremendously assisted in the publication of this book.

Finally, I would like to acknowledge the following organizations and institutions who have given permission to quote or reproduce materials:

Drew University Library (each citation will be followed with "Reproduced with permission of Drew University Library").

The General Commission on Archives and History of the United Methodist Church.

The New York Public Library (each citation will be followed with "Reproduced with permission of Manuscripts Division, The New York Public Library, Astor, Lenox and Tilden Foundations).

The United Library of the Garrett-Evangelical Theological Seminary in Evanston, Illinois.

Chapter 1

The Class Meeting in Early British Methodism: 1738-80

I. INTRODUCTION

The Methodist movement in England (and later in America) gained numerous adherents, and is distinguished from the other groups in the Evangelical Revival[1], because of its weekly class meeting which was required for prospective and full members of its societies as this study will show.[2] Despite the success of Methodism, scholars disagree as to what impetus led to the founding of the movement. For instance, some cited the weak spiritual conditions of the Established Church while others believed earlier revival and catechetical movements in England and Wales had spiritually prepared the people for Methodism. Again, some scholars asserted that Methodism's unique features such as itinerant preaching, use of laypersons as class leaders, and small groups which fostered faith-sharing and accountability led to its success. Granted, while scholars may disagree on the reasons for its earliest beginnings, they all agree that Methodism provided pastoral oversight to its members through the large Sunday evening society meeting, the twelve member weekly class meeting[3] which both explained Christian doctrine to prospective members and spiritually nurtured veteran members, and the more intimate band meeting[4] in which deeply committed members confessed their sins to one another. Although weekly class attendance fluctuated widely during Wesley's lifetime, the class meeting accomplished its two principal tasks because the Methodist leadership supported the class leaders in two significant ways.   First, Wesley instituted weekly leaders' meetings which provided collegiality and helped the class leaders, as a body, to carry out their pastoral duties.   Second, a number of Methodist preachers published "class manuals"[5] which gave practical advice and encouragement to class leaders.   On the other hand, the high expectations which were later placed on the class leaders, especially in the early nineteenth century, and the increasing tensions which developed between many class leaders and traveling preachers began to adversely affect the governance of the local Methodist societies.[6]

II.   REVIEW OF THE LITERATURE

Scholars differ on what led to the founding of Methodism in eighteenth century England.[7]   For example, Anthony Armstrong asserted that four major impulses infused the Methodism movement. First, Armstrong attributed the rise of Methodism to the weak spiritual condition of the Church of England which included Latitudinarian theology[8], an absence of personal religious sharing, a greater accommodation to society, and intellectual preaching.[9]   The second impulse which helped give Methodism its start was the itinerant field preaching[10] conducted by several Anglican clergy and laymen in both England and Wales in the early 1700s which led to widespread revivals of religion.[11]   Third, Armstrong believed that the Moravians whom John and Charles Wesley[12] met in Georgia, and later in London, gave to Methodism its strong emphases on the doctrine of "justification by faith" and personal, heart-felt religion.[13]   Fourth and last, Armstrong believed that Methodism flourished because of its appeal to the lower classes in the new industrialized cities such as the West Riding, the Black Country, Cornwall, London, Bristol, Manchester, and Newcastle-upon-Tyne. In this vein, Armstrong noted that the inhabitants of these cities were open to Methodist preaching because "they were new conglomerations, destitute of all those influences - agrarian regulation, or the rule of squire and parson - which prevailed in settled communities."[14] Moreover, Armstrong stated that the size of Anglican parishes was inadequate to seat the surrounding urban population. To illustrate, he showed that the city of Manchester

> had a population of 100,459 in 1817, and accommodations in church for only 14,850. In 1811, there were 60,000 inhabitants in Marylebone and there were seats in the parish church for only nine hundred.[15]

In contrast, Christopher Hill attributed the rise of Methodism to two somewhat different causes. First, Hill suggested that the complacency of the Church of England created ideal conditions for a revival movement. For example, in the late seventeenth and early eighteenth centuries, parish positions offered security and good wages because of a strong agricultural economy. Since most priests and curates were appointed because of political connections, they tended to support the government and the possibility of church reform was rare. Moreover, since 1717, Convocation had been suspended which further added to the church's inertia. The second impetus to the founding of Methodism, Hill asserted, was John Wesley's ability to reach the poor with the Gospel message; indeed, in the early 1700s, neither the Established Church nor the Dissenting Churches made that a priority. Into this lethargic and self-satisfied situation, Wesley preached an egalitarian message of God's grace offered to all, often called Arminianism,[16] which offended some members of the upper classes who resented being told they were just as sinful as a poor person. Hill, however, criticized Wesley for concentrating only on eternal rewards at the expense of changing unjust social conditions.[17]

Similarly, Norman Sykes believed the impetus for Methodism was also due to theological concerns. Like Hill, Sykes also felt that the Arminian doctrine of free grace offered to all had much greater appeal to people (not just the poor) than the Calvinistic doctrine of predestination which many Anglican clergy held.[18] In addition, Sykes felt that many people preferred the evangelical, personal faith which Methodism offered as opposed to the rationalism which currently existed in the Established Church. Sykes noted that

> the two Evangelical Revivals, led respectively by John Wesley and Charles Whitefield, although differing sharply and deeply from each other on the theological points which separated Arminianism and Calvinism, had arisen definitely in reaction and protest against the dominant rationalistic and Latitudinarian tradition in the church.[19]

Moreover, like Hill, Sykes believed that Methodism was able to establish itself as a growing movement because the Anglican clergy were generally not reaching out evangelistically and pastorally to the new industrial areas. In some cases, no Anglican parishes even existed in these areas and the Methodist plan of going to the people led to many converts who were then formed into societies. In addition to the itinerant system, Sykes noted that the use of lay preachers

was essential to the effective propagation of the Methodist revival,
for throughout its course the number of ordained clergy attracted to
do service was small, at first because of its unpopularity aroused by
Wesley's preaching, later by reason of the strongly Calvinistic
conviction of the leading Evangelical clergy within the Church of
England.[20]

On the other hand, the use of lay preachers eventually contributed to
a schism with the Church of England because many of the new
converts wanted their preachers to administer the sacrament of holy
communion in the Methodist chapels rather than receive it in the
Anglican parishes on Sunday as Wesley had suggested.[21]

In contrast to the others, E. P. Thompson saw Methodism as a
movement which repressed workers who were struggling to gain better
working conditions. He believed that the impetus for Methodism had
come from a combination of Wesley's authoritarianism and democratic
lay participation in the local societies. Tensions, however, were
continually present between the local societies and the centralization
embodied in the Conference[22] and in Wesley's letters and personal
visits.[23] In addition, Thompson criticized Methodism because it did not
stress social change, even though unjust working conditions prevailed
in many English factories.[24] Methodism took this position because
Wesley aligned himself with the conservative Tory party which led him
to oppose both economic and political revolutionary movements and to
urge submission to civil authorities and loyal obedience to the
Established Church.[25] Thompson noted that the Methodists "fell
ambiguously between Dissent and the Establishment, and did their
most to make the worst of both worlds, serving as apologists for an
authority in whose eyes they were an object of ridicule or
condescension, but never of trust."[26] Moreover, Thompson felt
Methodism succeeded because, while it eliminated almost all of the
radical elements of earlier Dissent, it placed "between the people and
their revolutionary heritage a callow emotionalism which served as
auxiliary to the Established Church and yet the Methodist rebel was
marked by a special earnestness and vigor of moral concern."[27]

William R. Ward believed that the Methodist societies flourished in
London, Bristol, and Newcastle (the three major Methodist centers)
because of "anti-court sentiments" and the lack of respect shown to the
clergy. Another factor in the rise of Methodism, according to Ward,
was the London religious societies. He noted that Wesley and George
Whitefield (both former members of the Oxford Holy Club) had
preached in them in 1737-38; from there Wesley and Whitefield spread
what Ward called "the religious society movement."[28] Furthermore,

while Whitefield was the more dynamic preacher, Wesley's organizational skills solidified the movement for he "did what he did with an intensity and regularity which was something new in the eighteenth century."[29]

Michael Watts also believed that some of the impetus for Methodism's founding came from its outreach to the poor, to the miners, and to those persons who crowded into the cities during the Industrial Revolution. Watts noted that both Methodism and the earlier Quaker movement had reached out successfully to the poor because they used itinerant lay preachers. In the case of Methodism, these lay preachers were drawn from the lower middle class and often had no grade school or higher education. According to Watts, their lack of education actually made them more effective since they were drawn from the people to whom they preached and could relate better to them. Although their education was limited, many of them were artisans who had particular skills.[30] Watts said these lay preachers

> were overwhelmingly men of modest means and humble circumstance, but to describe them as 'the disinherited' is wrong, for the term obscures the skills, the potential for economic advancement, and, in the case of masters, the economic independence which distinguished artisans from mere laborers.[31]

Moreover, Watts attributed Methodism's success to its "audience." Many of the people who heard the Methodist outdoor preaching were ordinary, uneducated common people whose geographical isolation from the cities probably also contributed to their openness to the message. Wesley and the other lay preachers did not usually preach to sophisticated city crowds.[32] Wesley apparently preferred preaching to the simple country folk for he wrote in his journal that "I bear the rich and love the poor; therefore I spend almost all my time with them."[33]

Another impetus for the founding of Methodism, according to Watts, came from its insistence that conversion was a gradual process rather than a one-time experience involving spectacular phenomena. For example, Watts stated that many of the early Methodist preachers had a conversion experience praying with others, at a meeting (probably a class meeting), or even alone at home while reading the Scriptures.[34] In addition to Methodist insistence on gradual conversion, Watts asserted that the standard themes of "fear of death, judgment, and damnation" in Methodist preaching contributed to its successful beginning. Watts felt this approach succeeded because death occurred so frequently from sickness, starvation, and war; death also featured prominently in the literature of that period. Similarly, the unusually high number of natural disasters in the first third of the eighteenth century also made the English people more favorably disposed to religion.[35]

Furthermore, Watts believed that the charity schools[36] in England and Wales prepared many people for the later Wesleyan revival which began in 1739. These charity schools reached out especially to the poor, and taught them various aspects of the Christian faith. Watts saw the charity school movement as the seeds of faith which the Evangelical Revival brought to fruition. In addition to the schools, Watts included the pious influence of many Christian homes throughout England.[37] Finally, Watts believed that another impetus for Methodism was its position within the Church of England. He pointed out that the Methodists and the Anglican evangelicals were able to lead revival efforts because the Toleration Act of 1689 had severely limited what the Dissenters[38] could do. Also, since the Methodists and the revival-minded Anglicans represented the state church, they were not seen as a politically subversive group as were the Baptists and the Quakers. Indeed, Wesley himself believed that a greater number of people could be reached by working within the Established Church; their credibility was simply that much greater than those on the outside. Moreover, Methodism gained strength from its itinerancy; none of the dissenting congregations had anything like it.   In addition, these dissenting congregations did not actively reach out to the non-churched since many were Calvinistic and, hence, believed in predestination. Another factor which limited the influence of the dissenting congregations was their deliberate separation from what they believed was a corrupt church; they were content to remain apart in their own congregations.[39]

Finally, A. Skevington Wood emphasized two factors in the rise of Methodism. First, Wood attributed the origins of Methodism to Welsey's contact with the Moravians[40] in Georgia who especially influenced him in the use of "band meetings" as a means for spiritual growth. Second, Wood believed that another impetus for Methodism was the lack of close-knit, interpersonal fellowship groups in the Established Church which Wesley "regarded as the most serious deficiency in the Established Church of his day."[41] Indeed, he told his Anglican critics to

> look east, west, north, and south, name what parish you please; is Christian fellowship there? Rather, are not the bulk of the parishioners a

mere rope of sand? What Christian connexion is there between them? What intercourse in spiritual things? What watching of others' souls?[42]

On the basis of the above, it seems more likely that the spiritual deficiencies in the Church of England such as the intellectual preaching and the lack of close-knit fellowship groups, rather than the effects of the Industrial Revolution, created a deep spiritual hunger which led to the founding of Methodism. Moreover, the earlier evangelical preaching and catechetical classes most likely had prepared many people in England and Wales for an even more intensive religious experience. Also, the powerful, fervent preaching of the Wesleys and George Whitefield went directly to the hearts of the people in language which they could understand. In addition, Wesley's plan of society, class, and band provided smaller pastoral structures which the Church of England apparently could not match. Finally, the unwillingness and inability of the Anglican clergy, with the exception of those involved in the Evangelical Revival, to promote renewal left the people even more vulnerable to the Methodist outreach.

III. THE PASTORAL STUCTURES OF BRITISH METHODISM

Notwithstanding these different understandings of the impetus for the founding of Methodism, scholars are agreed that the movement provided strong spiritual support to its members through its three primary pastoral structures.[43] First of all, the society meeting brought together on a weekly basis all the Methodists in a particular town or city. Second, every society member was encouraged to join a small band for more intimate sharing. Third and last, every prospective and full member was required to attend a weekly class meeting in which members described their spiritual progress under the guidance of the class leader.[44]

A. THE SOCIETY

The first pastoral structure, the society meeting, began in London in 1739 when several persons who had been affected by Wesley's evangelical preaching asked him for additional instruction.[45] This idea is shown by Wesley's response in which he urged that

if you will all of you come together every Thursday, in the evening, I will gladly spend some time with you in prayer, and give you the best advice I can. Thus, arose, without any previous design on either side, what was afterwards called a society.[46]

Eventually, these weekly society meetings spread to other towns and cities where Wesley had preached.[47] Also, as the Methodist movement became more organized, these society meetings were normally held on Sunday evening after the public preaching service; a typical meeting consisted of teaching, disciplining errant members (or disciplining the society as a whole), and internal matters, such as the reception of new society members.[48] An example of a society meeting is found in the diary of Thomas Hardy, a Birmingham merchant, who attended a five p.m. Sunday evening preaching service at the New Meeting House on City Road (London) which began

> with extempore prayer, then a hymn, and the sermon, etc., the same as, at most other Methodist meeting Houses, is commonly the practice. The public service being ended, Mr. Wesley spoke for some time to the society, and many others as well as myself who were not in connexion.[49]

Initially, society meetings were held in private homes; later, as the movement grew, they were held in Methodist "chapels," such as the "Foundry"[50] in London and the "New Room" in Bristol. Moreover, Sunday evening society meetings were regularly held until the early nineteenth century when the public "prayer meeting" replaced it.[51]

At the same time, in forming his societies, Wesley apparently drew upon the earlier Anglican "religious societies" in several ways.[52] First of all, both religious societies had a set of written rules governing admission, attendance, frequency of meetings, conditions for expulsion, and members' behavior.[53]   Second, like the Methodist societies, Horneck's included a talk as well as prayer, spiritual reading, and a psalm.[54] Third, both societies met weekly, usually in the evening.[55] Exemplifying this was the religious society at Epworth led by Wesley's father, the Reverend Samuel Wesley, which met every Saturday night to discuss his sermon for the next day. Eventually, when this society grew to forty members, it was subdivided into two societies.[56] Fourth, only those who were members of the societies could attend the meetings. Significantly, Horneck's fourteenth rule required that the minister approve every new member.[57] Wesley, however, required an additional probationary period before a person could become a full member.[58] Moreover, in order to enforce a "members only" attendance, Wesley gave out "class tickets"[59] once a quarter to those who were in good standing. In this vein, at one of his annual conferences of preachers, Wesley told his lay preachers to give tickets to none till they are recommended by a leader, with whom they have met at least two months on trial. Give notes to none but those who are recommended by one you know, or till they met three or four times in a class.[60]

Fifth, continued non-attendance at society meetings or improper moral behavior were grounds for expulsion in both societies.[61] An example is found in the Poplar society whose rules stated that anyone who missed four consecutive meetings without a legitimate excuse should be expelled.[62] In the same way, the Methodist "general, though unwritten rule, was that three consecutive absences constituted self-expulsion from a class, and leaders were required to keep a record of attendance on a special class paper, or later, in a class book."[63] Finally, both societies emphasized actively helping the poor. To demonstrate, Samuel Wesley's religious society, in the Horneck tradition, required each member to pledge a certain amount of money, part of which went to assist the poor.[64] Similarly, the fifth section of Wesley's General Rules for the United Societies exhorted society members to help the poor in the Biblical language of the twenty-fifth chapter of Matthew's gospel. Moreover, both societies had lay "stewards" who handled financial matters such as the allocation of funds to the poor.[65]

Besides Horneck's societies, the Society for Promoting Christian Knowledge, which was formed in 1698, may also have influenced Wesley. From 1700 to 1720, this organization founded many small societies throughout England; after 1720, however, it began to decline. In contrast to Horneck's societies, these later ones put a greater emphasis on social outreach rather than on Christian fellowship, teaching, and prayer; most of their activities involved teaching poor children, assisting the sick and visiting prisoners.[66] Similarly, at about the same time, the Society for the Reformation of Manners started religious societies. Contrary to those of the Society for Promoting Christian Knowledge, these societies sought only to improve morals in various ways.[67]

At the same time, Wesley also apparently drew upon his own personal experience in establishing the Methodist societies. This idea is shown by his experience as the leader of the "Holy Club" at Oxford University from 1729-1735 in which the members met regularly for prayer, Scripture study, and spiritual discussion, fasted twice a week, and received the sacrament of holy communion every Sunday. Furthermore, they also visited prisoners and the poor who lived in the area around Oxford.[68] Another personal experience which most likely influenced Wesley was the Fetter Lane society in London which Wesley and several others organized after his return from Georgia in 1737. This society, however, differed from the Holy Club and Horneck's religious societies in that it was further subdivided into smaller "bands."[69] Thus, Wesley's personal experience led to some changes in the structure of the religious society then current in England; Wesley was shifting it more in the direction of intimate personal sharing of one's spiritual life. In contrast, the earlier societies had not required these detailed spiritual conversations.[70]

In addition to the structural similarities, Wesley wanted his societies to renew the Established Church from within rather than to have them cause a schism. This idea is shown by his insistence that the Methodists should attend their parish churches on Sunday and receive the sacrament of holy communion from their parish priest, rather than from the Methodist itinerant preachers. Again, he deliberately avoided scheduling Methodist services at the same time as the Anglican ones were being held. Although the Methodist preaching services began to take on the characteristics of a separate denomination, Frederick Norwood has noted that

> on one matter the Wesleys were quite clear: these gatherings to hear preaching were not to be seen as substitutes for the liturgical services of the church. Sunday worship, morning and evening prayer, ought to continue unabated.[71]

Despite this, some Methodist lay preachers raised the question of separating from the Established Church at the annual conference of preachers in the early 1740s. Indeed, it was a question that simply would not go away, even though Wesley consistently rejected the idea. Moreover, some Anglican bishops and priests, instead of embracing the Methodist societies and incorporating them into the life of the church, rejected them, thus pushing them closer to formal separation. Exemplifying this unwelcoming attitude, Michael Watts noted that the "evangelical revival was initially an Anglican, not a dissenting, movement, but it was Dissent, not the Church of England, that reaped the ultimate benefit."[72] Furthermore, Watts believed that two factors ultimately drove out the Methodists from the Established Church. First, the Anglican hierarchy strongly doubted that Wesley would remain within the church. Second, the Methodist people themselves wanted separation. Also, some Anglican priests would not allow other ordained Anglican priests who were involved in the Methodist movement to preach in their parish churches nor would they allow them to preach in a Methodist "chapel" within their parish boundaries. To illustrate, in 1777, two Anglican clergy were forbidden to preach in a Methodist chapel in London when the local parish priest, William Sellon, protested their actions to a church court. The court agreed with Sellon that the two "outside priests" should not be allowed to preach "in a parish without the consent of its minister and in a building which had not been consecrated by a bishop."[73] Similarly, other Anglican bishops and priests wrote against the Methodists, refused to give them holy communion, and occasionally initiated (or at least tolerated) mob actions directed at their leaders or at a meeting.[74]

Despite Wesley's efforts to keep the societies loyal to the church, he sensed that separation was inevitable and did several things which seemed to set it irrevocably on that course. An example of this occurred near the end of his life, in 1788, when he wrote that the parish priest at Epworth, where his own father had served, was not preaching the true gospel message nor was he giving a good example to the flock. Because of this, Wesley wrote that

> I cannot, with all my influence, persuade them either to hear him, or to attend the sacrament administered by him. If I cannot carry this point, even while I live, who then can do it when I die?[75]

Besides his own pessimistic outlook, one modern scholar, Arthur Skevington Wood, asserted that Wesley also acted in a potentially schismatic way through

> the employment of unordained preachers; the planned invasion of parishes under the itinerant system; the setting up of a connexional organization as distinct from the Anglican constitution; the erection of rooms and preaching places, and from 1760, the administration of holy communion on such unconsecrated premises.[76]

Finally, Wood believed that two other acts of Wesley - the ordaining of three men for the American mission in the early 1770s, and the "licensing of the preaching places under the Toleration Act" - further pushed Methodism toward formal separation.[77]

B. THE BAND

The second pastoral structure which provided strong spiritual support was the "band meeting" which Wesley borrowed, with some modifications, from the Moravians.[78] Wesley had visited the Moravian community in Herrnhut in August, 1738, and attended a number of their community meetings, including several band meetings.[79] Indeed, Wesley's experience of the band meetings, as well as his overall impression of the Moravian community, was highly positive for he noted in his journal (possibly a letter to the Moravians) that "I greatly approve of your conferences and bands, of your method of instructing children; and, in general, of your great care of the souls committed to your charge."[80] Upon his return to England, he started bands which met weekly in the Bristol and London societies. Each band had a leader who was considered more spiritually advanced than the others. Also, the band leaders met weekly to discuss their members' progress.[81] Besides the small bands of three to seven members, Wesley or the itinerant preachers also held "band society" meetings twice a week - the men met on Wednesday evening and the women met on Sunday; these larger meetings consisted of additional teaching and members' testimonies rather than the usual spiritual examinations.[82]

The Methodist bands, however, differed somewhat from the Moravian model. For example, although Wesley kept them segregated by sex, he did allow the single sex bands to have both married and single members, unlike the Moravians who kept single and married persons in different bands.[83] Moreover, in December, 1738, he drew up his own Rules for the Band Societies in which each member was asked

> what known sin have you committed since our last meeting? What temptations have you met with? How were you delivered? What have you thought, said, or done, of which you doubt whether it be a sin or not? Have you nothing you desire to keep secret?[84]

Also, Wesley issued "band tickets" to the band members which admitted them to the private society meeting. Later, however, members were issued "class tickets" as band membership dropped off.[85]

In addition to the band meeting, the Moravians also apparently influenced Wesley's use of the love feast.[86] This idea is shown by his journal entry for 8 August 1737 when he most likely encountered the Moravian love feast for the first time in Savannah, Georgia. He recorded that their love feast, which was held after the Anglican evening prayer, "was begun and ended with thanksgiving and prayer, and celebrated in so decent and solemn a manner as a Christian of the apostolic age would have allowed to be worthy of Christ."[87] At the same time, Wesley again departed from the Moravian model. First, he allowed all society members to attend the love feast; the Moravians restricted attendance to only band members. Second, he put a greater stress on personal testimonies.   Third and last, he used it for evangelistic purposes.[88]

Despite the spiritual good which bands could accomplish, some Methodists as well as some non-Methodists criticized them. In this vein, some thought it improper for a husband and a wife to be separated by being placed in different bands. Moreover, others pointed out the awkwardness for a family member to answer these searching questions when a family servant was also present. Most important of all, many Anglicans compared it to the Catholic practice of confession.[89] Nevertheless, Wesley defended the confessional aspect of the bands by reminding his Anglican critics that confession to a priest

> is in nowise condemned by our own Church; nay, she recommends it in some cases.   Whereas, what we practice is, the confession of several persons conjointly, not to a Priest, but to each other. Consequently it has no analogy at all to Popish confession.[90]

Besides the criticism and suspicion of band meetings, Wesley had difficulty convincing Methodist society members to join a band or to faithfully attend the one they already joined. This idea is shown by his letter to the Bristol societies in which he urged that

> all of you who have faith meet in band without excuse or delay. There has been a shameful neglect of this. Remove this scandal. As soon as the Assistant[91] has fixed your band make it a point of conscience never to miss without an absolute necessity.[92]

Despite Wesley's strenuous efforts, band attendance remained low. To demonstrate, in June, 1745, only five hundred thirteen Methodists were in a total of eighty-five bands which was just twenty-five percent of the total membership for all the societies.[93]   In fact, William Dean has noted that "the most solid conclusion we can draw is that never more than twenty-five percent of the Methodist membership was in a band at any given time."[94]   Similarly, forty years later, in 1789, only one out of nine Methodists was in a band. Thus, "Wesley's ideal of a band society functioning as the heart of a Methodist society, providing guidance by examination and precept, stimulating the brethren to the wholehearted pursuit of godliness, ceased to be a motivating vision for the Methodists soon after his death."[95]   In short, the majority of Methodists resisted the deeper commitment which a band required.

C. THE CLASS

The third and final pastoral structure which provided strong spiritual support was the class meeting. In contrast to the society and band meetings which drew upon Anglican and Moravian practices, respectively, the class meeting developed entirely from events which occurred within the Methodist society in Bristol.[96] In fact, class meetings were not even part of the original Methodist structure; rather, they began three years later in 1742 in Bristol during a meeting in which Wesley and several other members were discussing how to pay off the debt on the new preaching house.[97] One of the members suggested that they divide the society into groups of twelve who lived near each other and that designated persons collect one penny a week from them; further, he asked that they

> put eleven of the poorest with me; and if they can give anything, well; I will call on them weekly; and if they can give nothing, I will give for them as well as for myself. And each of you call on eleven of your neighbors weekly; receive what they give, and make up what is wanting.[98]

At the same time, the classes quickly began to fulfil a spiritual function as well as a financial one. To illustrate, as the class leaders visited their members each week at their homes or places of employment, they became aware of various difficulties which their members were experiencing and tried to offer them counsel and encouragement. They found, however, that trying to speak to their class members at home or work was difficult since other persons were often present and some employers did not like their employees to be interrupted during working hours. Therefore, the decision was made for each class to meet together once a week with the class leader.[99] As a result, class members were able to form deeper bonds with each other and with their class leader. Thus, Wesley was soon able to write that

> it can scarce be conceived what advantages have been reaped from this little prudential regulation. Many now happily experienced that Christian fellowship of which they had not so much as an idea before. They began to bear one another's burdens, mutually to care for each other.[100]

In the same way, classes quickly spread to the London society when Wesley decided, with the concurrence of the leadership, that "there could be no better way to come to a sure, thorough knowledge of each person, than to divide them into classes, like those at Bristol, under the inspection of those in whom I could most confide."[101] Some

Methodists, however, questioned the new requirement of a weekly class meeting for several reasons. First, they were not explicitly mentioned in Scripture. Second, some did not like the idea of having an extra meeting to attend, especially one in which their lives would be so closely examined. Third, some resisted new developments in general and did not like change. Fourth and last, some opposed the class meeting because it was difficult to find enough good class leaders for each class.[102]

Furthermore, the class meeting, which Wesley praised so highly, followed a set pattern from week to week. In contrast to the band meeting, the "class meetings were much less intense, being a mixture of informality and firmness."[103] First, the class leader opened the meeting with a prayer and a hymn. Second, he gave an account of his own spiritual progress of the past week. An example of this is found in Joseph Barker's account, in which he related that the class leader "sometimes tells what trials he has met with, and what deliverances he has experienced" or "how he felt at the love feast, the prayer-meeting, or the fellowship meeting, what liberty he had in secret prayer, how he felt while reading the Scriptures, or hearing sermons, or while busy at his work, what passages have come to his mind."[104] Next, the class leader asked each member, in turn, questions such as "How has it been with your soul?" or "Well, brother, how do you feel the state of your mind tonight?" or "Sister, will you tell us what the Lord is doing for you?"[105] Then, in the words of one eyewitness, Joseph Nightingale, each "member then proceeds, without rising, to unbosom his or her mind to the leader; not, as has often been said, by particular confession, but by a general recapitulation of what has passed in the mind during the week."[106] Finally, the class leader responded to each member's report with suitable words of encouragement, exhortation, or correction after which the class sang a verse or two from an appropriate hymn.[107] Accordingly, it was precisely this emphasis on the sharing of personal religious experiences which set the Methodist societies apart from Horneck's; conversely, Horneck's societies had "expressed themselves in study and discussion, in the deepening of the spiritual life of their members, and in the extension of their theological knowledge."[108]

Besides fulfilling financial and "spiritual growth" roles, the class meeting also performed an evangelistic function. Indeed, William Dean has described the class meeting as the preeminent "evangelistic structure of Methodism at least until around 1830"[109] and noted that the "basic purpose of the class meeting was designed not so much to benefit the converted person (who could be invited to join a band

meeting) as to benefit the unconverted seeker."[110]   Indeed, the 1820
Liverpool Conference stressed the evangelistic use of the class meeting
by urging that the long established local societies "attempt the
formation of new classes in suitable neighborhoods, where we may
hope by that method to gather some persons who are 'not far from the
kingdom of God,' but who need special invitation, and are not likely to
give themselves fully to the Lord"[111] unless extra efforts, such as a class
meeting, were used.   Moreover, this idea is seen in the early
Methodists' belief that conversion was a gradual process containing
several distinct elements which could take days, weeks, months or,
sometimes, years. First, the "early Methodists believed that the goal of
preaching was not conversion, but 'awakening' - "the stirring of a deep
religious sense of condemnation and judgment for having broken God's
laws."[112] Next, both clergy and laity tried to guide the newly awakened
person, or "seeker," into a class where they could receive further
instruction on the doctrines of Christianity in preparation for baptism
and full membership in the society.[113] In this vein, Henry Goodfellow,
a Methodist "local preacher,"[114] who, after preaching, for the second
time in the same place

> invited "serious" persons to remain behind after the preaching service. He
> explained something of the organization of Methodism. He put fifteen
> persons into a class, and permitted several others to attend without
> enrolling them.[115]

Similarly, William Reeves was so affected by a Methodist preaching
service that he spoke to the preacher after the service who

> then tried to give me some comfort, and spoke many comfortable words to
> me: but alas! I could take no comfort. He then spoke to Mr. Shaw, to
> take me to his class which he did the next night.[116]

Again, some evangelistically-minded class leaders, such as William
Carvosso, actively recruited persons for the class meeting after the
Sunday preaching service had ended.[117]
    Last of all, after attending class meetings for a period of time, the
seeker usually experienced a conversion as a result of the class leader's
weekly instruction and the veteran class members' personal testimonies.
Exemplifying this is the fact that of all the Methodist biographical
accounts before 1820, more than half reported conversion occurring
either in a class meeting or in talking with the class leader. Moreover,
none of these accounts indicated a conversion which occurred during a
preaching service.[118] In the same way, David Watson found that "time

and again early Methodist biography reveals that the fellowship of the class meeting was a major influence in bringing people to the point of Christian commitment as well as confirming them in it afterwards."[119] To be sure, the role of the class leader was viewed as critical in the process of conversion. An example is seen in the Reverend James Wood's advice for class leaders in which he wrote that

> great care should be taken to prevent their resting in the drawings of the Father, on the one hand; and, on the other, to keep them from being discouraged by a sight of their guilt and misery. They should be exhorted to lay hold on the hope set before them, and to wash away their sins, calling on the name of the Lord.[120]

Weekly class meeting attendance, however, did not end with a conversion experience since all members were required to attend class. Furthermore, class leaders were required to keep a record of weekly attendance on a "class paper"[121] which the traveling preacher examined weekly and quarterly. The class paper, however, included more than simply recording each member's attendance. Besides attendance-keeping, a symbol was also placed next to the members' names to indicate their spiritual state. To demonstrate, the letter "a" meant "awakened," a period meant the member "professed justification," a colon meant the member claimed he or she had experienced "entire sanctification," and a question mark meant the member had doubts about salvation. To be sure, Wesley probably borrowed this practice from the Moravians who also spiritually classified their members as either "dead, awakened, ignorant, willing disciples," and "disciples that have made a progress."[122]

At the same time, Wesley personally met once a quarter with every class in every circuit to personally check on their attendance and behavior. As an illustration, Wesley recorded the time at Reading when he "began examining the classes, and every person severally, touching the bane of religion, evil-speaking, as well as touching their manner of life before they heard this preaching; and, by comparing what they were with what they are now, we found more abundant cause to praise God."[123] On the other hand, at some quarterly examinations, Wesley had to be severe such as the seven-day examination in which he excluded one hundred twelve members.[124] In addition to this examination, a class member was issued another "class ticket"[125] if his attendance and Christian discipleship were satisfactory; those, however, whose discipleship was unsatisfactory did not receive one. Besides indicating that the member was in good standing, the class ticket admitted the member to the weekly society and class meetings for the next quarter. On the other hand, those interested in Methodism, but who did not possess a class ticket, could only attend a few society and class meetings before they had to decide if they wanted to enroll in a class on a regular basis. Furthermore, doorkeepers were posted at the doors to these meetings in each society to make sure that the class ticket system was followed. At the same time, this strict policy brought criticism to which Wesley replied that if non-members were allowed to attend frequently, it would destroy the intimacy which was needed for these meetings.[126] To be sure, as the societies grew more numerous, Wesley delegated many of these quarterly examinations to his lay preachers. These examinations, however, which were usually held in the chapel after the Sunday morning preaching service involved large numbers of class members (sometimes a small society in the countryside had only one class), making it difficult to spend much time with each person. Besides the large numbers, the preachers also had to collect one shilling from each member which further added to the length of the examination. An example is found in the diary of Samuel Bradburn, a traveling preacher, who wrote that "meeting the classes to renew the society tickets is not, strictly speaking, laborious work, yet, it is a work that requires much care and attention, and having to do with money among poor people, it never fails to be unpleasant to feelings, so that I am glad when meeting them is over."[127] In contrast to Wesley's diligence, a number of the traveling preachers apparently did not faithfully carry out the quarterly examinations. As a result, according to William Dean, this neglect caused the traveling preacher to become more distant from the members of the society.[128] Despite these efforts, many class members still did not attend their class meetings regularly. To illustrate, in 1759, Wesley met the London society

> at five, and explained the nature and use of meeting in a class. Upon inquiry, I found we have now about five hundred members, but one hundred fifty of those do not pretend to meet at all. Of those, therefore, I make no account. They hang on but a single thread.[129]

Thus, even with the quarterly examination and the threat of expulsion, many Methodists disregarded Wesley's rule on weekly class attendance.

IV. ROLE OF THE CLASS LEADER IN EARLY BRITISH METHODISM

Despite the gradual decline in class attendance, the early Methodist class meetings successfully carried on Christian initiation and lifelong spiritual formation because the Methodist leadership provided several supports, both structural and Biblical-theological, to assist the class leaders in these pastoral duties. First, the leaders meeting provided a collegial atmosphere in which the class leaders could fulfill their stated responsibilities to both their class members and to the traveling preachers to whom they themselves were also accountable. Second, a number of class manuals gave important, practical advice on the qualifications and duties for the office of class leader. On the other hand, as the Methodist movement progressed, higher expectations were placed upon class leaders which began to change their original role as Wesley had envisioned it. At the same time, tensions also began to develop, especially in the nineteenth century, between many class leaders and traveling preachers over authority and governance in the local societies.[130]

The first way in which the Methodist leadership supported class leaders in their pastoral duties was through the weekly leaders' meeting. This idea is shown in Wesley's directive to class leaders that they were to bring the weekly "class collection" to the meeting and give it to the stewards and also report to the preacher which of their class members had been absent, sick, or living in an unchristian manner.[131] Moreover, the minutes of a number of early leaders' meetings indicate that those who neglected their class meeting or behaved improperly were quickly visited by a team of class leaders or asked to appear before a leaders' meeting to explain their actions. Accordingly, those who remained unrepentant were often expelled. Thus, the class leaders, through the leaders' meetings, were able to hold their class members to a high degree of accountability. After 1825, however, expulsions were rare. At the same time, accountability was also extended upward to the class leaders since the traveling preachers examined the individual class books at each leaders' meeting[132] In contrast to Wesley's original intention for the leaders' meeting (i.e., the class collections and status reports on the members), the leaders' meetings in the early nineteenth century began to deal with a variety of administrative matters such as the discipline of members, the appointment of new leaders, and the approval (or disapproval) of prospective members.[133] In short, as Methodism evolved from a "religious society" to a separate denomination, the leaders' meeting still supported the class leaders' role while also taking on additional responsibilities.

The second way in which the Methodist leadership supported class leaders was through the publication of class manuals which Methodist clergy had written. An example of this is the way in which some manuals listed basic qualifications which class leaders should have such as personal piety, an ability to pray and exhort in the meeting, and knowledge. Furthermore, this knowledge which class leaders needed was, first of all, knowledge of Scripture and Biblical commentaries and, secondly, knowledge of Wesleyan history and doctrine. Also, class leaders were expected to read widely in these areas. Indeed, the knowledge of Scripture was especially useful in the class meeting itself since the class leader was encouraged to use the Scriptures in responding to his class members' reports.[134] In addition to personal qualifications, some manuals discussed ways in which class leaders could improve the weekly class meeting, a concern which Wesley had also addressed at an annual meeting of the Methodist preachers where he urged them to

> change improper leaders. Let the leaders frequently meet each other's classes. Let us observe which leaders are the most useful; and let these meet the other classes as often as possible.[135]

In this vein, one manual urged class leaders (and class members) to avoid using religious jargon and speaking in generalities.[136] Another manual stressed that class leaders should warn class members against speaking in a low tone of voice and to use "simplicity of speech" rather than "studied speech." Again, this manual told class leaders to encourage the class members to be as open as possible in their reports. Furthermore, this manual emphasized that class members had a co-responsibility in insuring a lively and profitable meeting by practicing individual spiritual disciplines of prayer and Bible reading on a daily basis; otherwise, they would only be repeating the same information week after week. Indeed, this prayer and Bible reading would yield new insights and suggest additional ways in which God wanted to transform their lives which could then be shared with the class.[137]

At the same time, higher expectations were placed on the office of class leader, especially in the nineteenth century. To illustrate, class leaders were now expected to be well educated, good teachers, and willing to devote extra time visiting absent class members, even if it meant leaving their jobs earlier and thus earning less money. Similarly, as the nineteenth century progressed, the way a person was selected to be a class leader changed from the eighteenth century when

> the leaders' meetings were more apt to select a member they judged to be capable and then hand him an empty class book with instructions to recruit a new class. The more formal examinations, scheduled in advance, and the public installation services for new leaders that became common around mid-century reveal the higher status of the class leaders.[138]

As a result of these changed expectations, fewer class leaders were appointed which further contributed to an already existing shortage of qualified class leaders.

Finally, tensions began to develop, especially after the death of Wesley in 1791, between the class leaders and the Methodist hierarchy. To be sure, Wesley himself had experienced conflict with some class leaders such as the time when he corrected the class leaders of the Dublin society who had exceeded their authority. In a letter to them, Wesley compared the Methodist society structure to a wheel and warned that

> in the Methodist discipline the wheels regularly stand thus: the assistant, the preachers, the stewards, the leaders, the people. But here the leaders, who are the lowest wheel but one, were got quite out of their place. They were got at the top of all, above the stewards, the preachers, yea, and above the assistant himself.[139]

This tension, however, became acute in the first half of the nineteenth century with the formation of the Wesleyan Methodist Church. This idea is shown by the pastors who took a high view of the pastoral office and the class leaders who felt they should have more prestige. Furthermore, some class leaders who were also local preachers actually saw themselves as "pastors," since they were performing a number of pastoral duties already. In contrast, the traveling preachers argued that they should retain control of administration and discipline of the local society since they were full-time members of the ministry, whereas the others were not.[140] In addition to the conflict between class leaders and traveling preachers, class leaders also clashed with other units of the Methodist structure. An example is seen in the conflict between the class leaders and the trustees in Brunswick over the placement of an organ in the Methodist chapel in 1825. Both the Brunswick local preachers, who had initiated the protest, and the Brunswick leaders' meeting opposed the organ on "spiritual grounds." Nonetheless, the trustees, with the backing of the Annual Conference, prevailed. The dispute, however, caused the class leaders to secede from the Brunswick society and to form the Leeds Protestant Methodists.[141] Again, in the 1830s, the Rochdale class leaders submitted a ten point resolution to their quarterly meeting which listed a number of their grievances such as the absence of open discussion at the quarterly meeting, the removal of class leaders without the agreement of a majority at the leaders' meeting, and the expulsion of class members against the wishes of the leaders' meeting.[142] Another conflict occurred when the Methodist hierarchy in Sheffield abolished writing lessons in the Sunday Schools. As a result, many class leaders then supported "opposition schools" where writing was taught until they were forbidden to do that.[143] Besides class leader conflicts, entire circuits often opposed the central Conference on such matters as the division of circuits and the installation of new organs.

At the same time, some Methodist clergy wrote pamphlets in support of a strong central church authority. As an illustration, John Beacham wrote a pamphlet entitled "An Essay on the Constitution of Wesleyan Methodism" in which he argued that the Conference was the legislature of Methodism and that traveling preachers should have more authority than class leaders and local preachers because they devoted themselves to the ministry on a full-time basis.[144] Similarly, some traveling preachers noted that the class leaders of an entire circuit, who rarely were changed, were difficult to govern. An example of this comes from a traveling preacher on the Hull circuit who complained, in 1835, that when a certain leaders' meeting met it was

> not to show their class-books, that the preachers may become acquainted with the state of their respective classes, and visit the sick and absentees whose cases may seem to require it, and give them such advice as their office as leaders often needs, but to vote in determining how this and the other shall be done - the governing of the society, and its affairs really being much more in the leaders' meetings, than in the Superintendent.[145]

On the other hand, the other smaller Methodist denominations, such as the Primitive Methodists and the Free Methodists who split off from the larger Wesleyan Methodist Church, did not experience a great deal of conflict between class leaders and traveling preachers. To illustrate, the Free Methodist denomination took a much lower view of the pastoral office, thus allowing their class leaders and traveling preachers to work more closely together as had been the case in the eighteenth century. Thus, in the Free Methodist plan, "the leaders, under the supervision of an itinerant preaching ministry, formed an eldership which functioned as a collective pastorate, handling matters like policy, finances, and the reception and discipline of the members."[146]

V. CONCLUSION

The weekly class meeting, which provided basic instruction and spiritual edification to both new and longtime members, apparently contributed to Methodism's steady growth from 1738 to 1780. To be sure, scholars have advanced a number of different reasons for its founding as a movement within the Church of England. First, some scholars believe that the intellectual theology and preaching of the Established Church made many people more receptive to the Methodist emphasis on faith discussions in small, closeknit groups which met regularly. Second, other scholars attribute the founding of Methodism to earlier religious revivals in England and Wales and the charity school movement's emphasis on religious education which prepared the way for Wesley's evangelical call to repentance. Third, still other scholars assert that Wesley's ability to mobilize a large corps of itinerants, which neither the Established Church nor the Dissenting groups could match, spread the message quickly and effectively. Fourth and last, some stated that Methodism's success came from its deliberate outreach to the lower classes at a time when most other groups were neglecting them and to Wesley's use of many of those mainly uneducated, working class people as traveling preachers and class leaders.

Although the English people were apparently ready for a renewal movement, Wesley's three basic pastoral structures - the society, the band, and the class meeting - ensured its permanency. Unlike the Reverend George Whitefield who preached but did not gather converts into groups, Wesley provided a way for "seekers" not only to come to faith in Christ, but also to grow in holiness through the society and class meetings which regularly gave additional teaching on the Christian life. Equally important, the smaller class meeting offered spiritual direction and kept members accountable for their weekly discipleship in an intensive small group setting. Above all, the class leaders served as "sub-pastors" in both spiritual and administrative capacities. Exemplifying this were their visits to absent or sick class members and their weekly leaders' meetings which were held on a circuit-wide basis. Nevertheless, in the early nineteenth century, after the Methodist "societies" had become the Wesleyan Methodist Church, declining class attendance, the higher expectations placed upon the role of the class leader, and the growing tensions between class leaders and traveling preachers all combined to weaken its earlier dynamism.

Chapter 2

The New York Society: 1768-1800

I. INTRODUCTION

The formative period of New York City Methodism occurred from 1766 to 1800.[1] From 1784 to 1800, the class system functioned extremely well as a catechumenate by instructing prospective members over a six month period, by accepting or rejecting them as full members of the New York Society (i.e., the John Street Methodist Episcopal Church), and by "reading into" the society those who had been approved. Moreover, the class system stabilized New York City Methodism by developing close relationships among the members of a class and also between the class leader and individual members, by developing local church leadership, and by monitoring behavior. At the same time, New York City class meetings differed from the British Wesleyan model in that they segregated classes by gender and race and allowed class size to climb to extremely high levels.[2]

Band meetings, like the class meetings, were successfully transplanted to New York. They met regularly and apparently spiritually strengthened those who attended. Moreover, they continued to serve as the primary place in which to experience "Christian perfection," although the number of bands never matched that of the required class meetings. On the other hand, society meetings experienced more difficulty because of an unauthorized "open meeting" policy, even though church leaders such as Francis Asbury, Thomas Rankin, and Ezekiel Cooper tried to make them conform to the English model.[3]

Even after it had become a church in 1784, American Methodism, in general, and New York City Methodism, in particular, remained a "sect." In order to examine this hypothesis, Ernst Troeltsch's *The*

Social Teaching of the Christian Churches will be used in three ways: to contrast his classic definitions of "church" and "sect," to state his view that British Methodism was a sect rather than a "religious society" within the Established Church, and to correlate his "sect-type" of Christianity with New York City Methodism.[4]

II. CLASS MEETING AS CATECHUMENATE

During the formative period of New York City Methodism, the class system functioned as a catechumenate similar to those of the early church in which candidates for baptism were instructed in the faith over a period of several months or even years. First, a prospective new member attended a weekly class meeting for six months or possibly longer. Second, upon completion of the probationary period, the class leaders voted, as a body, whether or not to approve the candidate for full membership in the New York Society. Third and last, an approved member was received as a full member of the John Street Methodist Episcopal Church.[5]

Prior to joining a class, a person was usually "awakened" as a result of fervent, evangelical Methodist preaching (see Appendix 1: Typical Weekly Schedule for New York Society, 1772-1774).[6] The first stage in the catechetical process occurred when a person joined a class and was officially "admitted on trial."[7] The second step in the process occurred at the end of six months. At the weekly leaders' and stewards'[8] meeting, the class leader either recommended that the person be approved for full membership or be continued as a probationary member for another six months.[9] Acceptance into the society was far from automatic, which indicated how seriously the New York Society understood membership. For instance, the first section of the "State of the Society" for 1791 was entitled, "First, of those who remain on trial." The terms, "kept on trial" or "brought forward," were also used to indicate an extended probation. Moreover, the New York Society's membership lists in the 1790s listed numerous persons who were kept on trial, including a future class leader, Moses West, who was "declined" after his first probationary period. Another future class leader, Ware Branson, was admitted on trial on 17 June 1790 and read into society on 5 July 1792, making a total of twenty-five months of probation, which seems extremely long (see Appendix 2).[10] For those who successfully completed probation, the third and final step of the process was to be "read into Society," usually at the next society meeting or love feast.[11] Thus, in this early period, the class system followed the Wesleyan concept of the catechumenate without any deviation. As in England, regular attendance at all class meetings, unless excused, was expected and those who came sporadically or not at all were eventually expelled.[12]

Moreover, the class system stabilized early New York City Methodism in three important ways. First, the class system fostered close bonds among the members of a class and also between the class leader and individual members. Second, the class system provided stability in the way it was able to develop new leadership for the local church. Third, the class system, as in England, monitored the behavior of its members and reached out to those who had lapsed. First, class meetings may have provided stability by developing close relationships, especially among those who remained in the same class for a long period of time. The class lists from 1785 to 1796 contain numerous examples of people being in the same class for years at a time. For example, Jane Hipp and Mary Sands were in Peter McLean's female class together from 1791 to 1796 and possibly longer. Similarly, Susannah Mercein and Sarah Riker were in John Staples's class from at least 1785 to 1795 (see Appendix 3). Since class lists are extant only for 1785, 1787, 1791, and 1793-1795, it is possible that these class members, and others, were in the same class for a much longer period than five years. This is further confirmed by class lists in the 1800 to 1832 period. These close relationships were not only present in the weekly class meeting but also at other times, especially during illness. Early Methodist records contain accounts both of classmates visiting a sick member of their class in order to pray for healing and of dying class members exhorting their fellow classmates to persevere in the faith.[13] In addition to developing close bonds among members of the same class, the class meeting was again able to foster an extremely close class leader/class member relationship. The class lists from this period show that a number of women had the same class leaders from five to eleven years. For example, Sarah Codington was in John Bleecker's class for ten years, Susannah Mercein and Sarah Riker were in Staples's for ten and eleven years, respectively, and Mary Sand was in McLean's for eleven (see Appendix 3).[14] Consequently, these class leaders might have found it easier to spiritually direct their long-term members. Over a five to ten year period, he would come to know their temperaments, their strengths and weaknesses, and the various kinds of experiences they normally encountered at home and at work. This personal knowledge, built up over many years, would enable him to provide necessary admonition, encouragement, or reproof. In addition to a personal knowledge of their discipleship, both inward and outward, leader and member would build up a deep level of trust.

At the same time, the class lists for this period indicate that the class leaders themselves were changed periodically. For instance, class lists show that six women had three different leaders, three women had four different leaders, and one had five (see Appendix 4).[15] A change in class leaders could have both a positive and negative effect. A long-term relationship might be affected, but a change of leader could often bring variety and enthusiasm to a lifeless class. In fact, Wesley had recommended the practice of frequently changing leaders, especially those who were ineffective.[16] Yet, the frequent changing of some leaders at John Street may have been due to more practical concerns such as a shortage of leaders or a rapidly expanding membership that required constant class realignment in the various neighborhoods. Occasionally, the practice of changing class leaders was abused when autocratic deacons and elders removed effective leaders without sufficient cause such as the incident to which Asbury referred in a letter to Ezekiel Cooper.[17]

Second, the class system stabilized early New York City Methodism by developing new leadership for the local church. Indeed, Thomas Coke and Francis Asbury, in their "Annotations" to the 1798 Discipline, had called the classes "our universities for the ministry."[18] Some class members did, in fact, become ordained elders in the traveling ministry, but the class meeting system continually produced class leaders, exhorters, and local preachers who remained permanently on the local level. Without this pool of lay ministry, New York City Methodism would have been unable to provide the pastoral oversight that it did. In fact, in the 1790s, the ordained elder appointed to John Street only stayed for a year or less. Thus, it fell to the laity to direct the spiritual and temporal interests of the church, assisted by the elder.

Spiritual formation and preparation for ministry occurred, not in the formal setting of the seminary, but in the Christian community. For example, future class leaders usually spent at least two years as a class member before being appointed to that important position. For the fourteen class leaders who were appointed between the years 1791 and 1796, it took an average of 3.3 years to go from initial membership in a class to class leader (see Appendix 5). Of the fourteen class leaders, five were appointed two years after being read into the society, five were appointed after three years, two were appointed after five years, and two were appointed after six years.[19] Similarly, an analysis of fifteen other class leaders during the same 1785-1796 time period indicated an even longer average time from class member to class leader. Using the year they first appeared on a class list (rather than the date on which they were read into society), it took these class leaders an average of 4.2 years to go from class member to leader. Henry Newton, John Sprosen, and John Cooper each spent six years, from 1785 to 1791, as class members before becoming class leaders. Sometimes, it took even longer, as in the case of Paul Hick.[20] As a result of this careful and extended preparation, the new class leaders were probably quite effective, as their service record reveals. More than twenty percent of the seventy class leaders appointed in the 1780s and 1790s served at least eight consecutive years. Indeed, four of these leaders served twenty years or more, extending their terms well into the nineteenth century (see Appendix 6).[21]

The development of class leaders, exhorters, and local preachers, in the minds of these "disciples," closely paralleled the New Testament understanding of ministry which also emerged from within the community. In the first two centuries, bishops, deacons, and deaconesses first demonstrated certain qualifications and then the elders of the local church commissioned them by the laying on of hands.[22] Similarly, class leaders in New York were selected because of their holiness of life and because they had gifts of exhortation and preaching. A class leader was also expected to pray, read the Bible daily, and to lead family worship. Failure to carry out one's spiritual duties could lead not only to removal as class leader but also to exclusion from the society.[23] Another striking similarity to New Testament origins is that most of the class leaders, as well as the general membership, in this early period, came from very ordinary, working-class occupations.[24] This idea can be seen by looking at the occupations of the class leaders of the New York Society in 1793 which are listed in Appendix 7. For instance, of the twenty-five listed, four were shoemakers, three were tailors, two were grocers, two were bakers, and two were carpenters.[25] In addition to the development and oversight of the class leaders, the class system also nurtured "exhorters" and "local preachers."[26] These positions were extremely important in the New York Society, since traveling preachers had not yet "located" in one particular congregation but were still appointed to a "circuit" of several preaching "stations." As in England, it was not unusual for a class member to advance first to class leader, then to exhorter, and finally to local preacher; the 1795 New York Society church leaders' list showed that four class leaders, Jonas Humbert, William Valleau, Jesse Oakley, and Robert Cuddy, had advanced from class leader to local preacher. Humbert had been a class leader from at least 1785 and

Valleau and Cuddy from at least 1791. The church's call to ministry came from one of two places: the weekly leaders and stewards meeting, which the "preacher-in-charge" also attended, or the Quarterly Conference, composed of the current lay leadership, the preacher-in-charge, and the Presiding Elder.[27]

Fourth and last, class meetings provided stability by monitoring behavior. Following the Wesleyan model, a class leader was required to report any "disorderly walkers" at the leaders and stewards meeting.[28] Wesley's *General Rules*, which listed specific unacceptable behaviors, clearly influenced the New York Society's decisions regarding exclusion. From 1787 to 1793, "disorderly walkers" were often excluded for quarreling, brawling, non-attendance, drinking spiritous liquors, immoral conduct, and an unspecified type of disorderly behavior.[29] Methodist procedure called for the preacher, class leader, or class member to speak to the person privately about his or her behavior. If the first warning did not produce a change, a second meeting was held with two or three church members and the offending person. If that also failed, a select group of local church leaders conducted a church trial with or without the offender present. A guilty verdict could still be appealed to the Quarterly Conference; if the appeal failed, exclusion followed.[30] Consequently, this intense scrutiny of fellow members through the class system helped maintain extremely high standards of church membership and moral behavior right up to 1800; these same standards, however, would be increasingly questioned and gradually reduced as Methodism continued its move from society to denomination.

III. CLASS SYSTEM DIVERGENCES BETWEEN NEW YORK AND ENGLAND

At the same time, the New York City class system differed from the original Wesleyan model in three significant ways. First, classes were either all-male or all-female as opposed to mixed neighborhood classes in England. Second, classes were either all-white or all-black, which ultimately led to the formation of a new black Methodist-related denomination, the African Methodist Episcopal Zion Church. Third, the leadership allowed classes to reach extremely large levels, which weakened their effectiveness.

First, class meetings in New York, unlike those in England, were either all-male or all-female, with a few exceptions possibly indicated in the class lists of 1785 to 1796. During those twelve years, only four exceptions to the single-sex classes appear likely: a 1785 Negro class of twenty-six members, which, incidentally, was the only Negro class that year, a class at "Two Mile Stone,"[31] and the 1793 classes of William Grant and Thomas Hutchinson.[32]   Grant's class met on Thursday evening from at least 1793 to 1795; Hutchinson's seventeen member class met at the Poor-House in 1793.   On the other hand, classes in England were more diverse and

> were divided more pragmatically, according to the topography of the society membership and the exigencies of available leadership. In new societies, for example, there might initially be only one class, consisting of all the members, men and women; in the larger societies, there would often be separate classes of men or women as well as those of mixed membership.[33]

It is unclear just why class meetings were segregated by sex, at least for the first forty years of New York Methodism. Asbury, Pilmore, and Rankin would have been used to mixed classes from their Methodist experiences in England. Asbury had come to the colonies in 1772 in his mid-twenties; Pilmore and Rankin were older, but no less experienced in the ways of British Methodism. Moreover, female class leaders, which were becoming more common in England about this time, were almost unknown in America, at least until the early decades of the nineteenth century. One notable exception was the appointment of Mrs. Mary Thorne as class leader in the Philadelphia society in the early 1770s, a move which Asbury noted with approval.[34] Single-sex classes may have struck the leaders as one way to compensate for the small number of bands, which had always been segregated by sex.[35] The leadership may have reasoned that in an all-male or all-female class more intimate sharing could occur. Another band-like quality of the classes was that they were divided according to marital status; there were classes of unmarried women, married women, unmarried men, and married men to apparently allow for intimate sharing and the confession of sins.[36] Yet, the single-sex class as band substitute seems unlikely since individual bands were limited to two to five members. In the period before 1800, some New York City classes had twenty-five to thirty-nine members, making band-like sharing an impossibility, given the fact that the normal length of a class meeting was one to one and a half hours.[37]

Another possible reason for single-sex classes may have been the concern that the mixing of men and women, especially young men and women, might give the appearance of scandal or lead to sexual improprieties. Indeed, men and women (including married couples) continued to sit on opposite sides of the John Street church until the late 1830s. For a time, Wesley Chapel had separate entrance doors for men and women. Moreover, the "List of Exclusions" from the years 1787 to 1793 reveal that a high number of members were excluded for "immoral behavior" (often unspecified) making it clear that Methodism, in its formative years, took matters of sexual morality very seriously. On the other hand, the real reason for single-sex classes may have been location: cities were often treated differently than the rural areas. In the country, travel was more difficult because of longer distances and weather conditions (i.e., floods, extreme cold, etc.). Also, classes were usually held immediately after Sunday morning worship when everyone was together and were conducted by the preacher, not the lay class leader.[38] Hence, mixed classes commonly occurred in small towns and villages, since

> the structure of the Methodist society in town was more complex than on the circuit. On many circuits classes were in effect small societies and societies large classes; that is, the preacher would have no more than one group to meet at any one place; and in some preaching places there was no organized group at all. In town the Wesleyan structure was reasserted.[39]

Second, class meetings in New York City, unlike those in England, were also segregated by race (see Appendix 8). To be sure, this forced separation, in all likelihood, meant that the black classes did not receive equal attention from the visiting preachers and local class leaders. Both Asbury and Pilmore described meeting black classes or at least meeting the black members as a group.[40] Another racially charged action, taken by the 1784 Conference, stipulated that every black class was to have a white class leader.[41] The rationale for segregated classes was, in all likelihood, an extension of the racial situation in New York at that time. After the southern states, New York had the highest slave population of any northern state in the eighteenth century. At the time of Methodism's beginning, tensions were running high in the city because of several slave revolts and also because of the brutal way in which the insurrectionists had been punished. A number of highly restrictive laws had also been passed, especially those banning large assemblies of blacks.[42] As the century drew to a close, New York blacks began to press for increased self-determination and expanded freedoms.[43] In this situation, New York City Methodism chose the way of accommodation.[44] Although Wesley, Asbury, and Coke all fiercely opposed it as being unChristian and inhumane, the local lay leadership apparently condoned it.[45] Even into the 1830s, some prominent lay members in New York backed the colonization movement, or the policy of returning the slaves to Africa.[46] Ultimately, the segregated classes (and the segregated seating policy) drove the unhappy black members to start their own worship services in 1796 with the permission of Bishop Asbury.[47]

Third and last, New York City class meetings differed from those in England because of the growing tendency, which would become critical in the first part of the nineteenth century, to form extremely large classes. At first, class size remained at the recommended level or very close to it. For example, in 1785 and 1787, the majority of New York City classes contained less than twenty members (see Appendix 9). However, the four extant class lists of the 1790s reveal an alarming pattern of increase: classes in the twenty to thirty-nine member range began to outnumber those which had nineteen or less by about two to one, except for 1796, when there was an equal number in both groups.[48] One reason for the large classes was, as in England, a lack of qualified class leaders, which prevented subdivision of the classes. In the New York Society, it took from two and a half to nearly three and a half years to be appointed as class leader. To partially compensate for this shortage, a number of class leaders were given two and, sometimes, three classes. Usually, these class leaders had one male and one female class, although that could also vary from year to year. Those who had two classes during the 1780s and 1790s were Philip Arcularius, John Bleecker, John Davis, Paul Hick, John Staples, William Valleau, and Elias Vanderlip. Only William Cooper had three classes: one male, one female, and one mixed.[49] Another reason that contributed to the large classes was the New York Society's resistance to using female class leaders, although a precedent for this had been established in Philadelphia in the early 1770s. At the same time, the class lists for this period seem to indicate that four women, Jane Barsary (a Negro), Catherine Kelly, Sarah Day, and Elizabeth Barnet, did serve as class leaders in the 1780s, but only for a one year term. It can only be inferred that they were class leaders from the fact that their names were listed first in their class lists; normally, the first name on the list was also that of the class leader and was followed by the designation "leader." However, in the case of all four women, the designation "leader" does not follow their names. This designation only began to be used regularly in the 1790s class lists.[50]

IV. BAND MEETING

Band meetings, like the Wesleyan class meetings, were successfully transplanted to New York. First, both kinds of band meetings, the individual band and the band society, met regularly from 1770 to 1800. Second, the band meeting, as in England, was viewed as the primary place in which to experience "Christian perfection" or "entire sanctification." Third, although the bands were highly effective, the total number never matched that of the required class meetings.

As in England, both individual bands, composed of two to five persons, and the combined bands were present in early New York City Methodism. The combined bands were variously called the "band-society," "bands," "body bands," "band meeting," or "select bands."[51] Band societies had originally been designed for additional teaching opportunities for those who had gathered around Wesley in London.[52] During the 1770s, the band-society usually met on either Friday or Saturday evening at John Street for testimonies, singing, and prayer, and both Asbury and Rankin found them to be powerful experiences.[53] The band-society at John Street continued to meet in the 1780s and 1790s with the same edifying results to which both the Reverend Ezekiel Cooper, who spent part of 1785 in New York, and Thomas Coke attested.[54] Further evidence that bands of various types continued to meet during this early period comes from the quarterly "band tickets," which were issued at least up to 1798.[55]

As in England, the band meeting and the even more advanced Select Societies were viewed as the primary places in which to experience "Christian perfection" or "entire sanctification," rather than in the classes where the spiritual sharing was at a more basic level.[56] Because of the difference between the two groups, the 1798 *Discipline* concluded that the band meeting was necessary to deepen the holiness of each member and asserted that

> when bands can be formed on this plan (and on no other plan do we form them) they become one of the most profitable means of grace in the whole compass of Christian discipline. There is nothing we know of, which so much quickens the soul to a desire and expectation of the perfect love of God as this.[57]

Despite the thirty year existence of bands and an apparent positive effect on those who attended, the total number of bands in New York City never matched those of the required class meetings. As in England, the majority of church members did not join a band since they required a more intimate, "confessional" sharing. An extant, undated New York Band Society list from the 1790s showed only nine bands with a total of twenty-eight persons. The bands on this list varied in size from two to five persons, which was in keeping with the Wesleyan model, and the average size of a band for that year was 3.1 persons.[58] If the 1793 membership of seven hundred ninety-three was used, it would mean that less than five percent of the members were also in bands.[59] Frank Baker observed that

> the intimate and searching fellowship of the band never fully took on in American Methodism, although it was explained in the *Discipline*, urged by Coke and Asbury, and maintained a struggle for existence in larger centers such as New York well in the nineteenth century. The slightly more easy-going friendliness of the class meeting proved more congenial, as indeed it did in Britain.[60]

Nevertheless, the Methodist leadership fully expected every member to attend band as well as class. From the start, Asbury assumed that every Methodist would attend both class and band and rebuked those in New York who failed to do so.[61] In addition, the 1798 *Discipline*, while it took note of declining band attendance throughout the denomination, pointed out its spiritual benefits.[62] Whether the tone was gentle or severe, motivating the membership to attend band was difficult and would become even more so in the first part of the nineteenth century.

V. SOCIETY MEETINGS

Unlike the class and band meetings, the Wesleyan society meetings were much more difficult to implement in New York because of an "open meeting" policy which lasted for nearly twenty years. In order to rectify the situation, church leaders such as Asbury, Rankin, and Cooper struggled, sometimes in vain, to bring the meetings in line with established Wesleyan practice. Finally, the 1789 *Discipline* put an end to the dissenting position in New York by reaffirming the standard entrance requirements.

Although society meetings were regularly held beginning in the 1770s in New York City, they did not strictly follow the Wesleyan plan. From the beginning, the society meeting and the love feast had been private meetings, while other meetings, such as early morning and evening preaching, were public affairs. The rationale for closed society meetings and love feasts was that it allowed the members to share more openly.[63] At one of his annual Conferences, Wesley had insisted that non-members be allowed to attend no more than three society meetings until they joined a class.[64] In New York, however, a lay preacher and some influential lay members were allowing their non-Methodist friends to attend society meetings.[65] Shortly after his arrival in the colonies, Asbury encountered the situation in August, 1772, when he observed how Richard Wright, an unauthorized English lay preacher, who had taken charge in New York until the English missionaries arrived, allowed non-members to attend a love feast.[66] Four and a half weeks later, on Saturday, 5 September 1772, Asbury took firm steps to stop the practice but found himself opposed by several lay leaders of the society. His word prevailed but it took a while for the tensions to die down.[67] New York was not the only large society in which open meetings were the norm; the Philadelphia Society had gotten off to the same "undisciplined" start. Without authorized lay preachers to guide the earliest beginnings of the Methodist societies in the colonies, aberrations of discipline had grown up like weeds in an untended garden.[68] Despite the combined efforts of Asbury and Rankin, this problem stubbornly continued into the mid-1790s. To illustrate, both the Reverend John Dickens and the Reverend Ezekiel Cooper, who were stationed at John Street in 1783 and 1794-1795, respectively, also took steps to "fence in the society."[69]

VI. SECT VERSUS CHURCH: 1784-1800

In its first sixteen years as a new denomination, from 1784 to 1800, New York City Methodism retained the sect-like qualities it had as a religious society. In order to show this, Ernst Troeltsch's classic work, *The Social Teaching of the Christian Churches*, will be used to contrast "church" and "sect," to assess Methodism as a sect, and to correlate his "sect-type" characteristics with New York City Methodism.

Troeltsch stated that Christianity was either expressed as "church-type" or "sect-type."[70] The "church-type" was large and inclusive and, since it it worked with society, primarily attracted the upper classes. It understood asceticism only in the sense of severe mortifications performed in a monastery rather than holiness achieved through an ordinary life. In addition, the church-type acquired members from infant baptism and taught that God's grace came through the sacraments, even if the priest was unworthy. Finally, the church-type only allowed ordained clergy to preach and teach. On the other hand, the "sect-type," since it withdrew from society, was smaller, appealed largely to the lower classes, and minimally related to the larger society (including the institutional church).[71] It believed that everyone was called to the ascetic life which Troeltsch described as

> merely the simple principle of detachment from the world, and is expressed in the refusal to use the law, to swear in a court of justice, to own property, to exercise dominance over others, or to take part in war.[72]

Membership in the sect, however, was based upon adult conversion and voluntary association; one could not be "born" into a sect. Moreover, the sect deemphasized the doctrine that grace came through the sacraments and stressed instead that holiness came through "personal effort." Unlike the church-type, any laypersons who demonstrated gift(s) for ministry were allowed to exercise them.[73] For Troeltsch, the sect was

> lay Christianity, personal achievement in ethics and in religion, the radical fellowship of love, religious equality and brotherly love, indifference toward the authority of the State, the separation of the religious life from the economic struggle by means of the ideal of poverty, the directness of the personal religious relationship, criticism of official spiritual guides, the appeal to the New Testament and to the Primitive Church.[74]

Troeltsch classified British Methodism as a sect. On the other hand, it differed from most sects since it was both a "religious order" and a "voluntary association." Like a religious order, it required unquestioning compliance from both its lay preachers and members; like a voluntary association, it fostered an intense community lifestyle by which the membership was continually built up in the faith.[75] While British Methodism formed small religious societies like the Moravians and the earlier Anglicans had, Troeltsch labeled it a sect because of its larger and more ambitious mission of preaching the Gospel throughout the British Isles. By doing this, Methodism sought to "awaken the masses which, under the influence of an 'enlightened' church and the pressure of industrial capitalism, had become indifferent, dull, and coarse."[76]

In addition to its missionary zeal, British Methodism exhibited five additional sect-type qualities. First, it stressed personal appropriation of the faith as an adult rather than the efficacy of infant baptism. Second, holiness was expected of all members. Third, lay ministry sustained the early societies and classes.[77] Fourth, Methodism often stood apart from society and from the Established Church, even though it urged its members to attend parish services.[78] Fifth and last, it gained its victories in the middle and lower classes, among the the miners and in the industrial towns. To the middle and lower classes it brought a new sense of the sacredness of personality; and awakened a devotion which found expression in a most self-sacrificing charity. From the aristocratic classes and the rural population, as well as from the educated professional classes, it remained, on the whole, remote.[79]

Troeltsch's "sect-type" and early New York City Methodism, like British Methodism, can be correlated in a number of ways. First, the lay ministry of the sect corresponded to the lay ministry of class leaders, exhorters, and local preachers. Second, the close-knit fellowship of the sect was present in the close relationships among class members and between the class leader and individual members. Third, the striving for personal holiness found in the sect was reflected in the "prudential means of grace" (i.e., the additional society, love feast, class, and band meetings). Fourth, like the sect, New York City Methodism reached a number of persons from the lower classes. Its early male members were carpenters, grocers, bakers, and tailors, while many female members worked as domestic servants (see Appendix 7). Fifth, adult conversions, another sect characteristic, normally occurred in New York City Methodism as a result of its fervent preaching and the evangelical effect of the class meeting.   Sixth, New York Methodists periodically criticized institutional church leaders (i.e., the priests at Trinity Church and St. Paul's Chapel).[80] Seventh, the sect-type's appeal to the early church found expression in the use of the class meeting as a catechumenate. Eighth and last, both the sect and New York City Methodism practiced the right to excommunicate members who did not live according to Christian moral norms.[81]

In short, early New York City Methodism, like its British parent, continued to act like a sect up to 1800. Even though Methodism had become a church in 1784, it had not yet undergone the "sect to church" process; that would occur in the nineteenth century.[82] Specifically, the "sect-to-church" process refers to the way in which new movements in Christianity eventually become established and lose many of their distinctive qualities. Moreover, they accommodate themselves to the surrounding society and, as they increase in numbers, they begin to drop their higher standards of religious practice and become more inclusive.[83] Significantly, Max Weber referred to this gradual change (which usually spanned one generation or less) as the "routinization of charisma." Furthermore, Weber noted that "charismatic authority" was present only in the beginning of the movement. So, with the death of the founder, many changes often had to be made within the movement, whether it was political, economic, or religious.[84] In the same way, Methodism could expect routinization now that it had become a church in 1784. To illustrate, before 1784 many Methodist laity had desired that their preachers (mostly lay) could administer the sacraments instead of receiving them in the Anglican parishes. To be sure, in some rural areas, no Anglican parish may have existed nearby. Conversely, the urban Methodists had easier access to the Anglican parishes. In fact, John Street Church had two Anglican churches within walking distance. Moreover, the issue of Methodist-administered sacraments became critical when the Revolutionary War caused many "loyalist" Anglican priests to return to England. One result, however, of ordaining their own clergy (as a new denomination) would be the loss of local lay ministry (i.e., local preachers, exhorters, and class leaders) as the new ministers assumed more and more control of the local congregation. Another "routinization," as Methodism grew larger and more acceptable to a broader range of people, would be a tendency to drop its emphasis on the extra meetings (in addition to Sunday worship) which cultivated that close-knit feeling among class members as well as personal holiness. On the other hand, Methodism, as Wesley had understood it, was gathering people (especially new converts) into societies and classes to deepen their faith and discipleship. Indeed, a Methodist originally had been someone who took on additional spiritual commitments to complement their parish involvement since early Methodism meant to supplement, but not replace, their parish involvement. Next, "routinization" would probably affect Methodism's initial desire to reach the lower classes of New York City society. In fact, it is possible that the better educated parishioners, such as Methodism was attracting, might have different priorities such as more learned ministers, bigger and more beautiful sanctuaries, and a diminished fervor in proclaiming the gospel message to those who needed to hear it the most. Finally, Methodism could expect further "routinization" as it dealt with the question which practically every new Christian movement has had to deal with--how to bring the members' children and grandchildren to a conversion experience. Indeed, how would the Methodist Episcopal Church transmit its evangelical message and intense program of spiritual nurture to those who were "born" into its membership, rather than personally choosing it as adults?

Nonetheless, from 1784 to 1800, the John Street Methodist Episcopal Church retained the same structure and terminology of the earlier New York Society despite the fact that "routinization" loomed ahead. To illustrate, probationers were still "read into society," (i.e., received into full membership) at a private society meeting, rather than at a public service such as Easter or Pentecost. Moreover, the persistence of private society meetings and love feasts also revealed an exclusive "religious society" mentality.[85] Regarding this situation, Frederick Norwood has written that Methodism's

> great need was to be raised up in the ways of being a church, not a 'society.' One is amazed to discover how very little Methodism in America after the organizing conference differed from its former state. The form of discipline, based on the Large Minutes of Wesley's British Methodism, remained virtually unchanged. From habit the societies were still called societies, as if nothing had happened in 1784.[86]

VII. CONCLUSION

During this formative period, New York City Methodism used classes and bands as a primary means of catechesis and pastoral oversight. Like their English counterparts, they understood conversion as a gradual process and made provision not only for the "new birth" experience, but also for continual growth in grace. The move from a society to a church did not, at this time, affect the theory and practice of the class system, although that would soon change radically with the advent of camp and prayer meetings at the beginning of the nineteenth century. For now, the class meeting fulfilled its function perfectly.

In addition to a highly dedicated corps of traveling preachers of which Asbury was preeminent, New York City Methodism consistently produced stellar lay leadership through the class system. This highly developed system of class leaders, exhorters, and local preachers (all laymen) carried on the essentials of pastoral ministry as traveling preachers came and went. In the class meeting, under the supervision of a seasoned class leader, embryonic gifts could be discerned and encouraged. The local church leadership (i.e., the monthly leaders and stewards meeting and the Quarterly Conference), authenticated an individual's inner call to ministry and then provided continual supervision, since class leaders, exhorters, and local preachers underwent annual review. Nevertheless, with the class system driving the evangelistic and pastoral activities of the New York Society, difficulties were experienced in two key areas: its policy of segregating classes by sex, which under-utilized the gifts of women and indirectly led to an increase in class size, and its policy of segregating classes by race, which eventually led the black members to form the African Methodist Episcopal Zion Church.

Although Methodism had become a "church" in 1784 as a result of the Revolutionary War, it still acted like a "sect" or the "religious society" it had been since the late 1730s. Its structure, requirements, and even its terminology remained unchanged. New York City Methodism continued the way it had since the early 1770s. Probationers and full members took class meeting attendance seriously. It still attracted the lower classes, rather than the business and political leaders of New York City. It did not close in on itself as some other sects had historically done. Its undiminished evangelistic fervor led to the formation of the Forsyth Street and Duane Street Methodist Episcopal Churches in 1792 and 1798, respectively.

While New York City Methodism grew slowly but steadily in the last fifteen years of the eighteenth century, its individual and corporate worship life probably continued to deepen. In the early nineteenth century, this well-cultivated spirituality would lead to the founding of several voluntary societies, such as the Bible, Tract, and Sunday School societies. Also, in the early nineteenth century, its evangelical outreach of preaching and class meetings would be supplemented by the new "prayer meeting" and "revival meeting," causing membership to increase one hundred twenty percent in less than fifty years. In its next important period, it would also begin to face the reality of its own institutionalization, along with changing patterns of class attendance.[87]

Chapter 3

The New York Circuit: 1800-1832

I. INTRODUCTION

From 1800 to 1832, the New York City churches were formally grouped into the "New York Circuit."[1] During these thirty-two years, despite the valiant efforts of the class leaders, growing "sect to church" tensions, the effect of the weekly prayer meeting on the Christian initiation process of the class meeting, and the loss of spiritual intimacy as the size of classes grew larger (while actual class attendance declined) indicated that the earlier spiritual vitality of New York City Methodism was lessening. A number of "church-type" characteristics developed during this time, such as the beginnings of a "settled" pastorate, a desire for greater social respectability, and a new emphasis on education for both young boys and future ministers. In addition to its growing institutionalization, the new evangelistic methods of the New York Circuit diminished the class meeting's traditional role in Christian initiation. Influenced by the "camp meeting,"[2] the new weekly "prayer meetings"[3] were highly emotional services, using set techniques, which stressed instantaneous conversions. Although the prayer meeting created a new way for many persons to experience "peace with God" in a shorter period of time, the role of the class leader remained highly important in evangelism, pastoral care, and church discipline. Class leaders not only conducted their weekly class, they also attended the monthly Board of Leaders meetings, ministered in other ways as need arose, and, along with the preachers, oversaw the behavior of their class members. Although preachers and class leaders faithfully carried out their pastoral responsibilities in this period, other trends - such as large classes and declining class attendance - significantly affected the Wesleyan class meeting concept of "growing in grace."[4]

II. SECT TO CHURCH TENSIONS

From 1800 to 1832, New York City Methodism began to shed some of its "sect-type" characteristics as it entered a process of institutionalization. First, the itinerant plan of traveling ministry was changed to a more "settled" type of pastorate. Second, the new debate over free or rented pews indicated that at least some Methodists favored greater respectability and status. Third and last, the request of the New York Circuit's Quarterly Conference to establish a conference-sponsored school pointed Methodism in the direction of seminary education.

The first "church-type" characteristic in New York City Methodism was its "modified itinerancy" which resembled "settled" pastorates. Normally, only one traveling preacher served a circuit, which was composed of a number of "preaching stations." In the course of one year, the preacher might go through the circuit a number of times. From 1800 to 1832, however, when the New York City Methodist churches were grouped into the "New York Circuit,"[5] five preachers, plus a "preacher-in-charge," were appointed each year.[6] While each preacher preached only once in the same church on Sundays and once every five weeks in the same church for the mid-week service, they also had pastoral oversight for the church near their place of residence.[7]

This modified itinerancy represented a big change, since Methodism had never emphasized settled pastorates. For example, Bishop Asbury had firmly resisted "locality"[8] as far back as the 1770s, when many preachers wanted to settle in the large eastern cities. Again, in 1813, three years before his death, he compared Methodist itinerancy to the early church leaders, like Paul, who continuously traveled.[9] Similarly, three years later, the 1816 General Conference attributed a decrease in preaching and home visitation to the unauthorized formation of smaller circuits. The Committee on Safety reported that

> circuits have been formed - divided, subdivided on the principle of
> accommodation to local circumstances. This course has reduced circuits
> almost exclusively to sabbath appointments. We cannot consider this
> among the least evils which threaten the connexion at the present crisis: it
> has a general tendency to locality.[10]

The Committee on Safety further recommended that the bishops and presiding elders stop the preacher-in-charge from subdividing his circuit.[11] Despite this, many church leaders, such as the Reverend Nathan Bangs, wanted to modify or completely end the itinerant method. As presiding elder on the Rhinebeck District prior to his coming to New York, Bangs had been frustrated because Methodism had not grown significantly in western Connecticut even though the traveling circuit riders had converted many. Since the itinerants left immediately after preaching, the converts usually joined the older, established churches in the area. Bangs concluded that Methodism should start using stationed preachers and build churches in each town and village.[12] In describing the nineteenth century changes in American Methodism, Nathan Hatch asserted that Bangs's

> career and influence typified the allure of respectability facing insurgent religious movements. As their constituencies grew in social standing, it became difficult to retain their pastoral identity as defiant, alienated prophets. Bangs envisioned Methodism as a popular establishment, faithful to the movement's original fire but tempered with virtues of middle-class propriety and urbane congeniality.[13]

A second "sect to church" tension on the local, conference, and denominational levels was the desire, among some Methodists, for greater respectability and status which probably came from renting or buying a pew, a practice found in other Protestant churches of this period. To illustrate, the New York Conference[14] dealt with this issue on three separate occasions between 1822 and 1830. The conference of 1822 considered the case of the Reverend William Thatcher of New Haven who had built a new church in which pews could be rented or bought. A committee of the conference decided he had acted in ignorance of the recent General Conference ruling on the question and did not take any disciplinary action against him; it simply reminded the members of the policy.[15] Again, in response to reports of churches which were still disregarding this policy, the 1828 conference resolved that all churches in the New York Conference should have free seats. Moreover, those churches which had already rented or sold pews were ordered to make them free, while other churches which had rented or sold pews for a temporary period were told to honor their word and make the pews free again. Also, the Conference requested that the presiding elders and local church leaders prevent any future churches from being built on that plan and that bishops not appoint preachers to those churches which disregarded the open seating policy.[16] Finally, the 1830 conference discussed the case of the Reverend Heman Bangs who had tried to build a church with rented pews but stopped after being warned; again, no disciplinary action was taken.[17]

A third "sect to church" tension was the growing emphasis on theological education. This idea is shown by the New York Circuit's Quarterly Conference petition to the 1818 New York Conference which urged that a "seminary" be built for Methodist children for two reasons. First, Methodist children who went to other private religious schools were required to study the theology of a different church tradition; a Methodist school would remedy that. Another reason for the school was that it could educate the sons of the preachers who often could not afford private schools. In addition, while not calling for required theological education, the petition pointed out that younger clergy awaiting appointment "might, under the direction of the Conference, employ their time in the acquisition of the most useful knowledge, and at the same time occupy an ample field for the exercise of their ministerial talents."[18]   Similarly, the 1816 General Conference strengthened the theological education requirement for new clergy; each annual conference was to draw up a "course of study" and assign an older preacher to tutor the younger one.[19]

Thus, during this period, the New York Circuit began its change from sect to church. In New York City and elsewhere, the tendency to "locate," at least partially, had increased. Although clergy were now closer to, and more involved with, congregational life, lay leadership still remained vital. The movement to rent and sell pews raised other questions. Was it solely to raise additional monies to pay for new church construction? Was it partly a desire to imitate the other more socially respectable Protestant churches? Finally, the campaign to open a school which also taught the Bible and theology revealed some "second generation" concerns: education for the children of church members and better theological training for new clergy, although the New York Quarterly Conference petition carefully added that this was not to be seen as a general requirement for all clergy. American Methodism, in general, and New York City Methodism, in particular, were taking on more "church-type" characteristics as they gradually accommodated to society. Regarding this process, Roger Finke and Rodney Stark wrote that

> new religious bodies nearly always begin as sects and that, if they are successful in attracting a substantial following they will, over time, almost inevitably be gradually transformed into churches. That is, successful religious movements nearly always shift their emphasis toward this world and away from the next, moving from high tension with their environment toward increasingly lower levels of tension.[20]

III. ALTERATION OF CLASS MEETING'S CATECHUMENATE FUNCTION

In addition to acquiring more "church-type" characteristics, the new evangelistic methods of the weekly "prayer meeting" altered the Wesleyan process of Christian initiation through the class meeting. Unlike the class meeting, the prayer meeting strongly appealed to the emotions and used set, and even contrived, practices to induce conversion. Most important, the prayer meeting expected conversion to occur in one evening; this new approach de-emphasized and devalued the traditional six-month process of weekly class meetings in which "seekers" were questioned, instructed, and finally accepted or rejected as full members of the church.

The Wesleyan process of Christian initiation through the class meeting had simply trusted that conversions would gradually occur during the six month probationary period, although some actually took several years.[21] Up to the beginning of the nineteenth century, Methodist preaching was intended to solely "awaken" people to their need for salvation.[22] As in the formative period, a person "under conviction" either joined a class or was asked to join one. Regarding this process, the Reverend Tobias Spicer wrote that

> I offered myself to the Methodists, was admitted on probation as a seeker of religion. Reverend Elias Vanderlip was the preacher in charge, who received me into society, and John Craw was the leader to whose class I was assigned.[23]

Similarly, the Reverend Alonzo Selleck

> joined on probation the Willett Street Methodist Episcopal Church, and was assigned to the class of Brother Abram Rile. At the end of his probation he was baptized by Reverend Daniel Ostrander, and was received into full membership.[24]

Emotional appeals and mechanical methods to achieve conversion were never used. This idea is shown by the sensitivity and patience of the class leaders which allowed the probationer to experience the weekly class meeting in a non-threatening and non-judgmental way. Moreover, class leaders did not force probationers to give detailed answers to the questions which were asked of them each week; instead they tried to discern the spiritual level of each probationer and act accordingly.[25] Regarding this patient approach the Reverend John Bangs wrote

> that before my conversion I was permitted when under deep concern of mind, to take a seat in a class meeting, far back, feeling lonely and dejected. When the minister had spoken to the rest of the people, he did all in his power to administer consolation. I answered his questions as well as I was able, but could not fully explain the deep feelings of my heart.[26]

At the same time, more rapid conversions did occasionally occur in the class meeting, but not as a result of pressure; usually the person had been actively seeking God for some time previously. An example is the experience of Mrs. John Bangs who had been awakened earlier by Methodist preaching and

> continued to seek, and one sabbath she requested to join the class as a seeker, and was admitted. After returning home her distress of mind increased until the next morning, when, while engaged in prayer and reading the Scriptures, her soul was brought into unspeakable enjoyment in believing.[27]

Elizabeth Janion also experienced "peace with God" after attending only a few class meetings. On the last day of a New York Circuit Quarterly Conference, she heard the Reverend John Reese preach on the text, "Awake to righteousness and sin not; for some have not the knowledge of God. I speak this to your shame." She was "convicted," joined a class, and was converted after the third meeting.[28]

On the other hand, the weekly "prayer meeting" sought to initiate a "seeker" into the Christian faith in just one evening. In order to understand how the prayer meeting developed as it did in the New York Circuit, it is necessary to examine the origins of the camp meeting which preceded and influenced it. Camp meetings began at the Cane Ridge Presbyterian Church in Bourbon County, Kentucky, in August, 1801.[29] The Methodists who had participated at Cane Ridge very quickly began to hold camp meetings of their own and, by 1810, almost every Methodist circuit had their own.[30] Camp meetings, however, were not just limited to the south and west. According to Richard Carwardine, "the camp meeting had been transferred to eastern areas as an adjunct and a spur to city revivalism."[31]

Three steps were involved in the prayer meeting's initiation process. First, fervent evangelical preaching and exhortations often "convicted" persons of their need for reconciliation with God. Next, unlike the six month probationary process, those awakened were invited to make an immediate response by coming to the altar for prayer where the minister and other appointed church members offered sustained prayer for them.[32] A short time later, as a direct result of the camp meetings, New York City Methodists also used a "mourners' bench" or "anxious seat."[33] Third and last, great pressure was placed on the "penitents" to experience a heart-felt conversion. This idea is shown by James P. Horton's account of a Willett Street prayer meeting in which the "mourners" who were invited forward

> came flocking to the altar and in a short time the Lord converted all that came to the altar. We continued our meeting until nearly 11:00 o'clock, and there were twenty-five, I believe, soundly converted during the meeting. I never saw people get religion so easy as they did that night.[34]

Besides the new emphasis on instantaneous conversions, the prayer meeting succeeded as an evangelistic tool because of two other reasons. First, the prayer meeting had an informal structure which consisted of extemporaneous prayers and exhortations which were often led by laypersons. In contrast, the class meeting could become routine and dull because of its repetitive question-and-answer format. Moreover, the prayer meeting allowed women to exhort and pray, a practice which was not allowed in the other Protestant churches. These ideas are shown by the Reverend John Clark's recollection of his first prayer meeting where

> after several prayers had been offered, the exercises were changed, and exhortations were given by several persons in succession. At length, Mrs. Richards, the wife of the class-leader, addressed the little assembly in an affectionate and powerful manner.[35]

Another reason for the prayer meeting's evangelistic success was its ability to easily adapt itself to different settings and groups. In addition to church sanctuaries, some prayer meetings were held in private homes and smaller rooms at the churches.[36] Furthermore, since prayer meetings were so flexible, they could be directed toward specific constituencies, such as the "seekers' prayer meeting" held at the John Street parsonage every Monday afternoon. The Reverend Heman Bangs praised the meeting

> which we find very profitable; those wounded on the Sabbath, we gather up here. Many were present today. Some wept aloud for

mercy; others shouted for joy. It was the most powerful time I have
seen since I have been in New York.[37]

Similarly, "camp meeting prayer meetings" were often held in
Manhattan churches for those who had either been "awakened" or
converted at the out-of-town meetings to encourage them to join a class
where they could receive a fuller presentation of the Gospel message
and begin the process of assimilation into the body of Christ.[38] In
short, the revivalistic techniques of the weekly prayer meeting and the
effort to convert "penitents" in just one evening represented a sharp
break from both the practices of Wesley and early New York City
Methodism. The catechumenate function of the class meeting which
had produced lifelong disciples in the first generation of New York
City Methodism was increasingly deemphasized and devalued. The
original Wesleyan synthesis of justification and sanctification had
started to break down. In the eighteenth century, Wesley had seen the
futility in only converting people without joining them into a closeknit
community where they could grow in grace. New York City
Methodism, in particular, and American Methodism, in general, were
about to exchange a proven initiation process, with roots in the early
church, for a highly emotional and heavily contrived one which
produced questionable results.[39]

IV. THE ROLE OF THE CLASS LEADER IN THE NEW YORK
CIRCUIT

Although the prayer meeting had affected the way in which people
became members of the church, the class leaders of the New York
Circuit continued to foster Methodist spirituality and discipline in a
number of ways. Besides the weekly class meeting, class leaders
carefully examined the spiritual fitness of probationers at the monthly
Board of Leaders meeting. Moreover, they served on various
committees and assisted in other ministries of the circuit. Last of all,
they were chiefly responsible for their members' behavior and initiated
charges against those who failed to reform. At the same time, class
leaders' attendance at the monthly Board of Leaders meetings began to
decrease sharply in the 1820s, an indication that they were either too
busy with other church activities to attend regularly or simply growing
lax in their pastoral duties.

Without a doubt, the primary pastoral duty of the class leader was to
lead his weekly class. During this period, they were extremely
effective for two reasons. First, unlike the stationed preachers who

served only one or two year appointments, class leaders often led the same class for many years. For example, over a thirty year period, one third of the class leaders at John Street served three consecutive years, forty percent served six to eight consecutive years, and approximately twenty-six percent served fourteen to thirty years (see Appendix 2). As in the earlier period, class leaders who led the same class over a long period of time apparently developed close pastoral relationships with their members; encouragement, advice, and admonition could be easily given. On the other hand, the stationed preacher rarely developed close relationships and the class he led was usually the largest at each church, often consisting of fifty to seventy members.[40] In this period, it was the class leader who provided direct and effective pastoral care and not the stationed preacher, who often had to attend various committee and board meetings.[41]

Second, the class leader's effectiveness derived from an authentic call to ministry. This idea is shown in the way the leadership of the New York Circuit discerned gifts of ministry from within the local body of Christ which closely paralleled the method found in the New Testament.[42] The Board of Leaders meeting appointed new class leaders after observing them first as class members. Preachers "equipped" class leaders for ministry by meeting with them periodically, as the Discipline required.[43] Like the bishops and deacons in the New Testament period, the class leaders of the New York Circuit lived and worked among the people they served. Unlike the other Protestant clergy, they were not looked up to as the "learned person" in the community. They did not formally study theology like the other Protestant pastors; instead, like the Apostle Paul, they had a "tentmaker" ministry (i.e., full time secular occupations). This idea is shown by examining the occupations of the New York Circuit class leaders who served in 1812 and 1825. Of the 1812 class leaders, ninety percent were either artisans and factory workers, building trade workers, maritime workers, clothing workers, shopkeepers and dealers, workers in transportation, manufacturers, or proprietors. Only ten percent were in the professional workers or merchants category. Similarly, in 1825, seventy-five percent fell into the first category, while the percentage of professional workers and merchants had increased slightly to seventeen percent (in 1802 the actual number was five, in 1825 it was thirteen). The professional workers category, however, did not include anyone formally trained in theology; the category was composed of portrait painters, teachers, publishers, engravers, and one physician. At the same time, a few class leaders had changed occupations from 1802 to 1825, but these were relatively minor (see Appendix 3).[44]

In contrast, most of the other Protestant churches lacked both a small group system for spiritual nurture and a pastoral leadership which had emerged from the community. For instance, most of the Anglican, Presbyterian, Lutheran, Reformed, and Congregational clergy in America had received a college education.[45] Moreover, in the seventeenth and eighteenth centuries, practically all Congregational ministers were from higher levels of society and went to either Yale or Harvard for a general liberal arts education; these ministers were expected to have a sharp intellect and were looked upon by the community as "learned persons." Some Congregational students, however, stayed on at Yale and Harvard to study formal theology courses even though most graduates went on to live with other Congregational clergy for six months to a year where they could get more practical training.[46] Unlike the class leaders who were taken from among the people and remained in close contact with them, the college-educated Protestant clergy were usually separated and elevated from their parishioners. According to Sydney Mead

> the descendants of Europe's "right-wing" State churches maintained a position, a prestige, power, and dominance in America throughout the colonial period. And even though this was the twilight period of aristocracy, still the conception of learning verged on the ideal of universal knowledge, and was almost the exclusive privilege of the upper classes, automatically conferring prestige and social status on the educated man.[47]

In addition to having a university education, many Protestant clergy began to view the ministry as a "profession," rather than a "calling," in the early nineteenth century. This idea is shown by the number of seminaries which were established in this period; one of the earliest ones, Andover Theological Seminary, was established in 1808 and, by 1820, had one hundred students.[48] Three reasons led to the development of seminaries in this period: ministerial candidates now looked upon a college education as inadequate preparation for the practical aspects of ministry, the old system of living in a minister's home was not sufficient to handle the growing number of candidates, and each denomination felt a theologically-educated clergy was necessary in order to remain competitive.[49] Donald Scott believed that these new seminaries "represented both a formalization and standardization of ministerial training and a dramatically increased emphasis upon purely professional' training."[50] In short, while the older Protestant churches were now requiring further educational preparation for their ministerial candidates, Methodism only insisted upon heart-felt conversions and demonstrated piety for its lay pastors.

Another key pastoral function of the class leaders was the monthly examination of probationers whose six month terms had expired. Merely completing the probationary period did not mean automatic approval as a full member; probation was often routinely extended for another six months. Examples of this are found in the 1827 probationers' book in which Elizabeth Dayton was "carried forward" and Maria Friday was "laid over." Similarly, in the 1832 probationers' book, Horace Close was given a "new probation."[51] Moreover, during the five month period from January to May, 1814, only seventy-four out of one hundred twenty-four probationers, or approximately sixty percent, were approved for full membership; in that same period, twelve were "laid over," twenty were "dropped" (most likely for non-attendance at class meeting), and two were "read out" for repeated unchrisian behavior. Again, during the five month period from July to November, 1816, only fifty-one out of sixty-seven probationers, or approximately seventy-six percent, were approved for full membership; seven were "laid over" and nine were "dropped" (see Appendix 4).[52] Indeed, in the early 1830s, probationers had to be approved at both the "sectional" and "general" leaders' meetings.[53] For example, the probationers' list for 1831 recorded that Mary Ann Seely "passed" at both meetings whereas Jane Milliken "passed" at the sectional but was "dropped" at the general meeting.[54] Consequently, it was the class leader, and not the preacher, who truly knew the spiritual condition of the probationers and made the important decisions on who should be admitted into the church. In short, the preachers depended on the class leaders' knowledge of the people under their care, and not the other way around.

A third way in which class leaders provided pastoral oversight was by serving in various other leadership roles, such as the joint trustees-class leaders committees to carry out the disciplinary regulations on worship.[55] Moreover, class leaders had direct pastoral involvement in the three weekly prayer meetings held on Monday evenings. Specifically, at the 11 December 1811 Board of Leaders' meeting, ten class leaders were appointed to "attend" the prayer meetings and committees of class leaders from each church were appointed to conduct them.[56] Finally, class leaders also performed other administrative tasks such as arranging transportation to camp meetings, serving as secretaries and juries at church trials, and drafting petitions to General Conference.[57]

A fourth pastoral duty of the class leader in the New York Circuit was the administration of discipline. Class leaders visited absent members, reported the names of those who were not following the rules, brought "charges" (or "specifications") against unrepentant class members, and testified against them in church trials. An example of this "process" is shown in the "trial of Thomas Truslow (class leader) versus John Hoare" in which Truslow stated

> that he (i.e., John Hoare) had not attended his class for about one year, that he (i.e., Truslow) has called on him and requested him to attend his class which he promised to do, but did not fulfil his promise. He then reported him to Bro. Sandford (i.e., the preacher). Bro. Truslow says that he has not been to class since.[58]

Similarly, class leader Nathaniel C. Hart visited Arabella Hipwell who had absented herself from class for a year. Since she still did not come to class nor to church even after the preacher visited her, Hart charged her with "neglect of duty" and "superfluity of dress." He also testified against her at the trial where she was found guilty and expelled.[59] Besides visiting errant class members, bringing charges, and testifying, five or six class leaders also served as the "committee" (along with the preacher-in-charge) which decided each trial. To illustrate, in the trial of Hoare, the Reverend Peter P. Sandford presided, and class leaders Simeon Price, John Buckmaster, Thomas Fairweather, Abram Riker, and Nathaniel C. Hart composed the "committee." Again, in the trial of Hipwell, class leaders Price, Buckmaster, Fairweather, Keys, and Williams rendered the decision.[60]

A fifth and final key pastoral role for class leaders in this period was establishing new churches. For instance, in areas where no churches existed, persons who were awakened by Methodist preaching were placed in classes which met weekly. Until a decision was made to built a church (dependent on enough members to support it), the class(es) met in private homes or some other building. To illustrate, Bowery Village Methodist Episcopal Church was "built and dedicated in 1818; but the congregation had been collected, and classes formed, many years before."[61]

Although the role of the class leader was critical in the areas of spirituality, pastoral care, and administration, many class leaders only occasionally attended the important monthly Board of Leaders meetings. One extant, undated record of class leader attendance at the leaders' meetings over several months revealed that twenty class leaders were absent at the September meeting and forty-five at the November meeting.[62] Another extant record of class attendance for the twelve month period from October, 1827, to September, 1828, indicated that sixty-one of the one hundred twenty leaders (or just over half) attended six or more of the monthly meetings, while fifty-nine leaders attended zero to five meetings; in addition, only sixteen leaders attended seventy-five percent (or nine to twelve) meetings. Indeed, class leader attendance dropped even further the following year when only thirty-three leaders (just over twenty-five percent) attended six to twelve meetings and eighty-seven (or just under seventy-five percent) attended less than half of the meetings. Of the eighty-seven leaders who attended less than half, thirty-seven leaders attended from zero to two meetings. Also, no class leader that year attended more than seven out of twelve monthly meetings (see Appendix 8).[63] At the same time, the circuit leadership took some steps to correct this problem, such as the 1812 General Leaders' meeting's two-part resolution which stated that the preacher would visit any leader who missed two consecutive meetings and that his class would be given to someone else in the event of repeated absences.[64]

Although the stationed preachers were gaining more local pastoral responsibility in this period, the ministry of the class leaders was indispensable. The new denomination still understood preachers as being in the "traveling ministry." Class leaders had the advantage of living and working in the same community for long periods of time. Like the preachers, class leaders taught themselves doctrine and practiced personal spiritual disciplines and family prayer.[65] They were able to pastor those who had had a revivalistic-type conversion as well as those who were initiated more gradually. They demonstrated high levels of commitment to their "calling," taking on additional tasks as the needs arose. Yet, declining attendance at the monthly Board of Leaders meeting signaled that the class system was starting to take a less important role in the New York Circuit.

V. THE CLASS MEETING AND METHODIST SPIRITUALITY

Despite the highly dedicated efforts of the majority of class leaders, two changes in the New York Circuit's class meeting system adversely affected Methodist spirituality. First, larger classes made spiritual intimacy and home visitation more difficult. Second, declining class attendance indicated that many members, including probationers, had begun to disregard the Wesleyan emphasis on holiness. Still, the New York Circuit and Methodist periodical articles made efforts to call church members back to faithfully attending class meetings.

Large class size made it increasingly difficult for the class meeting to carry out its original spiritual function: providing each member with an opportunity to grow spiritually through directed "Christian conversation." In just one generation, class size had increased phenomenally. To illustrate, in 1785, seventy-eight percent of the classes had ten to nineteen members. In each succeeding period that percentage went down: in 1787 that figure had decreased to seventy-two percent, in 1791 it was fifty percent, and in 1793 it dropped again to twenty-five percent. Indeed, by 1826, only ten percent of the classes had ten to nineteen members. Moreover, it became common in the 1820s for classes to have forty, fifty, sixty, and even seventy members. For instance, in 1825, approximately eighty percent of the classes in the New York Circuit had twenty to forty-nine members and approximately eleven percent had fifty to seventy-nine. Likewise, in 1826, while the number of classes in the twenty to forty-nine member range had decreased to fifty-five percent of the total classes, the number of classes in the fifty to seventy-nine category had risen to thirty-five percent (see Appendix 9).[66]

Recognizing the difficulty large classes presented to Methodist spirituality, several attempts were made to reduce them to more managable levels. An example is found at a New York Circuit Quarterly Conference in which the presiding elder suggested having more classes meet on weekdays as a way to lower class size. Apparently, many members wanted to fulfil their class meeting requirement on Sunday so they would not be burdened with another meeting during the week.[67] Furthermore, in an apparent attempt to subdivide the classes or at least provide class leaders for new classes, the Board of Leaders

> resolved that it is the wish of this meeting, that all the Stationed, Located, and Local Preachers, and all the Licensed Exhorters of this city, take charge of classes, and that the President make this request known to them. The Ruling Preacher (i.e., the preacher-in-charge) is excepted.[68]

Another solution which was tried on a small scale was for class leaders to divide their classes into two sections. To illustrate, in 1826, the forty-one member class of Thomas Fairweather (of Bowery Village Methodist Episcopal Church) met in two parts: Sunday afternoon and Tuesday evening. The plan apparently worked; three years later, his class had fifty-one members and was still meeting on the two different days.[69] Some class leaders who subdivided their classes used female class members to conduct the other section. An example is Mrs.

Heman Bangs, a member of John Street, whose class leader was the Reverend John Summerfield. She related that

> he had divided his class, and wishes me to lead one half. He speaks to a part, than asks me to speak to the rest. I dislike to refuse, so I have tried a few times.[70]

Subdividing a class, however, could be difficult, as the Reverend Ezekiel Cooper found out when he made three classes out of one large one; many members resisted the change because they didn't want to be separated from their friends.[71] On the other hand, the New York Circuit showed an apparent lack of urgency in dealing with the extremely large classes. As an illustration, the Board of Leaders minutes reveal that only thirty new class leaders were appointed between 1811 and 1832, an average of one and a half new leaders per year. Five were appointed in 1811, one in 1812, seven in 1813, four in 1818, and thirteen in 1829 (see Appendix 13).[72] In addition, the New York Preachers' Meeting was empowered to recommend new leaders but apparently did that infrequently, if at all.[73] In short, although the New York Circuit grew steadily in this period, spiritual intimacy had been sacrificed. Surprisingly, the leadership of the New York Circuit accepted the new situation. The Board of Leaders minutes, over a twenty-one year period (1811-1832), revealed no resolutions, committees, or even discussions on the subject of large classes. Thus, the original Wesleyan attempt to join justification with sanctification within the small group setting of the class meeting had all but disappeared by the mid-1820s.

The second change which adversely affected Methodist spirituality was the decline in weekly class attendance which was especially noticeable in the New York Circuit throughout the 1820s and early 1830s.[74] Exemplifying this was the 1825 "observations on the members" on five classes at the Allen Street Methodist Episcopal Church. In the first class, the leader, Henry Stiles, observed that only forty-two percent attended half or more of the meetings, while fifty-eight percent attended less than half. In addition, the highest attendance recorded for this class was a member who attended "two thirds" of the time.[75] The attendance of the second class appeared to be even lower. William Doughty, the class leader, recorded the terms "seldom," "very seldom," or "rather seldom," next to every name.[76] Likewise, of Eliphalet Wheeler's thirty-one member female class, only one third (eleven members) attended half or more weekly meetings while two thirds (twenty-two members) attended less than half. Further observation of his comments indicate that only one member was "constant," one was "pretty good," eight attended "half" the meetings, and seven were described as "formerly attentive," "inattentive," or "seldom" (see Appendix 14).[77]   Conversely, the fourth class listed showed higher attendance figures.   To demonstrate, in Stephen Rockwell's twenty-nine member "mixed class," twenty-one members (or just over two thirds of the class) attended half or more of the meetings while only eight members attended less than half the time. Of the twenty-one who attended half or more of the meetings, one had perfect attendance (fourteen out of fourteen meetings), and seven attended "constantly."   Since Rockwell used notations like "5/14," "8/14," and "10/14," it is probable that this was a quarterly attendance record (see Appendix 15).[78]   The fifth class, like the first three, also had low weekly attendance. The class leader, Cornelius Polhemus, simply listed the number of times class members had attended, unlike the first four class leaders who had recorded the attendance in words or phrases instead of numbers. Taking into account the two weeks which were left blank because of bad weather (the quarter was from January to March), only twenty-eight percent of the class members attended half or more times while seventy-eight percent attended less than half the time (see Appendix 16).[79] Significantly, the class leader himself attended only six times in the quarter.

Another indication that class attendance was declining came from Thomas McFarlan's 1831-1834 "class book." McFarlan had a twenty-seven member class at the Forsyth Street Methodist Episcopal Church. For the year 1831, only thirteen members attended twenty-five to fifty meetings while fourteen attended twenty-four times or less. Moreover, only two members attended ninety percent of the time, in addition to McFarlan. The largest group of class members, seven, attend sixty percent of the time. On the lower end, six members attended ten or fewer meetings (see Appendix 17).[80] Even more startling was the attendance of probationers in McFarlan's class. Of the fourteen probationers who joined his class between 21 February 1831 and 5 October 1832, their combined average attendance for the six months of probation was just over fifty percent (or two to three meetings per month). Only five out of fourteen probationers attended an average of three or more meetings each month while another five attended an average of less than two per month (see Appendix 19).[81]

At the same time, some individual, circuit-wide, and denominational efforts were made to stop the decline. Individual preachers in the New York Circuit gave sermons on the necessity of the class meeting for sanctification, such as the Reverend George Coles who preached five "class meeting" sermons over a three year period. Coles, and others, based their sermons on three or four standard Biblical texts for "Christian conversation"; two of the most popular were Malachi 3:6-8 and James 5:16.[82] A circuit-wide effort occurred on 17 July 1826 when the New York Preachers' Meeting resolved that the preachers indicate at each meeting the number of classes they met during the previous week. This resolution may have sought to make the preachers more accountable for this aspect of their pastoral work or it may have been intended to spur them on to greater pastoral zeal as the decline became more pronounced.[83] Also, at the denominational level, articles began appearing which both defended the class meeting and criticized those who were neglecting it for a variety of reasons. An example is found in the 1818 article, "On Christian Communion," which began with the standard Methodist scriptural justification of class meetings, then described the qualities needed in class (i.e., simplicity, humility, and honesty), and ended by criticizing those who neglected it.[84] Another defense of the class meeting of a slightly different type was the partial reprint of Charles Perronet's English class manual entitled, *The Advantages of Class Meetings*. Besides giving practical advice on how to structure and conduct the meeting, he called a decline in class attendance a falling off in spiritual fervor and said that those who thought they no longer needed class meetings had simply grown cold in spiritual things.[85] At the same time, the response to declining class attendance stopped short of expulsion. Although the Discipline required it for those who neglected their class, church trial records for 1824-1827 indicate that only those who neglected class for one to one and a half years were tried and expelled (see Appendix 22).[86] Only the most obvious and long-term offenders were being punished (see Appendix 23). The members whose class attendance was sporadic were now accepted.

Besides the class attendance records, several periodical articles also confirmed that class attendance had declined both locally and denominationally. An example is found in the Reverend Laban Clark's article in which he wrote that the recent revivals in the New York Circuit had boosted low levels of class attendance.[87] Similarly, an 1832 article urged that the quarterly examination of class leaders continue because of the

> lax and careless manner in which classes are often met, and from the irregular and indifferent manner in which class books are often kept, in order to prevent class meetings from degenerating into mere forms. Many leaders never meet their classes; and some who do meet them, make it a kind of lovefeast meeting; others never mark their books or date the time of the meeting.[88]

Again, autobiographies and journal entries of New York Circuit clergy also noted lower attendance at the weekly class meeting, such as the Reverend George Coles who recorded that no one came to one of his class meetings.[89]   Indeed, declining class attendance had become a denominational concern as well.   For instance, at the 1816 General Conference, the Committee on Safety reported that

> our Love Feasts, Society, and Class Meetings, have not been observed in all parts of the work, with that caution and strictness which the letter and spirit of the *Discipline* require, and which is indispensably necessary to preserve harmony and spirituality of our Societies.[90]

The decline in class attendance and the New York Circuit's acceptance of it showed the difficulty of sustaining key "sect-type" characteristics into the second generation, a problem which many other renewal movements, religious orders, and denominations also experienced throughout Christian history.   The New York Circuit's difficulty in transmitting the faith and in leading new members to faithfully attend the weekly class meeting paralleled, in some ways, the difficulties of the Puritans in the late 1660s. Like the early Methodists, the Puritans had wanted to "purify" the Church of England by eliminating many abuses and expelling unworthy members.[91]   Again, like the Methodist societies and the first generation New York City Methodists, the Puritans took church membership very seriously.[92] From 1630 to the the-mid 1660s, these membership requirements worked well in New England; Puritan churches were "gathered churches" of holy people.   A problem occurred, however, when the adult children of the original members were not able to relate a personal conversion which then raised the question of whether or not their children (i.e., the grandchildren of the original members) could be baptized and if they could receive Holy Communion.[93]   In 1662, a synod decided that as long as the adult children affirmed the covenant, they were entitled to certain church privileges.[94]   The "half-way covenant," however, dealt only with the specific issue of how to treat the second generation children and not with an overall spiritual decline.[95]   According to many Puritan "election sermons" of the 1660s and 1670s, this declension had occurred because the people were not keeping the covenant.[96]   As a result of decreasing membership, the Puritans gradually began to be more concerned with the unchurched population and between 1669 and 1700 adopted more liberal attitudes for church membership.   In fact, by the early 1700s, many Puritan clergy were administering the sacraments to persons who professed faith in Christ but could not relate a definite work of grace (i.e., a conversion experience) in their lives.[97] The Puritan experience was now becoming the Methodist experience. Church membership requirements would be increasingly revised downward as the nineteenth century progressed.[98]

VI. CONCLUSION

From 1800 to 1832, the New York Circuit began to act more and more like a church. The preachers who were appointed to the New York Circuit had greater oversight of individual churches which was preparing the way for the "settled" pastorates of the late 1830s. As the church became more institutionalized, the preachers also shifted their primary focus from the "prudential means of grace" of the band and class meetings to the new voluntary societies: Bible, Tract, Sunday School, and Mission. Besides attending the meetings of these societies, the preachers also served as chairmen and as members of the board of directors. Their interests were now divided and the membership felt the effect, especially as preachers did not enforce strict class meeting attendance. Apparently, they had stopped believing in its necessity, too. New priorities on respectability and education also moved Methodism further and further away from the weekly small sharing groups.

In addition to a falling off of spiritual fervor, and perhaps even more damaging to the class meeting system, was the use of the prayer meeting as an evangelistic tool. The process of becoming a Christian through the class meeting was very quickly reduced to "coming to the altar for prayer." The careful preparation of the "seeker" for full membership into the church and the deeper, lifelong assimilation into the body of Christ had been deemphasized. Without the disciplined commitment to the class meeting, the emotional effects of a "prayer meeting conversion" soon wore away.

Although institutionalization and new forms of evangelism caused New York City Methodism to go in new directions, the class leaders of the New York Circuit labored heroically. Much more than the stationed preacher, the class leader truly pastored the members in his care by evangelizing new members, reaching out to the straying ones, and, when necessary, initiating proceedings against unrepentant backsliders. The class leaders resembled the early Christian leaders who also emerged and whom the community of believers then commissioned. In this time of transition, the class leaders remained deeply committed to their assigned tasks. Their oversight of other matters such as worship and church order allowed the preachers to concentrate on their primary tasks of preaching the Word of God, administering the sacraments, and ordering the life of the church. Like the first deacons of the Jerusalem church, the class leaders took care of a range of lesser tasks.[99]   No other lay group in the New York Circuit was as critical to the spiritual development of the membership as the class leaders.

In contrast, large classes and declining class attendance overwhelmed their dedicated efforts.   Classes of thirty to seventy members completely distorted the Wesleyan ideal of small group accountability and forced class leaders to rush through their meetings or allow the meetings to run late. Large classes meant superficial encounters each week and reduced the pastoral effectiveness of the class leader who could not possibly visit every inactive member. Moreover, declining class attendance meant that the Wesleyan emphasis on holiness was no longer taken seriously. The distinctiveness of Methodism, justification joined to sanctification, had broken down after only one generation. The next twenty-five year period would bring further transformation and an even greater loss of spiritual vitality.

Methodism, however, was not alone in experiencing a decline of spiritual fervor at this time. Indeed, a number of Protestant churches such as the Congregationalists and the Presbyterians also experienced both internal and external challenges which apparently affected their membership growth.[100]   To be sure, in seventeenth century colonial America, the membership standards of these other churches had remained high. Moreover, church attendance had also been high for several reasons. First, people went to church to worship God. Second, many felt the church provided community, especially in the outlying areas. Third and last, devout parents brought their children to church. At the same time, many churchgoers were not "communicants" because of the high membership standard.   Nonetheless, many "non-communicants" took part in many of their church's activities.[101]   In addition, the populations of the middle colonies (which included New York) grew five hundred percent between 1710 and 1760 which brought even more worshipers into the churches.[102] Although many of the established Protestant churches kept membership standards high at this time, several potentially harmful conditions were occurring. First, a "religious rationalism" had begun to affect many colonial churches both in the north and the south, especially the male political leaders.[103] Second, in the years leading up to the American Revolution, Deism had become popular among the higher classes.[104]   Third, Unitarianism, which had been developing since the 1740s in response to the first

Great Awakening, weakened Congregationalism in the eighteenth century.[105] Fourth, the theological move away from strict Calvinism to Arminianism affected both the Presbyterians and the Congregationalists. As a result, the Presbyterians split into New School (or New Divinity) and Old School factions. Eventually, this split caused some Presbyterians to leave the church.[106] Fifth and last, the Congregationalists, in particular, experienced a number of internal difficulties after the Revolutionary War. For instance, a split occurred between those who favored revivals and those who didn't, causing a number of Congregationalists to join other denominations. In addition, "there also had been an upper-class defection to Anglicanism; and by 1800 Methodists were making significant inroads."[107] Another split among Congregationalists occurred along liberal-conservative lines. Finally, the repeated efforts to disestablish the Congregational Church curtailed its effectiveness.[108] Thus, even though the Congregationalists and the Presbyterians had been two of the three largest Protestant denominations before the Revolutionary War, both internal and external factors affected their ability to retain high standards of membership and doctrine. Externally, America provided so much choice and freedom that if a member was upset with the church, that member could easily go elsewhere.

Chapter 4

The Rise of Denominationalism: 1832-70

I. INTRODUCTION

As New York City Methodism took on more mainstream Protestant church characteristics in the mid-nineteenth century, a large proportion of its members stopped attending class meetings for a number of reasons, among them being that many class leaders conducted ineffective and tedious meetings, and because these same leaders also failed to hold their absent members accountable by visiting and encouraging them to return to class. Also, from 1832 to 1870, the Methodist Episcopal Churches in New York City became more "church-like." When the New York Conference began requiring a four-year course of study for new ministers, its Sunday worship services also became more formal, and, for the first time ever, a "settled pastorate"[1] was introduced. Nevertheless, a number of New York City Methodists disliked the new "congregational" polity and, in the 1840s, sought to return to the former "circuit" system. At the same time, the settled pastorate began to gradually decrease the class leaders' role of pastoral oversight, although many leaders continued their personal involvement in the ministry of the local church.[2]

On the other hand, through the medium of the Methodist press, many clergy and laity offered recommendations for improving the meetings and gave personal testimonies about the good that class meetings had accomplished in their own lives over the years. Most significant, however, was a debate, carried out from the 1850s on, about whether or not class meetings should even be required any longer for church membership - a debate which centered on three key issues: Were they Scriptural? Should church members be "excommunicated" for neglecting class? How could a requirement for an eighteenth century "religious society" also be a requirement for a much larger and more inclusive nineteenth-century denomination?[3]

II. CHANGING NATURE OF THE MINISTRY IN NEW YORK METHODISM

From 1832 to 1870, New York City Methodism acquired several more denominational characteristics. First, a "course of study" was required for those seeking ordination as traveling elders. Second, the Sunday worship service became increasingly formalized. Third and last, New York City Methodism moved to a "Congregationalist" system of "settled" pastorates.

A. MINISTERIAL EDUCATION

The first "denominational" characteristic in this period was the institution of formal educational requirements for new ministers. In 1839, the New York Conference approved a four-year ministerial "course of study" which included readings in Bible interpretation, church history, theology, Wesley's sermons, and Methodist polity.[4] In addition, candidates for the ministry also had readings in rhetoric and logic, plus a required written sermon (see Appendix 1). Moreover, approximately twenty New York Conference clergy were appointed each year as "examiners" in the various subjects and an elder's ordination depended on successfully passing the courses.[5] Also, in 1854, the New York Conference required that all candidates for "local preacher"[6] must successfully pass a similar course of study before being ordained deacon or elder.[7] At the same time, a number of individuals (usually clergy) and periodical articles recommended that class leaders undertake an "unofficial" course of study.[8] For example, an article entitled, "To Class Leaders," advised them to read a number of Wesley's own writings such as his *Journals, Sermons, Notes on the New Testament, General Rules of the Society*, and *Appeals to Men of Reason and Religion*, as well as several biographies of Wesley, and a history of the Methodist Episcopal Church.[9] Besides this article, the Reverend Charles Keys, a minister of the New York Conference offered another, more extensive "unofficial" course of study for class leaders in his 1851 Class Leader's Manual in which he recommended the following: English grammar, geography, arithmetic, scriptural commentaries, the *Discipline*, commentaries on the *Discipline*, Methodist history, the Methodist hymn book, systematic theology, practical theology, and Christian biography.[10]

Eventually, however, formal theological seminary education replaced the ministerial course of study. This idea is shown by the New York Preachers' Meeting of 14 June 1858, which discussed "the establishment of a Theological Seminary in New York or vicinity."[11] Subsequently, ten years later, in 1868, Drew Theological Seminary in Madison, New Jersey, was established and, early in the following year, the New York Preachers' Meeting heard Dr. Foster report that the seminary then had "fifty-one students there and that in a few months they expected the number would be increased to nearly one hundred."[12] In short, within exactly one hundred years (1768 to 1868), Methodism had joined all the other major American denominations in requiring formal seminary training for its ministerial candidates.[13]

In addition to seminary education, New York City Methodism also supported secondary and college education in this period. For instance, in 1834, the Conference voted to start a school in Middletown, Connecticut, to prepare students for Wesleyan University, which was also located there; a Methodist secondary school already existed at White Plains, New York.[14] In 1838, the New York Conference also resolved

> that the preacher in charge of each circuit and station in the Conference be and is hereby directed to preach a sermon on Education in all their congregations and take up collections for the benefit of the Wesleyan University which collections shall go to the credit of the circuits and stations towards the fund of twenty-five thousand dollars to be raised by this Conference.[15]

Moreover, the New York Conference also created an Education Committee to oversee these activities.[16] Thus, New York City Methodism was putting a much higher value on secondary and college education than it had in its first sixty years.

B. SUNDAY WORSHIP

The second "church-type" characteristic of New York City Methodism in this period was the way in which Sunday morning worship had been transformed in three significant ways. First, pew rentals or sales occurred intermittently, usually because almost all of the Methodist churches in lower Manhattan struggled continuously with debt. To illustrate, in 1849, the Eighteenth Street Church reversed its policy against pew rentals and began charging from five to twenty dollars a year, a decision which caused some members who objected to leave the church.[17] This new policy, however, lasted only a short time; in 1861 when the church was renovated, pews were again rented and almost every one was taken.[18] Another major change in Sunday worship was the gradual introduction of musical instruments and choirs which partially replaced the traditional congregational singing. For example, the 1834 New York Conference noted these new tendencies with concern and issued a resolution stating

> that this Conference deem it of great importance to preserve the order, simplicity, and solemnity of the public worship of Almighty God in all our churches, and with these views we affectionately request all concerned to use their influence against the introduction of instrumental music into our Congregations as a part of divine service.[19]

Moreover, David Terry, a local preacher, told the Local Preachers' Association of New York City that

> among ourselves there is a manifest departure from the simplicity of our original character - a neglect of those simple observances that are calculated to minister to the faith and piety of the people and the introduction of expensive machinery in our public worship that in no degree improve our spiritual condition. Among these may be noticed the use of musical instruments in our churches.[20]

Again, that same year, the Eighteenth Street Church hired a chorister; in 1855, a bass-viol and a flute were added and, in 1871, a large organ was installed. Similarly, another "downtown" Methodist church had added two violins to its Sunday worship.[21]

Third and last, a much more serious innovation, and one which drew some criticism, was that some Methodist preachers now read their sermons from a manuscript.[22] For instance, the 1851 *Christian Advocate and Journal* article entitled, "Sermons, Written and Unwritten," took a strong stand for extemporaneous ones. The article described three ways to prepare a sermon. The first way was to pick a Biblical passage and then think about an outline for the sermon, including illustrations. Since this was an example of the "extemporaneous" sermon, it was not to be written out. The second way was to write an outline, including phrases. The third way, which was to be done occasionally, was to write it out entirely; this was considered the least desirable. Besides its clerical detractors, many laypersons also objected to the reading of sermons; Mrs. Mary Mason wrote that after hearing a Methodist preacher read a sermon she "would prefer hearing Gospel preaching fresh from the heart, and not from notes written studiedly."[23] Again, four months later, on Sunday, 7 October 1855, after she heard the minister read his sermon in the morning she decided to read "Watson's Commentary in the evening, thinking I might as well read at home as to be listening to reading in church."[24] Likewise, the second way of writing only an outline also had difficulties, since it restricted what the preacher could do. Ideally, the article stated, the preacher should not use any notes. While acknowledging that this method could be difficult, it was generally considered to be more effective.[25] Despite its unpopularity, it apparently increased to the point where the New York Conference passed a resolution stating that

> this conference (i.e., New York), looks with deep regret upon the introduction of this practice, and expresses our disapproval of it as an injurious innovation upon apostolic Methodistic usage, and recommend to all our members the abandonment of this practice, and the continuance of the method pursued so successfully by our Fathers, of extemporaneous preaching.[26]

C. THE BEGINNINGS OF A SETTLED MINISTRY

The third, and most important, denominational characteristic in New York City Methodism was the replacement of the circuit system, or "modified itinerancy," with a "congregational" polity. First, in 1832, due to the continual growth of Methodism, the New York Circuit was subdivided into the New York East and New York West Circuits. The following churches comprised the West Circuit: John Street, Duane Street, Greene Street, Bedford Street and Twentieth Street; those of the East Circuit were Forsyth Street, Willett Street, Allen Street, Second Street, and Seventh Street (formerly Bowery Village).[27] Meanwhile, the four or five stationed preachers in each of the two circuits still rotated to the different churches in their circuit. This plan, however, only lasted until 1837-1838 when, for the first time, one minister was appointed to only one church, a practice which was also occurring more frequently throughout the denomination.[28] At the same time, individual stations were also becoming more common throughout the denomination. In this vein, an 1841 *Christian Advocate and Journal* article entitled, "Itinerant Arrangements - Stations and Circuits," acknowledged the growing number of both city and country "stations" served by one preacher. To be sure, stations had occurred earlier in New York City and other large cities because of a higher population density. Still, the article expressed concern that, in the course of a two year pastoral appointment, the preacher's sermons would grow tedious.[29]

Individual "stations," however, were a near total reversal of Wesley's original intention for his preaching corps and an innovation which a number of New York City Methodists did   not easily accept. To illustrate, Wesley had consistently understood his "helpers"[30] as "extraordinary messengers (i.e., not of the ordinary way) designed to provoke the regular ministers to jealousy and to supply their lack of service, toward those who are perishing for want of knowledge."[31] Moreover, Wesley had said at one time that he viewed "the world as my parish" and also felt that it was "his bounden duty to declare unto all that are willing to hear, the glad tidings of salvation."[32] Accordingly, he saw both his own ministry and that of his helpers as traveling evangelists rather than parish pastors. Indeed, one of his rules for helpers stated that they were to spend their time "partly in preaching and visiting from house to house and partly in reading, meditation, and prayer;"[33] such was the same way that Wesley spent his time. Again, the exclusively evangelistic nature of their work can be seen in the three principal duties of a helper: preaching twice a day, meeting the classes and bands weekly, and attending the leaders' meeting.[34] At the same time, this demanding vocation presupposed that the helpers would be young, unmarried, and healthy enough to withstand the rigors of constant traveling and occasional violence. Last of all, in the Wesleyan itinerant system, each traveling preacher was assigned to a different circuit every six months or, sometimes, every quarter.[35] Thus, Wesley's plan for his preachers was one of evangelism rather than one of pastoral care.

Similarly, early American Methodism, including New York City Methodism, had closely followed the Wesleyan model. In America, also, the full-time traveling preachers functioned as evangelists rather than parish-based clergy since the local preachers, class leaders, stewards, and trustees attended to the day-to-day pastoral concerns. From 1770 to around 1835, in New York City, the preachers retained a "messenger" role.   Furthermore, the early American general superintendents like Asbury consistently resisted a "settled ministry" among their traveling preachers. In this vein, Asbury happily wrote that "all are movable at the pleasure of the superintendent whenever he may find it necessary for the good of the cause."[36] Besides the bishops' favorable outlook on itinerancy, the ordination ceremony for new elders required that they each pledge to go wherever the bishops should send them.[37] In addition to the bishops, the 1798 *Discipline* extolled itinerancy because "everything is kept moving as far as possible; and we will be bold to say, that, next to the grace of God, there is nothing *like this* for keeping the whole body alive from the center to the circumference, and for the continual extension of that circumference on every hand."[38]   Last of all, some Methodist traditionalists saw the itinerancy as defining and differentiating Methodism from the other Protestant denominations.[39]   Granted, a number of other American Protestant denominations had used a traveling form of ministry, especially as the country moved westward, but the American Methodist itinerancy differed from them because it remained totally identified with the British Wesleyan model. For these reasons, it is evident that both American and New York City Methodism had initially highly valued and closely adhered to Wesley's original intention.[40] To be sure, the Wesleyan itinerant plan had been shifting since 1784, when the Methodist societies formed themselves into the Methodist Episcopal Church. To demonstrate, the traveling preachers were expected to function more pastorally than before, especially in the administration of the sacraments. Another change which occurred was that appointments were no longer made on a national basis but on a smaller, conference-wide one. In addition, many traveling elders were now marrying and "locating" in order to raise a family.[41]   In fact, the high number of married preachers in the period from 1800 to 1820 caused Asbury to lament that

> marriage is honorable in all - but to me it is a ceremony awful as death. Well may it be so, when I calculate we have lost the travelling labours of two hundred of the best men in America, or the world, by marriage and consequent location.[42]

As a result of the high marriage rate, local preachers soon began to outnumber the full-time traveling preachers by as much as three to one.[43] Thus, when individual stations were approved in the New York West Circuit in the late 1830s, the evolution from an itinerant, evangelistic circuit rider ministry to that of parish pastor was complete.[44]

Although a number of New York City Methodist churches were moving to a "one pastor - one church" arrangement, some New York City clergy and laity still favored the former "circuit" plan. This idea is shown in the instance of the 4 March 1844 Forsyth Street Board of Leaders' meeting when the Board of Stewards[45] requested the class leaders[46] to suggest ways that the itinerant system could be restored. Accordingly, the Board of Leaders resolved that the stationed preachers should rotate at least once a week or even more than that. In addition to the resolution, a three-member committee of class leaders was appointed to discuss the matter with the pastor.[47] Similarly, some of the stationed preachers themselves submitted another plan which was approved at the 6 January 1845 Forsyth Street leaders' meeting.[48] Furthermore, three years later, the same leaders' meeting discussed the possibility of petitioning the General Conference to restore the circuit system in both the city and county of New York.[49] A month later, an article criticized the system of appointing pastors to individual churches. Significantly, the writer, an unnamed layman, observed that

> as a rule, to which I have never yet found an exception, that just in proportion as our ministers and members have lost their adherence to the peculiarities of Methodism and contracted Congregational attachments just in that proportion their piety, their zeal, and their usefulness have diminished.[50]

Specifically, the writer suggested that three to six ministers should itinerate on circuits which had from three to four stations; one minister would be the preacher-in-charge, and the rest would be his assistants. Moreover, the circuit system could utilize the older preachers who could still preach effectively once, but not three times, on a Sunday. As a result of the restored circuit system, the three to four churches on the circuit would be drawn closer together, the various "gifts" of the preachers could be shared, and the strong preachers would balance the weaker ones.[51] Finally, in the spring of 1848, a petition from New York City was sent to the 1848 General Conference in Pittsburgh requesting that the bishops restore the circuit system to the metropolitan New York area, since they believed that a restored circuit system would lead to "a more just and equal distribution of talent, as well as a higher degree of good feeling among the Churches thus associated and bound together, and in strengthening, by means of mutual and united effort, the cause of Methodism here."[52] The Committee on Itinerancy, however, rejected the petition. On the basis of the above, it is clear that the Methodist churches of New York City did not wholeheartedly accept the new "congregational" arrangements.

D. OTHER INSTANCES OF "DENOMINATIONALISM"

Besides the move to individual, independent churches, the "appointing process" in New York City Methodism also became more "congregational." For instance, instead of the bishop unilaterally assigning a preacher every year, the individual churches now began to make their own arrangements directly; the bishop, however, still had to ratify the choice.[53] A visitor to New York City in 1863 noted that the local churches, rather than the "cabinet,"[54] had made the necessary arrangements and that "it is yet five weeks to the sessions of the New York and New York East conferences; but all the appointments for New York City and Brooklyn are already fixed, and a matter of public notoriety."[55] Despite this, the New York Conference apparently took a more guarded approach to the practice of churches calling their own pastors. In this vein, the 1836 New York Conference proposed the following two resolutions: a church could request that its next minister have certain specific ministerial talents but not ask that a specified individual be appointed and that ministers were not to ask to be appointed to a specific church.[56] In addition to the bishop's reduced role in the appointment process, it also became harder for him to deploy ministers where they were most needed since many "traveling elders" were now buying homes. As a result, most of the preachers, especially if they had families, were more reluctant to move every two or three years.[57]

Besides the difficulty in moving preachers, it had become nearly impossible to transfer a minister from one conference to another since conferences no longer wanted to accept them. Previously, a minister could be assigned to any annual conference.[58] Yet, some Methodists thought that preachers who remained in one annual conference for their whole career grew apathetic and became discouraged in their preaching, since people would grow tired of hearing them repeatedly; they thought that moving to another conference might renew their preaching.[59] In short, from the late 1830s to 1870, a majority of New York City clergy and laity apparently preferred a more autonomous local church approach in issues relating to pastoral appointments.

"Denominationalism", however, did not just happen to the New York Conference nor to New York City Methodism; apparently, they embraced this movement from sect to church, especially in this period, for several reasons. First, the second generation New York City Methodists were generally better educated and cultured. Exemplifying this is a visit that the Reverend George Coles and his family made to another Methodist pastor's home on Pearl Street in which the pastor's daughter

> entertained us with several fine pieces on the piano. We also had singing and other pleasant sources of enjoyment. Praise the Lord for the kindness and good will of those who are both pious and affluent. I could not but

think of the great difference in the temporal circumstances of many of Christ's followers.[60]

Again, three months later, Coles described the seven persons present at his Thursday morning class meeting as "all ladies, all rich, all pious."[61] As a result, many apparently desired a more learned and cultured ministry like those of the other mainline Protestant denominations. Second, the New York City and the New York Conference leadership had had a new vision since 1810, the year in which the Reverend Nathan Bangs had been appointed preacher-in-charge of the New York Circuit. In addition, the minutes of the weekly New York Preachers' Meeting indicated a drift away from evangelistic and "spiritual life" concerns to more refined literary, theological, and philosophical concerns. In fact, the New York Preachers' Meeting in this period became more of a weekly intellectual seminar than a meeting directed to the urgent promotion of evangelism and holiness. Of course, the membership of the New York Preachers' Meeting was comprised not only of local church pastors, but also college professors, visiting Methodist bishops and preachers, and publishing executives such as Dr. Bangs.[62]

Finally, the higher numbers of married clergy and the desire of some churches to keep a successful and well-liked pastor beyond the two year limit put an additional strain on the itinerancy. Moreover, there had always been clergy, from the 1780s on, who had preferred to be in large urban areas such as New York. To be sure, only Asbury's authoritarian approach to itinerancy had prevented more preachers from settling permanently in places like New York and Philadelphia. In the 1830s, however, the total opposite had occurred as many Methodists no longer viewed it as a problem. In brief, this rise of denominationalism was not so surprising since many of these policy changes had been present for some time; the New York Conference was simply acting in a cautious manner - as most institutions have done in a time of change.

III. THE CLASS LEADER IN AN ERA OF TRANSITION

At the same time, "denominationalism", and especially the settled pastorate, began to gradually modify the role of the class leader since the individual church members could now go directly, if they wished, to their stationed preacher for help with their spiritual problems instead of discussing them at their weekly class meeting.[63] On the other hand, as the class leaders' role of direct spiritual oversight gradually grew less important, they continued to perform a number of administrative duties, including some that originated in response to new pastoral concerns.

Besides its effect on itinerancy, the settled pastorate meant that the primary spiritual role of the class leader, which was to provide edification and correction, was in danger of becoming obsolete since the preacher was theoretically available to his flock on a daily basis for counseling and prayer, instead of only once every four or six weeks. Granted, declining class attendance in this period, which was a completely different issue altogether, was also a factor in the class leader's weakened "spiritual" role in the local church. Yet, this shift to clergy pastoral care apparently occurred slowly since the Manhattan-stationed preachers allowed the class leaders to function as they always had. Indeed, records of this transitional period from "circuit to station" indicate that the preachers' priorities were not so much focused on providing direct pastoral care to their congregations as on their weekly sermons, church administration, and social visits.[64]   Again, David Holsclaw has noted in his denominational study of the class meeting that

> Methodist values had changed. Ministers defined their duties in terms of pulpit performance and the administration of Sunday School, missionary, tract, Bible, and temperance societies. Close pastoral supervision and the cultivation of disciplined fellowship were no longer priorities.[65]

Although "stationed preachers" represented a potentially significant change in pastoral oversight, both the regional annual conferences and the denomination still viewed the class leader's role in spiritual terms. For instance, it was the class leaders, rather than the preachers, who were expected to visit absent and sick class members. Indeed, part of the Pastoral Address of the 1858 New Jersey Conference stated that

> much, very much, too, depends upon the class leader. If he is diligent in looking after the delinquent members, not resting till he knows the cause of their absence from class, and then endeavors, with all that solicitude which the love of Christ inspires, to lead them back to God, few if any, need be lost.[66]

In addition to visitation, many class leaders remained in key ministry roles. Exemplifying this is that four out of the five exhorters in the Forsyth Street Church in 1842 (five years after many Manhattan churches became "independent") were also class leaders.[67]   Similarly, the Board of Leaders at some of the Manhattan Methodist Churches periodically appointed a committee of class leaders to supervise their church's weekly prayer meeting.[68]

Although the class leaders' spiritual oversight role was about to undergo some change, they continued to perform a number of administrative duties, such as attending the weekly leaders' meetings.[69] Also, many class leaders retained administrative positions as stewards, trustees, and members of church building committees.[70] In this vein, in 1852-1854, at the Forsyth Street Methodist Church, thirteen out of sixteen trustees and three out of six stewards were also class leaders.[71] Again, Methodist obituaries of this period indicate that some class leaders had other local church administrative responsibilities besides being stewards and trustees. Specifically, William S. Hunt, the founder of the Eighteenth Street Church, had been a class leader, trustee, steward, and Sabbath School superintendent over a forty year period.[72]

In fact, even after 1838, class leaders sometimes took on new roles of service. For example, the Reverend Charles Keys, in his *Class Leader's Manual* published in 1851, compared the new social outreach of Methodist class leaders to that of deacons in the early church.[73] Also, the minutes of several Board of Leaders' meetings in the 1830s and 1840s reveal that small committees of class leaders were specifically appointed to care for the needs of the poor in their areas. On 2 July 1838, the Forsyth Street leaders' meeting appointed a committee of three class leaders to see which church members needed help. In addition, all class leaders had to give the names of any church members they knew who were in financial need.[74] Again, on 3 May 1841, the same Board of Leaders' meeting appointed a committee to visit those members who had requested financial help; three class leaders plus the needy member's own class leader comprised the committee.[75] Furthermore, five years later, the Forsyth Street Church class leaders "were requested to hand the names and residences of the poor of their classes to the stewards previous to their next meeting."[76] Finally, class leaders occasionally worked together with their stationed preacher on specific, short-term quasi-administrative projects such as the temperance cause. An example of this occurred in February, 1849, when the New York Preachers' Meeting contacted the Forsyth Street leaders' meeting about the possibility of forming a committee comprised of the preacher and four class leaders. This committee was to propose ways to achieve temperance and also to meet periodically with all the other local church temperance committees.[77] In summary, although most Manhattan churches now had their own ministers, the class leaders of each church still provided some pastoral oversight although their main role now seemed to be administrative; moreover, their pastoral oversight role apparently decreased because of the decline in class meeting attendance rather than the clergy explicitly or implicitly taking on more pastoral care of the membership.[78]

IV. THE DECLINE OF THE CLASS MEETING

As New York City Methodism was acquiring more denominational qualities, many members apparently no longer supported the weekly class meeting concept. From 1832 to 1870, a number of New York City Methodist class books indicate that class meeting attendance levels, on the average, were consistently low. Three principal reasons, drawn especially from numerous articles in the *Christian Advocate and Journal* over a forty year period, apparently account for this change.[79] First, class meetings were too long and became tedious because they often went beyond their normal one hour length. Next, the heart of the class meeting, the-question-and-answer-format, had become "unedifying". Finally, many class leaders failed to visit and encourage their absent members, which lessened the members' accountability and also gave the impression that the leaders were not concerned for their spiritual well-being.

A. EXTENT OF CLASS MEETING DECLINE IN NEW YORK CITY

Extant class books[80] in this approximately forty year period reveal a consistently low weekly attendance pattern. To demonstrate, the weekly average attendance in Anthony Tieman's class at the Seventh Street Church for thirteen "quarters",[81] ranged between 14 and 40 percent, but was mostly around 20 to 25 percent.[82] Similarly, a class at the Eighteenth Street Church had a 25 percent weekly attendance from 1850 to the first half of 1851, but, in the next two years, it dropped from 20 to 8 percent.[83] Also, Henry Wicker's class at Allen Street Church averaged from 15 to 33 percent from September, 1855, to July, 1858.[84] Likewise, Henry Moore's class, also at Allen Street, averaged from 17 to 50 percent, with most of the average quarterly attendance around 30 to 40 percent.[85] Another Allen Street class, conducted by Samuel R. Spelman, averaged 12 members out of a total of 35, or one-third of its members, from 2 April 1858 to 10 December 1858. In 1859, William Bennett took over the class and average weekly attendance fell to 20 percent.[86] Again, the Allen Street "preacher's class" (usually the largest class in every Manhattan Methodist Church) averaged only 6 members out of 60, or just over 10 percent, from 5 May 1859 to 3 November 1859.[87]

This trend of poorly attended classes is further confirmed by several other Allen Street Church classes in the 1860s, such as Samuel H. Smith's class which had an average weekly attendance of 15 out of 65 to 70 members, or approximately 20 percent of the class.[88] In the same way, James H. McIntosh's Allen Street class averaged about 2 out of 8 to 9 members, or approximately 25 percent.[89] Finally, almost a decade later, the class book of Richard Newton revealed nearly identical figures; from 18 May 1871 to 25 April 1872, his 28 member class averaged a little more than 7 members, which was slightly over one quarter of the class.[90] Besides the Allen Street figures, the New York District reports at the annual New York Conference meetings further confirmed that New York City class attendance had continued to decrease into the mid-1870s. In this vein, the 1874 New York district report stated that "inquiries have been made in regard to the attendance on class meeting, and it has been found that only about one half of the members of our churches habitually attend class."[91] Class attendance figures, however, for New York City churches were apparently higher in 1880 as the churches tried to get class members to come voluntarily, without the threat of expulsion, thus indicating a total shift from the original Wesleyan discipline. To demonstrate, the "Report of the Brooklyn District" stated that

> an effort, quite general and somewhat persistent, has been made to secure better class meeting attendance. The effort has been so far successful that the attendance is increasing rather than falling off on the district, and it is shown that as good an attendance can be secured on the voluntary plan as was secured by the attempted compulsory one.[92]

In short, both city and district records show that class meeting attendance had dropped from previously higher levels.

B. FIRST REASON FOR DECLINE: LENGTH OF MEETING

At the same time, three main reasons were advanced for this pattern of low attendance.[93] The first "internal" class meeting problem was that meetings sometimes lasted from one-and-a-half to three hours instead of the normal one hour for several reasons. First, class meetings did not always start on time. Second, the class leaders often had a long opening prayer which sometimes lasted for thirty minutes followed by a long "opening address" in which he recounted his past week's spiritual experience. Then, a long opening hymn might be sung. Finally, some class members took ten to fifteen minutes to relate their spiritual progress while some class leaders took the same amount of time to respond.[94]

Apparently the problem was recognized because a number of recommendations were given to keep the meeting to its original length of one hour. First, some urged that the opening prayer, the opening address, and the opening hymn be shortened. Next, some advocated that hymns should not be sung after each member's testimony, and when they were sung, only one verse should be used. Moreover, a number of articles stressed that the responses of class leaders and members should be restricted to only a few minutes. Equally important, the Reverend James Finley, in his article, "Rules for Leading Class," stressed that the class leader must follow the regular pattern of calling upon each member in turn who then should speak so all can hear. He also recommended that if the class leader could not call on all the members in one hour, he should begin with the others first at the next meeting.[95] Finally, another article suggested that class leaders should not respond to each class member individually, but only exhort at the beginning and end of the meeting. Eliminating individual responses, the writer felt, would have a positive effect since

> the present custom (with us at least) is, after hearing one speak, to give an exhortation to him or her, as the case may be; and so on throughout the class, so that necessarily there is a great deal of repetition, which, in most cases, is productive of stupor, precisely repugnant to the design of the institution.[96]

Accordingly, the difficulty in calling on everyone to speak in one hour because of large classes was readily evident in New York City Methodism. For example, in 1842, John Street Church had five classes in the 10-19 member range and five which were 20-29 members; just a few years later, however, only two classes had 10-19 members while ten now had between 20 and 50 members.[97] Similarly, in 1842-1843, Forsyth Street Church had seven classes with 10-19 members and twenty-one with 20-49 members. A year later, only three Forsyth Street Church classes had 10-19 members while twenty-four had 20 to over 50 members.[98] Furthermore, in 1838, Allen Street Church had five classes with 10 to 19 members and thirty-five, or 87 percent, with 20 to over 50 members.[99] On the other hand, in 1837, Seventh Street Church had the same number in both the 10 to 19 and the 20 to 29 member categories: five in each. In 1845, when its number of classes had doubled, the percentage still remained about the same: eleven classes in the 10 to 19 member category, nine in the 20 to 29, and one each in the 30 to 39 and 40 to 49 categories (see Appendix 5).[100]

Despite the many helpful recommendations offered to class leaders in this period, these two and three hour meetings were causing many members to come reluctantly or to stop attending altogether. This is shown by the experience of many young, unmarried women who boarded at other people's homes; evening meetings which went past ten o'clock caused problems with their landlords.[101] Similarly, long meetings affected young married women who had small children at home. A woman who hadn't been attending her class meeting told her minister that

> the class hour is a source of great comfort to my soul; I would seldom, if ever miss it, but my good leader keeps me for two to three hours every time I go. You see my charge. There are four little children, one quite young, and I have no one to leave with them, except my husband. Occasionally I could leave them for an hour; but it is impossible for me as a mother to leave them and do my duty.[102]

In brief, class leaders who lacked attention to detail and who were not sensitive to the schedules of their members, especially the female ones, apparently were the cause of some of the steady decline in class meeting attendance.

C. SECOND REASON FOR DECLINE: BOREDOM WITH MEETING

In addition to lengthy meetings, the second internal problem of the class meeting was the increasing superficiality of the "class leader - class member" dialogue, which made the meetings dull and unedifying.[103] Furthermore, this problem had three distinct components: the class leader's questions to the member, the response of the class members, and the class leader's individual exhortations. As a result of these unsatisfying and repetitive meetings, a number of articles were published in the *Christian Advocate and Journal* containing suggestions on how to enliven the discussions. Thus, class leaders were advised to ask more specific questions than the traditional "How does your soul prosper?" or "How is it with you?" General questions tended to elicit vague answers, thus preventing the leader from determining their true spiritual state and giving them the appropriate advice.[104] Another article suggested that the class leader ask the class members to conduct a kind of spiritual examination by asking specific questions which dealt with various aspects of discipleship such as

Do you read the Bible daily? Do you pray in private? Do you fast? Do you enjoy religion? Do you feel that you that are progressing in grace from day to day? Do you feel the remains of anger, pride, self-will, the carnal mind which is enmity against God.[105]

As a result, class members would have to think beforehand how they had fulfilled their responsibilities. In the same way, the article, "Formality in Class Meetings," suggested that the class leader ask specific questions which bore on that particular individual's circumstances, such as "Can you tell us what discouragements these have been?" or "What leads you to think you have been making progress?"[106] Equally important, the class leader should stress "conversational" responses from each class member rather than "speeches," since an open sharing would break the monotony. Finally, the article instructed class leaders not to have their class members simply focus on inward feelings, but also upon their outward duties since a focus on feelings could quickly lead to antinomianism. Moreover, a focus on outward discipleship was especially important for persons who had been converted in revivals and who needed to understand that feelings were secondary to the "fruits of the Spirit," or the actual practice of Christian virtue.[107] Consequently, class leaders were being urged to try new approaches to enliven classes which had grown repetitive and dull.

At the same time, class members were criticized for responding to the leader's questions with vague words and phrases such as "prospering, getting on, pressing forward, careless, lukewarm, neglected private prayer, neglected reading the Scriptures, broken resolutions, and listened to the voice of the tempter."[108] Also, some class members did not simply relate their spiritual experience of the past week, but spoke about other things.[109] To be sure, a successful class meeting depended on the class member's faithful attendance and prior preparation. Exemplifying the "model" class member was the description given in the 1846 article, "Backsliders," which told how these members

> do not tell the same old stereotyped story over and over from week to week; but being in the way of cultivating their minds and hearts, by a regular course of reading, meditation and prayer, they always have something new to say at every meeting. There is a freshness and interest in their testimony which show they are growing in grace.[110]

Similarly, class leaders were urged to respond to each individual class member with very specific advice. As an illustration, another article noted that if the leader is always "dealing in general terms of encouragement or of caution, and never coming to particulars, the members are not drawn out, they will learn to speak in like general terms; many of them will by and by say as little as possible."[111] Of course, individualized replies were dependent on knowing each class member personally; this could only occur if the leader visited his absent members. Similarly, the article, "Responsibilities of Class Leaders," compared a class leader speaking to his class members to a surgeon operating on patients who had different sicknesses.[112] Besides knowing their class members on an individual basis, class leaders were also urged to develop a comprehensive understanding of the Scriptures in order to use them as the basis of their replies, as well as in their prayers during class.[113] At the same time, these personalized replies, based on the Scriptures, had to also be able to touch the heart and to inspire each class member since a class meeting was not the place to discuss theology.[114] Finally, a class leader was advised to speak prudently and "weigh a matter before he pronounces an opinion, or proffers counsel, more desirous to give a safe answer than a ready one, and to offer a weighty saying than a smart one."[115] In short, a profitable class meeting depended both on the creativity, sensitivity, and spirituality of the class leader and the spiritually-prepared class member.

Besides the recommendation to shorten various elements of the class meeting and improve the "class leader-class member" exchange, four other "internal" improvements were suggested. First, the article, "Interchange of Leaders," advised leaders to meet each other's classes, in order to keep the meetings lively.[116] The article also compared the interchange of leaders to the itinerant ministry: both preacher and leader should be rotated to avoid repetition. Otherwise, to meet the same class "every week, with as many addresses, short and suitable, is no small task; and the wonder is, with this task so often recurring, not that our leaders fail in its performance, but that they perform it so acceptably, and preserve the interest, and add to the utility of our classes."[117] In contrast, some believed that class leaders who rotated would not be able to give appropriate advice since they didn't know the class members well. Granted, the class leader's knowledge of each member was limited, but he could still advise those members who were open to him.[118] A second suggestion aimed at the internal working of the class meeting was that unsuitable class leaders should be promptly removed from office so that the class would not be ruined. A leader, however, should only be changed when the problem was severe, since it was difficult to find good replacements.[119] Obviously, removing a leader could be a delicate matter, and one Methodist writer in this period recommended that setting a two-to-three year limit for class leaders would make it easier to eliminate the ineffective ones. In addition, a two-to-three year limit would also eliminate the boredom that could come from having the same leader for many years, since "what leader has the ability to interest his class for the life-term; his hearers are the same, his topics are the same, he is the same."[120] Also, a term limit would prevent the situation of a long-time leader gradually accepting the faults of his class members without correcting them.[121] Third and last, another *Christian Advocate and Journal* article entitled, "Class Meetings: Existing Evils - Remedy Proposed," suggested a return to single-sex classes and the appointment of female class leaders to female classes. As a result, female class leaders would make up for the shortage of male leaders and also for the incompetent ones who could be removed when this new plan went into effect. Besides, a female class leader could more easily discuss temptations particular to women; female class members could also speak more freely to a woman. Furthermore, a female leader could visit her class members without the difficulty a male leader would have. In brief, a number of other ideas were suggested in this period to deal with the persistent problems of boredom and ineffective leadership.[122]

D. THIRD REASON FOR DECLINE: FAILURE TO MAKE HOME VISITATIONS

Besides these two problems, there was the third problem that class leaders no longer visited their absent members. This apparently contributed to the growing decline in class meeting attendance both in New York City and throughout the denomination. For instance, the lack of class leader visitation at mid-century caused the Reverend

Charles Keys to write that, from what he had observed, most class
leaders did not visit their absent members.[123] Also, the unnamed writer
of an 1845 *Christian Advocate and Journal* article noted that some
class leaders were not visiting absent members.[124] Similarly, the 1845
article, "Do You Visit Your Delinquent Class Members?" urged class
leaders to fulfil this responsibility since statistics showed that twenty-
five percent of all probationers never completed their probation.[125]
Equally important, the ministerial non-enforcement of the class
attendance rule also signaled a further laxness and lowering of
standards for membership which some called an "accommodation"
rather than an "improvement" in Methodism.[126] One writer to the
Christian Advocate and Journal asserted that the lessening of discipline
was weakening Methodism; the church might gain new members but
these same members would not develop a sound spirituality and would
also remain "worldly" because the accountability on discipleship had
been lowered.[127] The writer asked

> has the non-enforcement of plain "old fashioned" disciplinary
> requirements, such as refer to dress, class meetings, love feasts, band
> meetings, etc., "improved" it? True, the accommodation principle - the
> becoming of all things unto all men - may gain more readily the great, the
> learned, and the wealthy, and their addition to our numbers, and perhaps to
> our wealth: but does it "improve" Methodism?[128]

At the same time, some circuits and conferences attempted to restore
higher standards. Exemplifying this was the unified decision of the
Philadelphia Preachers' Meeting in 1834 to enforce the rule on non-
attendance.[129] To be sure, expelling a "nominal professor" who gave
money to the church but did not attend class meetings could be
difficult, but it should nevertheless be done. Several Methodist
observers noted how a number of consecutive preachers at the same
church tolerated non-attendance; obviously, they preferred leaving the
unpleasant task of disciplining the members to their successors. While
enforcing the rule might anger some long-time influential members, a
number of "traditionalists" believed it would ultimately prove
beneficial to the church.[130]

To be sure, these isolated efforts by some individual groups such as
the Philadelphia Preachers' Meeting did some good in boosting
attendance, but many believed that the solution to low attendance was
diligent class leader visitation which would, in turn, make class
members more accountable. In 1845, the Reverend Finley wrote that
leaders should

inquire at the close of your meeting about those who are absent. Never omit this. And if possible, go right from your class room to see the absentees, and you will not have to do this more than twice or thrice until your delinquent brother or sister will say, "I must go to class, or my leader will be after me."[131]

Likewise, a Brooklyn, New York, class leader attributed his high weekly class attendance to his practice of faithfully visiting absent members. For instance, over a one year period the average class attendance for his eighteen member class was sixteen and a half. This leader did not view visitation as a means of putting pressure on them to attend, but as an expression of how much he cared for them; gradually, this pastoral concern made them take their commitment seriously.[132] Accordingly, he could say that

> they may at first stay away on trifling excuses; but when they find you are faithful, that you never fail, they will come. Your practice will force upon them the conviction that you care more for their soul's welfare than they themselves do.[133]

In the same way, he gave an example of a woman in his class who, in previous years, had missed many classes, but in the past year had missed only two. Her attendance had dramatically improved because she knew her class leader would visit if she was absent.[134]

Besides the encouraging reports of class leaders who visited their absent members, a number of class members also related how significant a visit from their class leader had been in helping them remain active in both class and church. As an illustration, one man recalled a time, forty years before, when he had become upset with another member of his class. Accordingly, he did not go church nor to class meeting that week and was planning to give up Christianity altogether. His class leader, however, who thought his absent member had been sick, came to see him on the following Monday and discussed his problem. As a result, the class member decided to come back to the church because "this affectionate care and kind attention of the leader broke the snare of the fowler, convinced the writer that he had got among the right kind of Christians, whose economy was well calculated to help the feeble and build them up in their most holy faith."[135] In the same way, a young man from Baltimore had had an argument with his employer in which he

> felt condemned and did not go to class that week, and concluded not to go anymore. On the next Sunday, while in church, I reflected on what my

leader had said, and concluded to go to class again, and did go; and to this day I am holding fast, and shall ever thank God that my leader visited me.[136]

Likewise, another class leader's visit helped a member, who had stayed away from class for four weeks, to return. The member had been struggling with the idea that he had never truly been converted; during the visit, the leader encouraged him and, on the following day, he spoke with him again and also gave him a book to read on the subject. In addition, they arranged to go together to the next class meeting.[137] On the basis of the above, faithful class leader visitation apparently produced higher levels of accountability on the part of their class members.

Conversely, class leaders who did not visit gave the impression that they did not care about their absent members. An 1845 article entitled, "Class Leaders II: Their Duties," reported how a minister visited someone who had been neglecting class. The minister said that this behavior had made the class leader unhappy. The class member replied that his class leader had never even visited him and when they met at church or in the neighborhood, the leader still did not bring up his repeated absences. Since the leader apparently didn't care about his spiritual condition, the class member was losing interest in the church.[138] Of course, the problem of declining class attendance often went beyond "accountability issues" to a radical shift in the way New York City Methodists viewed the life of discipleship. To demonstrate, during this period, the rise of the "voluntary associations"[139] apparently adversely affected weekly class attendance as many Methodists joined one or more of these organizations since these "new missionary, tract, Bible and Sunday School associations offered the same (if not better) opportunities for service and enhanced status as traditional Wesleyan institutions."[140] Most significant, these new associations required less accountability on the part of the members (unlike the class meeting) while, at the same time, they demanded much time and effort which probably reduced the time available for members to attend their class meeting and for class leaders to visit their absent members.[141]

Of course, some class leader visitation was still conducted in this period for specific disciplinary reasons, rather than pastoral outreach to those who had failed to attend. Exemplifying this was the action taken by the Forsyth Street Board of Leaders' meeting on several occasions. First, at an 1837 leaders' meeting, three committees made up of two to three class leaders each, reported the results of their visits to errant members. Class leaders Donaldson, Higgins, and Truslow reported that the brother whom they had visited had responded positively to their admonition. Abraham Riker and Lancaster Burling also reported that they had seen Abijah Abbott, and a third committee reported a positive outcome with a brother who had been drinking intemperately.[142] Again, on 7 November 1842, three Forsyth Street class leaders were appointed as a committee to visit a member who was selling spiritous liquors, and on 6 February 1843, another committee of class leaders recommended after their recent visit that a probationer (the same one?) be dropped for the same offense.[143]

V. REQUIRED CLASS MEETINGS: THE DEBATE

Besides the class meeting's problems in the mid-nineteenth century, numerous voices in both New York City Methodism and in the denomination at large wanted to abolish completely the rule concerning required class attendance as a condition of church membership for several reasons. First, they opposed it on the grounds that the requirement was not scriptural. Second, they did not believe a member should be excommunicated for a matter which was not considered essential for salvation. Third and last, they argued that class meetings should not be required since they were originally part of a commitment to a "religious society" and not to a more inclusive "church." At the same time, supporters of the rule on class attendance countered with arguments of their own. The debate, which was carried out primarily in the Methodist press, in the class manuals of that period, in the deliberations of the New York Conference, and in the New York Preachers' Meeting, was ultimately resolved when the 1908 General Conference of the Methodist Episcopal Church (north)[144] abolished required class attendance.

A. CLASS MEETING NOT SCRIPTURAL REQUIREMENT

The first argument against required class meetings was that they were not scriptural, unlike the sacraments of baptism and holy communion which had been expressly commanded. As in the earlier period, supporters of the class meeting requirement admitted that Scripture did not require them, but that numerous passages in the Old and New Testaments appeared to provide a strong rationale for them.[145] In this vein, several Scriptures seemed to support the creation of class meetings by their admonition for leaders to watch over the flock.[146] Moreover, the Reverend Charles Keys believed that the classes were the way in which the Methodist leadership carried out this admonition to provide pastoral care contained in Jesus' words to Peter, "Feed my sheep."[147]   Keys noted that other denominations might approach pastoral care differently but that they were all striving for the same general goal. In addition, the pastoral relationship went both ways; the Scriptures, specifically Hebrews 13:17 and 1 Corinthians 16:15-16, also exhorted church members to accept the oversight of their leaders. Finally, Keys compared Methodist classes to the "teachers" and "helps" mentioned in the list of ministries in 1 Corinthians 12:25; he argued that the class leader was someone who taught others.[148]   Another justification for class meetings drawn from the Scriptures was the New Testament admonition for Christians to grow in their faith.   To illustrate, the article "The Scriptural Basis of Class Meetings," admitted that while they were not specifically mentioned in Scripture the churches had been free in every period to devise ways to help their members achieve holiness.   Moreover, the Biblical view that a Christian must separate from the world and that the church was a distinct group within the larger society confirmed the need for a support system.[149] For these reasons, Methodism had chosen class meetings as its key pastoral structure.[150] Hence, against the argument that Scripture did not require class meetings, Methodist traditionalists stressed that some mechanism was essential for the spiritual growth required in the New Testament, and that class meetings appeared to fit the broad guidelines given in the Scriptures.

In addition to the articles in the Methodist press on this subject, the New York Preachers' Meeting also spent four meetings in the fall of 1868 discussing the question, "Are class meetings authorized by the Holy Scriptures?"   To be sure, the discussions were lively, with preachers taking both sides of the issue. For instance, at the 11 October 1868 meeting, ten preachers spoke to the question and "on motion of the Reverend E. E. Griswold it was ordered that the same subject be taken up for discussion at our next meeting."[151] Also, at the last three meetings in which the question was discussed, the length of the preachers' meeting had to be extended so that all those who wanted to could speak.   Besides the high number of speakers, it was unusual for one question to be extended over several weeks.[152] Thus, in addition to a "denominational" discussion, the New York City preachers also struggled with the question.

B. *SALVATION POSSIBLE WITHOUT CLASS ATTENDANCE*

A second, and much more compelling, theological argument against required class meetings was that church members should not be excommunicated for something that was clearly not essential for salvation. In arguing that position, the Reverend Hiram Mattison of New York City asked

> What right, then, have we to make the door of Christ's church on earth more strait than the gate of heaven? Think of it. Turning persons out of the Methodist Episcopal Church, whom Christ is ready and willing to welcome to paradise? Who hath required this at our hands?[153]

Moreover, the rule was then virtually unenforced since many Methodist clergy could no longer accept excommunicating members for neglect of class. Therefore, opponents of the rule began to suggest that they be optional; but keeping an unenforceable rule in the Discipline, they argued, only made the church lose credibility.[154] Exemplifying this change of attitude on the part of many clergy was Reverend Mattison's account of a New York Preachers' Meeting where he stated that he

> once heard the venerable Dr. Bangs say, at the close of a preacher's meeting in New York, where the subject had been discussed, that he never excluded but one person from the Church merely for not attending class, and that he was always sorry for that. And so many pastors feel; they are not clear that Christ will justify the enforcement of such a rule.[155]

Conversely, supporters of the rule admitted that salvation was not dependent on class attendance; rather, they viewed this argument in terms of church membership. To demonstrate, supporters of required class attendance argued that since every Christian church was free to make its own rules, members of the Methodist Episcopal Church had to abide by the particular rules of the denomination or risk expulsion. In their opinion, a Methodist who did not attend class had effectively withdrawn from the pastoral oversight of the church.[156] Furthermore, supporters of the rule noted that expelling members for neglect of class did not cut them off entirely from the church as "progressives" had argued; they were still free to join another church.[157] Again, traditionalists also argued that the Methodist Episcopal Church was entitled to set high standards for members since these standards were intended to help them grow spiritually. If church members neglected this important "prudential" means of grace, so the argument went, then they should follow their behavior to its logical conclusion and leave the church and join another which did not require these meetings.[158]   In short, Methodist traditionalists believed that the membership "covenant" took preference over an individual's feelings about the necessity of class meetings.

C. CLASS MEETINGS APPROPRIATE TO "RELIGIOUS SOCIETY" ONLY

Third and last, the progressive-minded Methodists believed that required class meetings were certainly appropriate for a "religious society" which existed within a Christian church, but not for the members of an entire denomination.[159]   In this vein, Charles Adams asserted that a religious society could make strict rules for its members who had joined voluntarily, but that a church had to be more inclusive (i.e., set easier membership standards). Furthermore, Adams stated that he had

> long been unable to account for the apparent want of discrimination between the ecclesiastical status of Mr. Wesley's societies and that of the membership of the Methodist Episcopal Church. As Bro. Mattison has faithfully shown, the societies alluded to were but *societies* - societies in contradistinction from a *church* (societies in the sense precisely of temperance or anti-slavery societies).[160]

In contrast, supporters of required class meetings did not directly answer that objection but continually warned that eliminating them would weaken the spirituality of the church. Exemplifying this were the many Methodists who wrote articles and editorials in the *Christian Advocate and Journal* over a forty-year period linking regular class attendance to spiritual vitality and, conversely, neglect of class with spiritual decline.[161]   Similarly, traditionalists argued that a Methodist Episcopal Church, without the class meeting rule, would probably have a larger membership but one that was more worldly and less inclined to discuss their spiritual lives. Besides, a large increase in numbers was actually to be guarded against since numerical success "of this sort could only be a strain and incubus on the energies of God's people."[162] Consequently, even though Methodism had shed most of its "sect-like" traits, supporters of the rule maintained the necessity of high standards in order to retain spiritual fervor among the membership.

VI. CONCLUSION

New York City Methodism had clearly entered mainstream American Protestantism by the end of its first one hundred years. The number of New York City Methodist churches and its total membership had grown rapidly from 1832 to 1870, but its structure and spirituality had undergone a number of changes.[163] To illustrate, it was no longer persecuted and looked down upon, nor distinctive for its fervent, evangelical preaching and spirited worship. It more easily attracted persons from the middle class of society as its formerly high membership standards were relaxed, especially the expectation of weekly class attendance. Its settled pastors began to resemble the clergy of the other Protestant churches in theological training and preaching style, although a seminary degree was only beginning to be required. In fact, even its local preachers and class leaders were also expected to be well-read in Bible, church history, and theology.

To be sure, the settled pastorate, which began in 1837-1838, did not totally, at first, eliminate the sub-pastoral role of the class leaders since many of the stationed preachers concentrated primarily on preaching and administration. Moreover, many New York City preachers spent a considerable portion of their time attending meetings: the Board of Leaders, the New York Preachers' Meeting, the voluntary boards (i.e., the Tract Society, Bible Society, Sunday School, Missionary Society, and Juvenile Missionary Society), and special, ad-hoc committees which often arose in response to specific needs such as the local temperance committees. Although the New York City preachers no longer traveled a circuit, pastoral visitation was still regarded as the responsibility of the class leaders. In fact, the New York City class leaders, to judge from the Quarterly Conference and Board of Leaders' minutes of the various churches from 1832 to 1870, seem to have been involved in slightly more pastoral and administrative tasks, rather than less. The difference, however, in this period was that these tasks had little or nothing to do with the weekly class meeting.

At the same time, class leaders seem to have had difficulty fulfilling their responsibilities to the class meeting. Granted, large classes probably prevented many New York City class leaders from visiting absent or sick class members, but the problems of over-extension and a lack of pastoral zeal seem to have also contributed to a breakdown in the class leader-class member relationship. The lack of class leader visitation most likely contributed to a lowering of accountability among the membership, as it became easier to routinely miss one's class meeting without the class leader or the local congregation (through a church trial) taking any corrective action. Without direct, personal admonition to keep seeking holiness, it was easier for neglectful class members to drift along, perhaps going to church but not striving for a deeper transformation in Christ which could occur in the weekly class meeting. Since the class leaders had the direct pastoral oversight of their class members and many apparently let these duties lapse, it seems safe to say that they should bear some of the responsibility for declining class attendance. To be sure, there must have been some leaders who conducted their class meeting duties in traditional fashion and faithfully attended their leaders' meetings, but the class books of a number of New York City Methodist churches reveal consistently low weekly attendance.

Besides the apparent lukewarmness of the class leaders, the very nature of the class meeting system was increasingly being called into question. Since many of the articles which were critical of required class attendance were printed in the Methodist press, it seems likely that, even on the highest levels, the Methodist Episcopal Church was permitting both sides to be heard. As "institutionalization increased", Methodism seemed less certain about what it was supposed to proclaim and also how it was supposed to help its members, especially its new converts, grow in grace. The class meeting, once the strength of Methodism, had now begun to sharply decline, and the majority of its preachers and class leaders in New York City, as well as throughout the denomination, seemed unable or unwilling to restore its former glory.

Conclusion

The Class Meeting and the Churches Today

I. INTRODUCTION

Although Methodism has been consistently declining, along with other mainline Protestant denominations, for the past thirty years, a reintroduction of the class meeting can revitalize the church's efforts to initiate people into the faith and also to assimilate them into the body of Christ in such a way that they can progressively grow in holiness. To be sure, the period from 1870 to 1890 saw Methodism complete the move from "society to church" as it became even more bureaucratized and its membership and doctrinal standards continued their liberalizing tendencies causing a decline in membership and an exodus of some of the more "traditional" members into new Methodist-type sects. Despite this downward trend, an examination of the "Wesleyan synthesis" (i.e., justification by faith and holy living) and the twin Wesleyan emphases of a carefully prepared initiation into membership and disciplined spiritual nurture (both accomplished in the weekly class meeting) can guide present-day church renewal efforts. Indeed, the newer, mostly unaffiliated churches which began in the late 1960s and early 1970s have used a number of "Methodist" pastoral strategies, including the weekly small group meeting, to both evangelize and ground their members in the faith.

II. 1784: THE CRITICAL TURNING POINT

The decision to become a church in 1784 greatly affected Methodism's ability to set and enforce high membership standards. At the same time, the move from "society to church" paralleled, in some ways, the fourth century legalization of Christianity from a persecuted religion to an accepted one. Eventually, however, the consequences of denominationalism caused Methodism to both lower its doctrinal standards and to enter a sustained period of membership loss beginning in the 1850s. Finally, new "reform movements" within the Methodist Episcopal Church split off from the main body to retain earlier Wesleyan principles and practices.[1]

A. METHODIST PARALLELS WITH CONSTANTINIAN CHRISTIANITY

Obviously, the decision to withdraw from the Church of England to form an entirely new denomination was the significant turning point for Methodist spirituality as expressed particularly in the pastoral structures of society, class, and band.[2]   Subsequently, American Methodism was forced to turn its collective attention to other things, such as building churches and parsonages, developing a denominational-wide Sunday School curriculum, and raising funds. To be sure, the number of churches and members grew in New York City during the nineteenth century (although the denomination as a whole started to decline in membership after 1850) but it was a different church to which these new members were added. Moreover, this change that Methodism was soon to undergo was analogous, in some ways, to the change which Christianity experienced after its legalization in 313 A. D. To illustrate, pre-313 Christianity and pre-1784 Methodism had a number of common characteristics. First, both groups initially required a high level of commitment to become a member. Another similarity was that both pre-313 Christianity and pre-1784 Methodism required prospective members to go through a stated period of doctrinal instruction (i.e., the catechumenate). At the same time, once Christianity had been legalized and Methodism had become a denomination, membership standards were gradually relaxed and both groups began to tolerate a much higher number of "nominal" Christians in their midst. In fact, in referring to the church of the late fourth century, Saint Augustine compared it to the parable of the wheat and the tares growing together, implying that the church was now "mixed" and that God would sort it out at the judgment.[3] Again, in the post-313 period, church membership was seen as the socially acceptable thing to do for both business and social purposes.

B. CONSEQUENCES OF DENOMINATIONALISM

Methodism's new identity as a church forced it to be more inclusive of a multitude of differing views on polity, practice, and spirituality. These differing views, however, resulted in the lowering of both doctrinal and moral standards. In fact, Finke and Stark have shown how difficult it is for a "church" to hold its spiritual and institutional lives together since "churches serve the segment of the market with less need for a strict and otherworldly faith; sects serve the segment seeking those features."[4] A second consequence of Methodism's denominational identity in the nineteenth century was that new people were no longer being drawn to Methodism now that its message, clergy, and local church organization were indistinguishable from the other Protestant churches. Indeed, apparently it is the religious groups which set the high standards, rather than the more relaxed groups, which keep their veteran members and attract new ones.[5] Moreover, Dean Kelly noted the same phenomenon in the late 1960s: "conservative churches" (his term), who put high doctrinal and moral demands on their members, were growing while the mainline denominations were declining. Furthermore, not only did the mainline denominations not grow, they began to lose members in a fairly significant way.[6] Mainline decline, however, had actually been occurring since the 1850s.[7] Indeed, it was around 1850 when the Methodist Episcopal Church first began to drop from its position as the largest Protestant denomination in America. To illustrate, in 1776, the Methodists had only three percent of the nation's church membership and, by 1850, they had increased to thirty-four percent. Yet, after 1850, as "denominationalism" set in, they had difficulty in drawing new members and late-nineteenth century schisms further depleted the membership. [8]

C. METHODISM IN THE "GILDED AGE": INCREASING BUREAUCRATIZATION

Moreover, from 1870 to 1890, Methodism became even more bureaucratized and centralized in three principal ways. The first way was the transformation of the presiding elder's role from that of a nurturer of junior clergy and a powerful evangelistic preacher to that of a "middle-management" church administrator. For instance, once the "voluntary boards"[9] became official Methodist agencies, the presiding elders were expected to raise the necessary monies from the churches in their districts. To illustrate, the 17 January 1884 *Christian Advocate and Journal* reported that the Committee on Ways and Means of the Missionary Board (now an "official" church board) met for five hours with the presiding elders of the New York, New York East, Newark, and New Jersey conferences to consider ways in which they could help raise money in their districts. Furthermore, a Missionary Board official suggested that the presiding elders preach on missions once a year at each of their district churches.[10] Besides the New York area meeting, the chief subject of a Presiding Elders' Convention[11] the following summer was missions and their role in raising funds from the district churches.[12] To be sure, in the nineteenth century, American Protestant churches strongly emphasized mission, especially overseas ones, but Methodist presiding elders were also now responsible for the "budget askings" of the other central agencies as well. Indeed, practically every presiding elder convention held in the 1880s dealt with these post-Civil War aspects of centralization. Exemplifying this is the December, 1884, Presiding Elder Convention held at the Park Avenue (Manhattan) Methodist Episcopal Church (to which presiding elders of seventeen other annual conferences were invited) in which the following papers were read and discussed: "How can the presiding elders promote the general benevolences (i.e., offerings) of the Church?" "What are the changes in the duties of the presiding elder, and the causes therefore?" "What are the duties of the presiding elder to the temporal cause?" and "What can the presiding elder do to forward the Sunday School interests of the Church?"[13] Of course, some of the topics discussed still dealt with spiritual concerns such as "How can the presiding elders assist in the promotion of revivals?" "How may the presiding elders inspire the preachers with enthusiasm for their work?" "How can we promote spirituality in our Quarterly Conference?" and "What can the presiding elder do to maintain the peculiarities of Methodism?"[14] Nevertheless, administrative and financial concerns predominated at practically all of these conventions. Moreover, David Holsclaw, in his denominational study of the decline of the class meeting in the nineteenth century, confirms this view. He concluded that, as Methodism sought to increase membership, it failed to call that membership to high standards of discipleship. Moreover, it concentrated on denominational tasks such as building new churches and raising money for the budgets of the various central boards.[15]

Thus, bureaucratization was further draining strength from one of Methodism's key spiritual offices. [16]

Second, centralization also occurred on the local, congregational level as stationed preachers assumed greater control of each individual congregation. To illustrate, from 1850 on, stationed clergy continued to replace the more mobile circuit riders throughout the denomination. At the same time, the General Conference began to allow the preachers to stay longer in one church. This idea is shown by the 1864 General Conference, which raised the time limit for preachers' pastorates from two to three years. Again, in 1888, it was raised to five years and, in 1900, the time limit was abolished. [17] Thus, longer pastorates and greater clerical control apparently caused Methodism to lose its popularity. Indeed, Finke and Stark asserted that Methodism became the largest Protestant denomination in the mid-nineteenth century precisely because it was organized "democratically" at the local level while "centralized" at the higher level. [18]

Third and last, the continued "professionalization" of the clergy marked American Methodism in this period as it did all mainstream Protestant denominations. For instance, by 1880, the Methodist Episcopal Church had eleven theological seminaries, forty-four colleges and universities, and one hundred thirty female educational institutions. [19] Also, higher theological education for Methodist clergy in this period was reflected in much higher salaries. To demonstrate, in 1907, the average Methodist salary was higher than the national average. [20] Besides attending a theological seminary, some Methodist clergy also did graduate theological studies in Germany which influenced their subsequent seminary teaching in a more intellectual and less evangelical direction. Indeed, Finke and Stark pointed out that the concept of evangelism itself was now becoming unclear. [21]

D. METHODISM AS THE "ESTABLISHED CHURCH"

As a result of this increased centralization and liberalization in the mid to late-nineteenth century, new Methodist sects formed. Granted, schism or the formation of a new sect often occurred when the original sect had become highly institutionalized (although the "traditionalists" usually made efforts to reform the group before they were either expelled or left on their own). [22] Exemplifying this in the Methodist Episcopal Church was the situation which occurred in the Genesee Conference (western New York) in the 1850s. First, a group of clergy and laity had objected to the new liberal doctrines and centralization of the church. Next, in 1857, the Reverend Benjamin Titus wrote an article entitled "New School Methodism" in the *Northern Independent* in which he argued that Methodism had been divided into two groups: "new school" and "old school." [23]   Moreover, the article, written by a self-styled "Old School Methodist," criticized the "newer" liberal theology and the worldiness of the Methodist Episcopal Church (i.e., the more fashionable clothing and some of the changes in church decor).   Eventually, the Reverend Benjamin Titus and other like-minded clergy were expelled from the Genesee Conference for their open criticisms.   As a result, the Free Methodist Church was formed in Pekin, New York, in 1860. [24]

Significantly, this same "sect to church to new sect" pattern has also been occurring recently in America, with hundreds of new churches (some within existing mainline Protestant denominations and some outside) forming since the 1970s as large numbers of mainline Protestants became dissatisfied with their churches. [25]   In addition, a recent survey found that "forty-three percent of American Protestants were raised in the mainline, but approximately one out of every five have moved on to the nonmainline bodies." [26]   Moreover, the survey revealed that those who have switched to non-mainline churches have brought higher levels of commitment (i.e., as shown in the number of weekly church activities in which they participate) which apparently indicates that the churches which have rigorous standards actually attract more people. [27]   This idea is shown by the Mariner's Church in Newport Beach, California, and others like it which are "drawing a flock of previously unchurched or unhappily churched people by being relentlessly creative about developing forms of worship - most symbolically and definingly, music - that are contemporary, accessible, and authentic." [28]   Besides the parallels to nineteenth century Methodist schisms, these newer, mainly unaffiliated churches bear a striking, direct resemblance to the early Methodist societies in four principal ways.   First, like the early Methodists, the newer churches are meeting the needs of those persons who are now thrown into new cities due to job changes and consequently need more secure attachments. [29]   Another similarity is the strong emphasis on small faith-sharing groups. To illustrate, many of these newer churches say that their goal is to make "Fully Devoted Followers of Christ," or FDFX for short, a goal which often utilizes additional small group meetings. [30]   Third, like the early Methodists, these newer churches offer multiple opportunities for teaching, worship, and close-knit Christian fellowship.   Again, some of their congregational gatherings resemble the early Methodist society meetings or love feasts. [31]   Furthermore, most of the "sermons" given at these newer churches resemble "messages" or "teachings," which was a feature of the early Methodist Sunday evening society meeting. Fourth and last of all, like the early Methodists, most of the pastors of these newer churches are not required to have seminary training. Indeed, like the early Methodists, most of these contemporary preachers and teachers have emerged from within the church community rather than sent from some hierarchy. For these reasons, these newer churches are phenomenally successful because, perhaps without realizing it, they are using the Wesleyan emphases of evangelism (although in several different forms), various "ports of entry" such as the small groups (as well as more specialized small groups for parents and Christian "singles," to name just two), and full assimilation into the body of Christ which includes significant lay ministries of teaching, counseling, and service. As a result of these "Wesleyan" pastoral tactics, these churches are overtaking the United Methodist Church of today in membership, "program," and ministry to the community.

III. "OLD THINGS AND NEW" - THE WAY TO RENEWAL

Despite its recent downward trend, two original Wesleyan emphases upon which this study has focused (i.e., the catechumenate and spiritual nurture, both of which occurred in the weekly class meeting) offer a guide for renewal of the United Methodist Church today. First of all, before these two emphases can be examined, it is important to review what the late Dr. Albert C. Outler called the "Wesleyan synthesis" of justification by faith and holy living. [32] Second, the importance of a gradual and carefully prepared conversion (i.e., the first Wesleyan emphasis) will be discussed. Finally, spiritual nurture (i.e., the second Wesleyan emphasis), especially as the newer, mostly unaffiliated churches practice it, will be studied.

A. WESLEY'S ESSENTIAL VISION

Before the two central Wesleyan emphases are reconsidered for the church today, it is necessary to review carefully how Wesley understood the Christian life in both its initiation and lifelong development. In this vein, in an important essay entitled , "The Place of Wesley in the Christian Tradition," Dr. Albert C. Outler asserted that "it was Wesley's distinctive undertaking to integrate 'faith alone' with 'holy living' in an authentic dialogue." [33] Specifically, Outler believed that Wesley fused the "Latin" (i.e., western) understanding of salvation as "pardon" with the Eastern concept of "participation" or "perfection." [34] Indeed, according to Outler, this contribution was especially significant for all of western Christianity because this connection had been ruptured in the Reformation in the theological disputes between Catholics and Protestants and among the various Protestant traditions as well. Catholics, too, had some internal battles over how to keep these two parts of the whole in balance. [35] Granted, this comprehensive approach to the Christian life has once again been considered at the highest levels of both the Roman Catholic Church and the mainline Protestant denominations. [36] In short, Wesley emphasized initiation and nurture as two parts of one whole. Indeed, initiation was not to be taken lightly nor was holiness seen as just for the Christian "elite" of monks and clergy, but for all believers.

B. SETTING A NEW BAPTISMAL STANDARD

At the same time, a recovery of the understanding of conversion as a process can enable the United Methodist Church to appropriate some of its evangelical past. Significantly, this study has pointed out that conversion in the original Wesleyan tradition generally was a four-step process involving evangelical preaching, weekly class attendance, an eventual change of heart (which often occurred either alone or at the class meeting), and baptism. Of course, "conviction of sin" and the "grace of repentance" can also occur in modern-day prayer groups and adult Sunday School classes as well as at revival meetings, as the "new paradigm churches" and the charismatic movement have demonstrated. While "public preaching" and the evangelistic quarterly conferences of early Methodism produced a change in many people's hearts, new methods are certainly acceptable and are to be actively sought. In fact, in the past thirty years, other Christian traditions such as the Roman Catholic Church have once again stressed the singular importance of the proclamation of the gospel message. For instance, Pope Paul VI wrote, in *On Evangelization in the Modern World*, that "we wish to confirm once more that the task of evangelizing all people constitutes the essential mission of the church." [37] Again, Pope John Paul II, in *Mission of the Redeemer*, wrote that

the moment has come to commit all of the Church's energies to a new evangelization and to the mission *ad gentes* (to the Gentiles). No believer in Christ, no institution of the Church, can avoid the supreme duty to proclaim Christ to all peoples. [38]

Of course, evangelism is something which lies at the very heart of Methodism - what is new, at least for the current period, is that it needs to be linked once again to a systematic plan of catechesis. [39]   To be sure, some United Methodist Church leaders have begun to grasp this concept and good results have followed their efforts. An example is seen in the revitalization of a large downtown United Methodist Church in Wichita, Kansas, in the mid-1970s. [40] First, the new pastor, Reverend Richard Wilke, tried a number of traditional evangelistic outreaches such as pastoral calling, "two by two evangelism," a telephone campaign, and a mass rally. These activities, however, did not draw people to the church. Later, the pastor realized that people were joining the church only after they had been attending for awhile, usually for six months. Indeed, he noted that

> they first came, got involved, made friends, and then were drawn into a commitment. *They were assimilated before they were received. They were part of us before they were converted.* Several became active in their classes or sang in the choir for six months before they were baptized and joined the church. [41]

Moreover, these new members often came to faith in Christ through the adult Sunday School classes. [42]   In fact, every new person who came to church in that mid-1970 period was personally invited to join an adult class.   At the same time, no one was asked to join the church immediately.   Eventually, after the new people had worshipped, studied, and eaten together, they were ready to make a commitment. As a result of this "assimilation" approach, church school attendance increased (over a ten year period) from 500 to 1000 (700 adults, 300 children) and the original eight adult Sunday School classes increased to twenty. Wilke noted, however, that it usually took two years to start a new adult class. In addition to the adult Sunday School classes as a "port of entry" for new people, the church also targeted specific groupings such as college students and single adults in order to draw them more deeply into the life of the community. [43]

Exemplifying this was the church's approach to the young married women in which they asked them what weekly activity they would like to have. For one thing, these young married women did not attend the "traditional" United Methodist Women's meeting.   In contrast to desiring a pastor-led Bible study, these women simply wanted to meet weekly (Thursday mornings at 10:30) at the church to share and pray. Significantly, they wanted to discuss their difficulties in raising young children and the challenges they faced being married in a society which seemed to devalue marriage. Eventually, that group grew to forty women. Moreover, the pastor, in assessing the effectiveness of the group wrote that "the effort cost the United Methodist Women thousands of dollars in nursery costs until the group became self-sufficient, and those young women never really understood the United Methodist Women's program, but they experienced healing and faith." [44] Similarly, the choir also reconfigured itself into a "port of entry" to reach out to the new members who were continually joining it. In this vein, the choir began discussing the scriptural texts of the hymns and anthems. Also, choir members were divided into groups of four so that they could provide spiritual oversight for one another. [45]

Finally, in describing this revitalization, Wilke made a distinction between "centrifugal" evangelism which reaches out and "centripetal" evangelism which draws people into the fellowship. While Wilke sees a place for "centrifugal" evangelism (i.e., pastoral calling, rallies, etc.), he believes "centripetal" evangelism is necessary because

> today, with people so fractured, so fragmented by life, the spiritual need is often the opposite. People are disoriented or, as we say, "going off in all directions." The need now is to pull in toward a center. [46]

Likewise, this centripetal witnessing parallels, in many ways, what the early Methodists did. Granted, they did go out to the people and preached in the open fields, churches, and homes, but they also immediately invited those who appeared to be moved to join a class. In fact, as this study has noted previously, new classes were sometimes started at the conclusion of the preaching service so that these "seekers" could be assimilated into the body of Christ (i.e., the local Methodist societies) where they could experience the intimate fellowship, singing, prayer, and doctrinal instruction. [47] Thus, some United Methodist Churches have already begun to link evangelism and catechesis through a variety of church settings such as Adult Sunday School classes, choir, and weekly sharing groups.

C. "RECEIVE NOT THE GRACE OF GOD IN VAIN."

In addition to reconnecting basic, "primary evangelization" (to use Pope John Paul's words) to instruction in the faith, a blueprint for church renewal includes the recovery of a systematic plan of spiritual nurture which could operate on several levels, as Wesley's did. Obviously, a call for deeper spirituality should be sounded with great care and sensitivity since Methodist parishes today contain persons who are at a number of different "spiritual" levels. Indeed, a re-evangelization (or at least a re-education in things "Wesleyan") of the local church members will often have to precede the call for intensive spiritual nurture. In addition, studying as many models of Christian "cell" groups, both past and present, can also be useful. In short, spiritual nurture can not be expected to "just happen" - it must be intentionally pursued. Certainly, one would expect that local church pastors are already providing key leadership for spiritual nurture programs; the reality, however, is that administrative duties, district or conference responsibilities, the weekly Bible study, and sermon preparation often overwhelm them.

Significantly, the success of the new, unaffiliated churches has come, in large part, from their highly developed systems of small groups which are variously called "Kinships, Mini Churches, Home Fellowships and Care Groups." [48] Indeed, many of the new members of the Mariner's Church in California find that the small faith-sharing groups help them feel like they are truly connected to this large church which averages 3,500 at its weekend services. [49] Again, the Willow Creek Community Church, which averages 15,000 persons at its weekend services currently has 1400 small groups, each with its own leader. [50] Besides the small group leader, many of these small groups also have an "understudy," or leader-in-training, who automatically becomes the leader of a new small group whenever the existing class grows too large. [51] Another striking similarity to the early Methodist class meeting is that new leadership "emerges" from these small groups. In fact, most of the new pastors for the Hope Chapel movement are identified in the setting of the small group. Significantly, these new paradigm churches see that their

> goal is to continually "disciple" new lay leaders. This training is done through mentoring relationships between home fellowship overseers, leaders, and understudies with the goal being moral and spiritual maturity rather than growth simply in cognitive knowledge of the faith. [52]

Moreover, Jim Mellado, the overseer of the small groups at Willow Creek Community Church said that new members are quickly invited to join a small group which "is the basic unit of church life." [53] At the same time, small group members experience not only spiritual benefits but usually call upon their "cell-mates," as the early Methodists did, for help with various tasks or in times of sorrow. As a result of today's highly mobile society, these new cell-mates often take the place of the relatives and neighbors of an earlier, more traditional period. [54] Also, like the early Methodist class meeting, the members of these small groups hold individual members accountable for living up to Christian standards. [55] Finally, even the relatively recent "Promise Keepers" phenomenon which encourages "male-only" small sharing groups is comparable to the single-sex "bands" (for both men and women) of early Methodism. [56] Thus, upon close examination, it is evident that these newer, often unaffiliated churches are drawing upon Wesleyan principles in their small group ministries, experiencing close relationships between small group members, and instituting male-only sharing groups.

In short, both the experiences of Bishop Wilke at the Wichita church and the pastoral strategies of the new paradigm churches reveal how central the class meeting or small group can be for church renewal today. For example, Wilke's experience at the Wichita church underlines how both an "informal" six month catechumenate and an intentional spiritual nurture program can prepare new people for commitment to Jesus Christ and to the church. Wilke rediscovered the same principle to which Wesley had been led: the little church within the larger church. In both cases, in England in the eighteenth century, and America in the late twentieth century, these smaller, weekly meetings (either voluntary or required) help connect new people to the larger "society" or church. In contrast, all the other "evangelistic" efforts which Wilke tried in Wichita failed totally. Similarly, Wesley had observed early in the Methodist movement that converts would quickly fall away unless they were placed into the smaller groupings of the class meeting. Indeed, the insights of Wesley and Wilke again point to the crucial importance of the class meeting (or the Adult Sunday School classes, in Wilke's case). In fact, the new paradigm churches also report that many members find the weekly small group meeting to actually be more significant than the large Sunday worship experience, which many new paradigm church pastors say is primarily for "seekers." [57] Thus, the Wesleyan class meeting appears as relevant and essential as ever for evangelization and nurturing purposes. In fact, Wilke's initial failures at evangelism in Wichita provide a strong argument for reinstituting the class meeting in Methodism. At the same time, the insights of Wilke and the new paradigm church leaders imply that highly emotional revivalistic methods will generally fail as they did in Manhattan in the 1820s and 1830s. To be sure, some people then, as well as some people today, may have been moved to "commit their lives to Christ," but without a smaller group to whom they are accountable, they can easily lose their initial fervor or even fall away from the faith. Granted, some United Methodist Churches have begun a number of small groups for Bible study, prayer, or spiritual growth which may or may not target specific groups like single adults and young married women as this chapter has already shown. Moreover, the Wesleyan class meeting concept has also been tried in "traditional" Methodist youth ministry. This idea is shown by the "McFarlin Youth I. C. U.," the regular Sunday evening youth group at McFarlin United Methodist Church in Norman, Oklahoma, which meets in smaller groups of six to nine teenagers with a leader for ten minutes at the end of each meeting. Moreover, in these ten-minute sessions, they share any difficulties with each other, take attendance of their "unit," and make plans to reach out to those who are absent with a phone call or card. [58]

Equally important, some United Methodist pastors have begun to select and train key lay people for small group leadership, teaching, and counseling, similar to the way in which class leaders, exhorters, and local preachers "emerged" from the early Methodist class meeting system. Indeed, a number of United Methodist Churches are beginning to put the emphasis on "making disciples" who can, in turn, form others in discipleship. This visionary approach is shown by Dr. William Hinson of First United Methodist Church in Houston, Texas, who met every Thursday morning at seven a.m. with key laymen and again at two-thirty p.m. with twenty-five key laywomen. Besides having a time of prayer and sharing, he also trained them to be "lay pastors" in the church. [59]   Again, Dr. Norman Neaves, pastor of the Church of the Servant (United Methodist) in Oklahoma City, Oklahoma, trained many of the laity to do hospital visitation, Bible study, counseling, youth ministry, and lead small groups. Furthermore, these lay "sub-pastors" at Church of the Servant, like the early Methodist class leaders, "see to it that the training programs are continual and comprehensive, and that every new inquirer is brought into the community of faith in such a way that he or she may be able to make a life-changing commitment and continue to grow in the fellowship." [60]

In addition, a partial recovery of spiritual nurture specifically involving the class meeting has already begun in the United Methodist Church. Exemplifying this is the 1988 General Conference's approval of an updated version of the Wesleyan class system in which the pastor, in consultation with the nominating committee of the local church, recommends a number of class leaders to be elected at the annual charge (or church) conference. [61]   Then, the new class leaders invite members of the congregation to join their classes while new church members are assigned to existing classes. [62] Furthermore, class leaders must meet every month with the other class leaders, the pastor, and the lay leader in the Class Leaders' Council to discuss the "spiritual state" of their class members. [63] Also, every class leader must be in a covenant discipleship group which is comprised of two to seven persons who meet weekly to discuss their own discipleship. On the other hand (and this is quite puzzling), the actual "classes" have a much looser structure. For example, the eight to ten members of a class are not required to meet together weekly; the only requirement is to have monthly contact with their class leader. Nevertheless, the members of a class may choose to meet together on a weekly basis if they should desire it. [64] Yet, without meeting together (!), the class leader is to develop in the class members "a regular pattern of doing acts of justice, compassion, devotion, and worship." [65] Moreover, the new class system departs from the Wesleyan model in several ways. First, classes do not have to be neighborhood groupings, and a number of other configurations are acceptable. Second, classes may be formed for purposes other than spiritual nurture, such as evangelism and social concerns. [66] Third, the fact that classes do not have to meet regularly raises the concern that spiritual nurture and accountability will be greatly lessened. Fourth and last, the new guidelines for class meetings do not seem to address the issue of instruction in the faith following an "awakening." Thus, while some attempt has been made to reintroduce the class meeting system from the denominational level, it seems that a higher "commitment level" like that of the new paradigm churches could make it more effective.

In addition to encouraging class meetings in the local church, the development in two more critical areas could help acquaint local churches with the class meeting system of initiation and nurture: seminary training and district resourcing. For example, United Methodist seminaries could offer several courses on the theory and practice of the Wesleyan class meeting. Besides the basic and advanced courses, Methodist seminaries could create a subspecialty called "Class Meeting Studies." [67] In addition, qualified experts on the class meeting could serve as "visiting professors" at the various Methodist seminaries. Also, Methodist seminaries might consider forming "class meetings" for their first-year seminarians to ground them in the actual practice. Besides the seminary possibilities, districts (under the direction of the District Council on Ministries) could provide training for clergy and laity in the theory and practice of class meetings. As a result of district training, selected clergy and laity could conduct similar sessions at cluster-level[68] "Lay Schools of Religion" and at the local church level. Moreover, district representatives could provide resources and, occasionally, the district could invite experts in the field to speak at a district location. Eventually, the local churches of a district could be encouraged to start a "study group" on the class meeting with the ultimate goal of starting one or more in their congregations. Finally, at an annual conference level, the bishop could ask each church to start two new class meetings a year and then recognize those churches who have done so at the yearly conference meeting.

IV. CONCLUSION

This study suggests that the Wesleyan class meeting, far from being a relic of the past, can enhance existing church efforts at initiation and assimilation into the body of Christ. For instance, a close examination of the new paradigm churches reveals that several basic elements of the Wesleyan class meeting still work well today. First, new paradigm churches either encourage or require that every member attend a weekly small group where close-knit bonds can be formed and individual members can minister to and be ministered to by other group members. In addition, the small groups which these churches offer seem to be meeting a deep need for authentic community which exists in America today. In the same way, the class meetings of early Methodism provided stability for those affected by the Industrial Revolution and urbanization. Second, recent research on these churches indicates that evangelism, spiritual growth, and accountablility also occur in these natural settings. Similarly, these three activities occurred abundantly in the early Methodist class meetings in England and Manhattan. Third, a leader oversees the small groups of these new paradigm churches and when the group grows too large it is quickly subdivided so that effective, personal ministry can continue. Significantly, the new paradigm churches have so far avoided the mistake of nineteenth century New York City Methodism in which the local Methodist churches let their classes grow so large that the meetings became superficial due to trying to hear each member's "report" in an hour or an hour and a half. Fifth, another higher body oversees the small group leaders in these new paradigm churches, much like the class leaders meetings in early Methodism. Last of all, these new paradigm churches experience new leadership (small group leaders, pastors, etc.) emerging from the weekly small group meetings which is exactly what occurred in the Methodist class meetings. Consequently, as the evidence for the new paradigm churches' small group meetings shows, an increased emphasis on the class meeting within the United Methodist Church today can begin again to draw new people into its local churches and strengthen existing members through the instruction, intimacy, and inspiration which the class meeting uniquely provides.

Appendices

Chapter 1. Appendix 1
Significant Events in British Methodism

Year	Event
1703	Birth of John Wesley, founder of the Methodist societies
1707	Birth of Charles Wesley
1714-1720	John Wesley at Charterhouse preparatory school, London
1720-1726	John Wesley at Oxford for Bachelor's and Master's degrees
1725	John Wesley ordained deacon
1726	John Wesley elected Fellow of Lincoln College
1727	John Wesley ordained priest of the Church of England
1729-1735	Holy Club meets at Oxford
1735-1737	John and Charles Wesley in Georgia; first contact with the Moravians
1738	John and Charles Wesley both experience a deeper conversion in May
1739	John Wesley preaches out-of-doors in Bristol and Kingswood
	Bristol Methodists build "New Room" (May-June)
	London Methodists purchase the "Foundry" (November)
1742	Class meetings begin at Bristol
1744	Lay preaching established; first "annual conference of preachers" held
1769	First "missionaries" sent to America
1788	Death of Charles Wesley
1791	Death of John Wesley
1795	Formation of the Wesleyan Methodist Connexion; Methodist societies are no longer part of the Church of England
1797	Formation of the Methodist New Connexion

Chapter 2.   Appendix 1
Typical Weekly Schedule for New York Society

Day	Time	Type of Meeting
Sunday	Early morning*	Public preaching
	Mid-morning	St. Paul's Chapel
		(Anglican) for Holy Communion
	Afternoon	Public preaching
	Evening	Society meeting (private)
Tuesday	Evening	Public preaching
Thursday	Evening	Prayer and Praise Service
		Public Preaching
Friday	Evening	Intercession**
	Evening	Class Leaders' meeting
Saturday	Evening	Exhortation
	Evening	Band-society meeting

*   Early morning preaching also occurred on weekdays at 5:00 or 6:00 am.
**   The "Intercession" was a meeting for prayer and was introduced by Joseph
      Pilmoor. It later developed into the mid-week prayer meeting.
+   Class meetings were also held at regularly scheduled times during the
      week.

Source: Francis Asbury, *The Journals and Letters of Francis Asbury*, ed.
          Elmer T. Clark (Nashville: Abingdon Press, 1958), vol. 1.

Chapter 2. Appendix 2
Length of Time to Become a Member

NAME	ADMITTED ON TRIAL	READ INTO SOCIETY	CLASS(ES) ATTENDED	YEAR
Bronson, Ware	17 June 1790	5 July 1972	S. Rudd W. Phoebus	1791 1791
Gourby, James	4 June 1793	26 Dec. 1793	E. Vanderlip	1793

Source: "John Street Church" (New York, NY: Manuscripts Division, NYPL, Astor, Lenox and Tilden Foundations, MECR, vol. 241, photocopied).

Chapter 2.   Appendix 3
          Class members Having the Same Class Leader

CLASS MEMBER	CLASS LEADER	YEARS IN CLASS
Sarah Codington	John Bleecker	1785-1795
Jane Hipp	Peter McLean	1791-1795
Susannah Mercein	John Staples	1785-1795
Sarah Riker	John Staples	1785-1796
Mary Sands	Peter McLean	1785-1796

Source: "John Street Church" (New York, NY: Manuscripts Division, NYPL, Astor, Lenox and Tilden Foundations, MECR, vol. 241, photocopied).

Chapter 2.   Appendix 4
Members Having Three or More Leaders, 1785-1796

CLASS MEMBER	CLASS LEADER	YEAR
Hannah Baldwin	John Bleecker	1785-1787
	Preacher's class	1791
	John Sprosen	1793
	John Davis	1795
	John Wilson	1796
Hannah Hick	William Tellers	1785
	Preacher's class	1791
	John Sprosen	1793
	John Davis	1795
Elizabeth Humbert	Abraham Russell	1785
	Peter McLean	1787
	Abraham Brower	1791
	Cornelius Warner	1795
Phebe Coutant	Andrew Mercein	1787
	John Cooper	1791-1793
	Andrew Mercein	1795
	Paul Hick	1796
Hannah Vanderlip	Peter McLean	1787
	Preacher's class	1791
	John Bleecker	1795
Ann Grant	John Bleecker	1785-1787
	Preacher's class	1791
	John Bleecker	1793-1796
Sarah Day	Abraham Brower	1785
	Henry Newton	1795
	John Brower	1796
Mary Dando	Abraham Brower	1785
	Henry Newton	1795
	John Brower	1796
Ann Sprosen	Abraham Brower	1787
	John Bleecker	1791
	William Valleau	1793
Cornelia Anderson	Peter McLean	1785-1787
	Preacher's class	1791
	John Sprosen	1793

Source: "John Street Church" (New York, NY: Manuscripts Division, NYPL, Astor, Lenox and Tilden Foundations, MECR, vols. 233 and 241, photocopied).

Chapter 2. Appendix 5
Number of Years between Membership in the New
York Society and Appointment as a Class Leader

Name	Read into Society	Classes Attended	Years	Year Appointed Class Leader
D. Carpenter	21 June 1789	-----	-----	1791
S. Bonsall	18 July 1790	A. Russell	1791	
		E. Vanderlip	1793	
		A. Russell	1795	1796
N. Morris	18 July 1790	J. Humbert	1791-1793	
		W. Cooper	1795	1796
W. Snyder	5 Sept. 1790	W. Cooper	1791-1793	1795
W. Henry	5 Sept. 1790	W. Cooper	1791	1793
T. Carpenter	3 Oct. 1791	W. Valleau	1791	1796
S. Elsworth	6 May 1792	W. Grant	1793-1795	1795
W. Bronson	5 July 1792	S. Rudd	1791	
		W. Phoebus	1791	1795
D. Renny	20 Aug. 1792	S. Rudd	1793	1795
R. Leacraft	20 Aug. 1792	A. Russell	1792	1794
J. Sharrock	10 Sept. 1793	E. Vanderlip	1793	1795
J. Wilson	-----	E. Vanderlip	1793	1796
J. Gourby	26 Dec. 1793	E. Vanderlip	1793	1796
J. Osman	-----	W. Cooper	1794	1796

The following persons were "admitted on trial" (i.e., as probationers) on these dates:

W. Bronson	17 June 1790	J. Gourby	4 June 1793
J. Wilson	21 Dec. 1793	J. Osman	15 Sept. 1794

Source: "John Street Church" (New York, NY: Manuscripts Division, NYPL, Astor, Lenox and Tilden Foundations, MECR, vols. 233 and 241, photocopied).

Chapter 2. Appendix 6
Years of Consecutive Service as Class Leader, 1785-1812

CLASS LEADER(S)	YEARS OF SERVICE*	YEARS
Abraham Russell	1787-1812	26
Philip Arcularius, Samuel Stilwell	1791-1812	22
John Davis	1793-1812	20
Paul Hick, Samuel Sears	1794-1812	19
Samuel Elsworth	1795-1812	18
Thomas Carpenter, Charles Gillman	1796-1812	17
Joseph Graham	1796-1812	17
William Cooper	1791-1802	12
Peter McLean, John Staples+	1785-1796	12
Elias Vanderlip	1791-1802	12
Abraham Brower, Jonas Humbert	1785-1795	11
Daniel Coutant	1787-1796	10
William Henry	1793-1802	10
Andrew Mercein	1787-1796	10
John Bleecker, George Courtney	1787-1795	9
Stephen Rudd	1787-1794	8
John Brower	1795-1802	8
Samuel Bonsall, William Dougal	1796-1802	7
John Sprosen	1791-1796	6
Richard Courtney, Robert Cuddy	1791-1795	5
Henry Newton, William Valleau	1791-1795	5

* These class leaders may have also served before 1785, which is the earliest extant class list.
+ Thomas Coke recorded in his Journal in 1792 that John Staples "has been a leader in our Society for about twenty years" which would mean he had been a class leader since 1772.

Source: "John Street Church" (New York, NY: Manuscripts Division, NYPL, Astor, Lenox and Tilden Foundations, MECR, vols. 233 and 241, photocopied).

Chapter 2.   Appendix 7
Class Leaders' Occupations, 1793

CLASS LEADER	OCCUPATION	ADDRESS
Abraham Russell	Builder	16 Crown Street
Stephen Rudd	Grocer	Gold and Beekman Streets
William Cooper	Dyer and fuller	74 Broadway
Jonas Humbert	Baker	16 King Street
Elias Vanderlip	Shoemaker	57 William Street
William Henry	Grocer	43 Cherry Street
Moses West	Boatman	27 Gold Street
George Courtney	Plaster of Paris Manufacturer	Cherry and Orchard Streets
Henry Newton	Shoemaker	31 Great-dock St.
John Cooper	Hatter	38 Little-dock St.
John Bleecker	China and earthenware store	28 Maiden Lane
Philip Arcularius	Tanner and currier, New York State legislator	22 Frankfort Street
John I. Staples	Watchmaker	5 Maiden Lane
Daniel Coutant	Shoemaker	52 Chatham St.
John Sprosen	Windsor chair-maker	20 Golden Hill St
William Valleau	Ship-carpenter	23 Prince Street
William Grant	Tailor	25 Fair Street
Daniel Carpenter	Comb-manufacturer	32 Cherry Street
Andrew Mercein	Baker	29 Gold Street
Abraham Brower	Tailor	66 Broadway
John Davis	Tailor	10 Catherine St.
Cornelius Warner	House carpenter	Barclay Street
Joseph Rice	School-master	37 Chapel Street
Robert A. Cuddy	Shoemaker	Vesey Street

Note: A second William Henry is listed as a ship-maker residing on 11 Slate Lane; two other John Coopers are listed: a mariner on 72 Cherry Street and a carman on 5 Church Street; five Abraham Browers are listed. For John Davis, two are listed: a ship-carpenter on 3 Pump Street and a mason on Barclay Street.

Source: "John Street Church" (New York, NY: Manuscripts Division, NYPL, Astor, Lenox and Tilden Foundations, MECR, vols. 233 and 241, photocopied.) David Franks, ed., *The New York Directory* (New York: Shepard Kollock, 1786), 45-77. William Duncan, ed., *The New York Directory and Register for the Year 1793* (New York: T. and J. Swords, 1793), 1-174.

Chapter 2. Appendix 8
Statistics of Black Membership and Classes, 1785-96

YEAR	BLACK MEMBERS	FEMALE CLASSES	MALE CLASSES	AVERAGE SIZE	LARGEST CLASS
1785*	26	0	0	26	26
1787	36	2	1	12	19
1791	124	3	2	20	34
1793	133	4	2	22.1	35
1795	155	6	2	19.3	22
1796	126	5	2	18	24

*Only one black class existed in 1785. This class was "mixed" (i.e., both men and women).

Source: "John Street Church" (New York, NY: Manuscripts Division, NYPL, Astor, Lenox and Tilden Foundations, MECR, vols. 233 and 241, photocopied).

Chapter 2.   Appendix 9
       Rate of Increase from 1785 to 1796

YEAR	TOTAL CLASSES	10-19 MEMBERS	20-29 MEMBERS	30-39 MEMBERS	LARGEST CLASS
1785	13	10	3	0	26
1787	18	16	2	0	24
1791	27	10	11	6	38
1793	28	8	11	8	45
1795	34	12	18	4	36
1796	39	21	16	2	32

Source: "John Street Church" (New York, NY: Manuscripts Division, NYPL, Astor, Lenox, and Tilden Foundations, MECR, vols. 233 and 241, photocopied).

Chapter 2. Appendix 10
Quarterly Band Tickets of Mrs. Hannah (Dean) Hick.

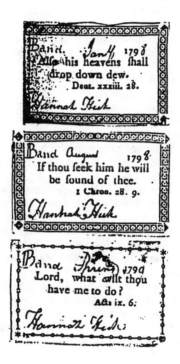

Source: Hannah Hick (Madison, NJ: UMCA – GCAH, "Drew
University Methodist Collection." Drew University).
Reproduced with permission of Drew University
Library.

Chapter 3.   Appendix 1
Chronology of Events in New York City Methodism,
1766-1866

Year	Event
1766	First Methodist preaching and class meetings of the New York Society
1768	Wesley Chapel established (later renamed John Street Methodist Episcopal Church in 1784)
1784	Methodist Episcopal Church (hereafter, M.E.C.) founded at Baltimore
1792	Forsyth Street Methodist Episcopal Church established
1797	Black Methodists begin to hold separate services and class meetings
1798	Duane Street Methodist Episcopal Church established
1800	New York Circuit formed
1811	Reverend Nathan Bangs appointed to New York Circuit Allen Street and Greenwich Village Methodist Episcopal Churches established
1813	New York Preachers' Meeting established African Methodist Episcopal Zion Church formed in Manhattan
1816	Death of Francis Asbury
1818	Bowery Village Methodist Episcopal Church established (originally called "Two Mile Stone" church since it was two miles north of the old city hall.)
1826	Willett Street Methodist Episcopal Church established *Christian Advocate and Journal* begins publication in Manhattan
1832	New York Circuit divided into New York East Circuit and New York West Circuit
1837	New York East Circuit divided into the following "stations" or "charges" - Forsyth Street, Allen Street, Seventh Street (formerly Bowery Village), Willett Street, and Ninth Street (at Avenue B)
1838	New York West Circuit divided into the following "stations" - John Street, Duane Street, and Bedford Street.

Chapter 3. Appendix 2
Class Leaders' Consecutive Years of Service, John Street Church, 1802-1832

CLASS LEADER	YEARS OF SERVICE	TOTAL YEARS
Joseph Smith	1802-1832	30
Stephen Dando	1812-1832	20
John Bartine	1812-1830	18
Abraham Knapp	1812-1830	18
Jonathan Lyon	1802-1818	16
John Westfield	1812-1827	15
Robert Tolefree	1812-1827	15
Francis Hall	1818-1832	14
Abraham Paul	1818-1826	8
Samuel Waldo	1818-1825	7
Thomas Brown	1825-1832	7
Safety Magee	1812-1818	6
Abraham Coddington	1812-1818	6
William W. Lake	1826-1832	6
Erastus Hyde	1826-1832	6
William Gale	1826-1832	6
John G. Horton	1825-1830	5
Thomas Roby	1825-1827	3
William Jewett	1825-1827	3
Abijah Smith	1826-1829	3
Ralph Mead	1829-1832	3
Joseph Higgs	1829-1832	3
James Gascoigne	1829-1832	3
Gabriel Disosway	1829-1832	3
John Dunn	1829-1832	3
William Haines	1830-1832	3

Note: Some class leaders like Abraham Russell, Paul Hick, and Thomas Carpenter served from the 1780s and 1790s into the early 1800s. See Chapter 2, Appendix 6 for their dates. Also, the class lists for the years 1802-1832 are not all extant; therefore, some class leaders may have served for a longer period of time.

Source: "Methodist Episcopal Church of New York. Classes. 1825-1826" (New York, NY: Manuscripts Division, NYPL, Astor, Lenox and Tilden Foundations, MECR, vols. 66-67, photocopied).

Chapter 3. Appendix 3
Class Leaders' Occupations, 1802 and 1825

OCCUPATION	1812	1825
Artisans and Factory Workers:	9	15
baker, upholster, cooper, tanner, bookbinder, fancy hairmaker, jeweler, fancy trimmings maker, packer, smith, stone seal engraver, saddler, printer, corkcutter		
Building Trades Workers	7	6
Clerks	0	1
Clothing Workers: hatter, shoemaker, tailor	10	6
Government Employees: inspector of customs	0	1
Laborers and Porters	0	1
Manufacturers: plaster, shipbuilder, nail manufactory, capmaker	3	2
Maritime Workers: chandler, sailmaker, ship carpenter, ship-wright, cordwainer, ropemaker, rigger, caulker	4	9
Merchants	3	4
Professional Workers: portrait painter, clergy, teacher, publisher, engraver, physician, academy	2	9
Proprietors and Custodians: street commissioner, boardinghouse	1	1
Shopkeepers and Dealers: dry goods dealer, food dealers, butchers, grocer, hat store, floor store, bookseller, hardware store	12	12
Workers in Transportation and Related Jobs: stonecutter, shipmaster	10	8
Miscellaneous Occupations: fisherman, gardener	0	3
Total	85+	102+

+   For 1812, 8 class leaders were not listed in the NYC Directory and the occupations for 16 other class leaders could not be determined since their addresses were not written in the Class Leaders' list and the City Directory listed several persons with the same name. For 1825, the totals were 17 and 5, respectively.

Source: "New York City Churches. Classleaders. 1825" and "John Street Church. Classes. 1802" (New York, NY: Manuscripts Division, NYPL, Astor, Lenox, and Tilden Foundations, MECR, vols. 204 and 237, photocopied). Thomas Longworth, *American Almanac. New York Register and New York City Directory* (New York: by the author, 1812, 1824, and 1825).

Chapter 3. **Appendix 4**
Number of Probationers Approved for Full
Membership in the New York Circuit, 1814-1816

DATE	APPROVED	LAID OVER	DROPPED	TOTAL
Jan 1814	23	3	9	35
Feb 1814	14	1	4	28*
Mar 1814	5	3	4	14+
Apr 1814	23	5	7	35
May 1814	9	0	1	10
Total	74	12	25	122

DATE	APPROVED	LAID OVER	DROPPED	TOTAL
July 1816	16	0	0	16
Aug 1816	8	2	2	12
Oct 1816	13	2	4	19
Nov 1816	14	3	3	20
Total	51	7	9	67

*	9 additional probationers whose terms had expired
+	2 additional probationers were read out
Note:	No minutes were taken from June, 1814 to June, 1816

Source: "Methodist Episcopal Church of New York. Board of
            Leaders. Minutes 1811-1823" (New York, NY: Manuscripts
            Division, NYPL, Astor, Lenox and Tilden Foundations,
            MECR, vol. 90a, photocopied).

Chapter 3.   Appendix 5
               Original Transcript of Church Trial of John Hoare

N. C. Hart)

John Hoare had been duly notified but did not appear. Complainant charges John Hoare with neglect of duty and immoral conduct.

As to neglect of duty. his Leader states that he has not attended his class for about one year, that he has called on him & requested him to attend his class which he promised to do, but did not fulfil his promise. he then reported him to Bro Sandford. Bro Sandford states that called on J. Hoare and conversed with him on the subject & informed him of the consequences of continuing to neglect, when he promised that he would go to class that night. Bro Truslow says that he has not been to class since.

On the Second charge. Bro Truslow states that John Hoare who is a member of the church informed him that, that his father, drinks to excess frequently & often uses wicked profane language. Bro Sandford states that he conversed with John Hoare on his intemperance, which he acknowledged had been the case frequently.

The committee are of opinion that John Hoare is guilty of both charges.

Signed   Simeon Price
            John Buckmaster
            Thomas Fairweather
            Abraham Riker
            N. C. Hart

Source: "Transcripts of Church Trials for New York Circuit" (Madison, NJ: UMCA – GCAH, "Drew University Methodist Collection," Drew University), 4 October 1824, 22. Reproduced with permission of Drew University Library.

Chapter 3. Appendix 6
Transcript of the Trial of Arabella Hipwell

N. C. Hart   New York Oct. 5, 1824
in behalf of the church
vs.
Arabella Hipwell

P. P. Sandford Presider
Sim. Price
David Keys
T. Buckmaster   Committee
T. Fairweather
S. Williams

Charge, neglect of duty and superfluity of dress.

Has been duly notified to attend - not present.

Her leader states that she has not been to class in a year - does not attend our church except that she may occasionally. Has been visited by her Leader. Also by P. P. Sandford who explained to her the consequence of neglecting her duties. Martha Hipwell says that she thinks her extravagantly gay in her dress.

The Committee judge her to be guilty of wilful neglect of duty and also of being gay and worldly in her dress.

Simeon Price
David Keys
John Buckmaster
Thomas Fairweather
Saml Williams
She is expelled from the M. E. Church for a breach of our rules.
New York   Oct. 4, 1824   P. P. Sandford

Source: "Transcripts of Church Trials for New York Circuit" (Madison, NJ: UMCA - GCAH, "Drew University Methodist Collection," Drew University), 26. Reproduced with permission of Drew University Library.

Chapter 3. Appendix 7
Transcript of the Church Trial of Parmelia Olmstead

The Church vs. Parmelia Olmstead   Rev. P. P. Sandford &
(formerly P. Burrows)   John Baily, Samuel Williams,
                                             Committee

Charge: Breach of Rules.
1. Neglect of duty. 2. Marrying an irreligious man.
She was notified to attend by David Keys, who carried to her an open letter from P. P. Sandford and read it to her. Letter stated the charge with its specifications. She does not appear. D. Keys says he did not think at the time she intended to appear.
1. Specification. Was last a member of Br. Rudman's class. Has not attended her class for more than a year and six months. Last fall professed to be reclaimed from a backslidden state. Talked of wishing to get into another class, but neglected to do so. Has not attached herself to any class.
2. Specification. David Keys states that he cautioned her against keeping company with and marrying the man to whom she was afterwards married. She paid no regard to it. Finally married him. He found a change in her conduct for the worse immediately after her marriage. Her husband told her of this attachment to another girl. She threatened to take Laudnum to destroy herself. Returned to brother. Was unsteady. Finally demanded all her wages that night though her month was not up and left the house promising to return in half an hour. Never returned until he sent for her to inform her to appear on her trial. The man to whom she is married is of bad character. Plays cards, &.
The judgment of the committee is that she is unworthy to be a member of the Methodist Church having forfeited her membership by her improper conduct. She is expelled from the Methodist E. Church.
                                 Signed   John Bailey, Michael
                                             Dixin, Samuel Williams,
                                             P. P. Sandford

Source: "Record of the Proceedings in the Trials of Members of the New York Circuit, 1824-1827" (New York, NY: John Street United Methodist Church), 28 February 1825, 33.

Chapter 3. Appendix 8
Attendance of Class Leaders at Monthly Board of
Leaders' Meeting of the New York Circuit from
October, 1827 to September, 1829.

Oct., 1827 - Sept., 1828 # of Class Leaders	Oct., 1828 - Sept., 1829 # of Class Leaders	Meetings Attended
1	0	12
3	0	11
4	0	10
8	0	9
15	0	8
11	17	7
19	16	6
12	17	5
13	19	4
10	14	3
10	12	2
7	9	1
7	16	0
120+	120*	

+   6 class leaders were crossed off the list, one withdrew from the society, and one died.

*   14 class leaders were crossed off the list. No explanations were given.

Source: "Forsyth Street Church. Board of Leaders. Minutes. 1825-
              1832" (New York, NY: Manuscripts Division, NYPL, Astor,
              Lenox and Tilden Foundations, MECR, vol. 212, photocopied).

Chapter 3. Appendix 9
Breakdown of Class Size for 1825-1826, New York Circuit

1825	No. of Classes	Size of Class				
		10-19	20-29	30-39	40-49	50-59
Allen Street*	18	1	7	4	3	1
Bowery Village	4	0	1	2	1	0
Duane Street	18	2	6	6	3	1
Forsyth Street	26	3	7	7	5	4
Greenwich Village	7	1	0	2	3	1
John Street	20	2	9	4	4	0
Willett Street	10	0	0	2	5	0
Totals	103	9	30	27	24	7

Note: John Street had one class with under 10 members. Willett Street had 1 class with over 80 members.

1826						
Allen Street	23	2	7	4	3	1
Bowery Village	4	0	0	1	2	0
Duane Street	21	1	4	5	5	2
Forsyth Street	33	4	6	8	4	8
Greenwich Village	11	2	2	0	0	2
John Street	16	0	1	8	0	6
Willett Street	22	2	0	4	2	9
Totals	147	11	28	34	20	29

Source: "Methodist Episcopal Church of New York. Classes. 1825-1826" (New York, NY: Manuscripts Division, NYPL, Astor, Lenox and Tilden Foundations, MECR, vols. 66-67, photocopied).

Chapter 3. Appendix 10
Class Size, 1785 and 1787

<u>1785 Classes</u>   <u>1787 Classes</u>

Class	Number in class	M/F*	Class	Number in class	M/F
1	12	F	1	14	M
2	14	F	2	18	M
3	18	F	3	12	M
4	18	F	4	16	F
5	22	F	5	17	F
6	15	F	6	19	F
7	13	M	7	20	F
8	14	M	8	18	F
9	13	M	9	14	F
10	18	M	10	14	F
11 (black)	26	M&F	11	16	F
12	14	M	12	24	M
13	23	F	13	12	F
			14	16	M
			15	NA+	NA
			16 (black)	9	M&F (?)
			17 (black)	18	F
			18 (black)	8	NA

* Male or female
+ Not Available

Source: "John Street Church. Classes. 1785-1787" (New York, NY: Manuscripts Division, NYPL, Astor, Lenox and Tilden Foundations, MECR, vol. 233, photocopied).

Chapter 3. Appendix 11
Class Size, 1791 and 1793

1791 Classes			1793 Classes		
Class Number	Number in Class	M/F*	Class Number	Number in Class	M/F
1	17	F	1	22	M
2	18	F	2	18	M
3	22	F	3	29	M
4	25	F	4	29	M
5	22	F	5	29	M
6	19	F	6	14	M
7	16	M	7	18	F
8	13	F	8	27	F
9	18	F	9	25	F
10	24	F	10	29	F
11	11	M	11	33	F
12	13	F	12	22	F
13	29	F	13	21	M
14	13	M	14	23	F
15	18	F	15	35	F
16	19	F	16	45	F
17	26	M	17	31	F
18	23	F	18	31	F
19	12	M	19	30	M&F
20	28	M	20	33	F
21	30	F	21	12	F
22	25	F	22	17	M
23	NA	M (?)	23	18	M
24	NA	F (?)	24	16	F
25 (black)	15	M	25	24	F
26 (black)	NA	F	26	33	F
27 (black)	22	M	27	35	F
28 (black)	NA	M			
29 (black)	24	M&F			
30 (black)	NA	M			
31 (black)	NA	NA			

*M/F = Male/Female

Source: "John Street Church. Classes. 1791-1796" (New York, NY: Manuscripts Division, NYPL, Astor, Lenox and Tilden Foundations, MECR, vol. 241, photocopied).

Chapter 3. Appendix 12
Size of Nine Classes at John Street Church, 1817-1832

Class #	Class Leader	M/F	1817	1825	1826	1827	1829	1830	1832
1	Preacher	F	NA	44	57	62	61	48	50
4	Thomas Brown	M	NA	16	23	28	24	24	24
5	Robert Tolefree*	F	NA	22	29	27	26	39	33
6	James L. Phelps	F	NA	24	24	26	25	32	27
9	Joseph Smith	F	51	48	25	42	38	39	43
13	Daniel Ayres	F	NA	29	39	45	42	39	41
14	Erastus Hyde	F	NA	NA	21	29	25	34	32
16	Francis Hall+	F	37	28	32	32	32	44	38
17	Stephen Dando+	F	14	NA	20	20	16	19	19

* Joseph Higgs became the class leader in 1829.
+ Classes 16 and 17 were listed on the class lists as "colored classes."

Source: "Methodist Episcopal Church of New York. Classes. 1825-1826" (New York, NY: Manuscripts Division, NYPL, Astor, Lenox and Tilden Foundations, MECR, vols. 66-67, photocopied).

Chapter 3. Appendix 13
Number of New Class Leaders Appointed in the New
York Circuit, 1811-1832

Date		Number of new class leaders appointed
May	1811	1
Nov	1811	4
Oct	1812	1
Apr	1813	1
Sept	1813	2
Dec	1813+	4
Oct	1813	4
Sept	1829	7
Oct	1829	6
Total		30

+   No minutes were taken from 1814 to 1816

Source: "Methodist Episcopal Church of New York. Board of Leaders.
              Minutes. 1811-1823" and "Forsyth Street Church. Board of
              Leaders. Minutes. 1825-1832" (New York, NY: Manuscripts
              Division, NYPL, Astor, Lenox and Tilden Foundations, MECR,
              vols. 90a and 212, photocopied).

Chapter 3.   Appendix 14
Eliphelet Wheeler's Observations on Class Attendance
in his Female Class of 31 Members at Allen Street
Church, 1825

Number of Class Members	Frequency of Class Class Attendance
1	constant
1	pretty good
1	more than half
8	half, about half
5	nearly half, not quite half
3	not half
1	tolerable
3	formerly attentive - not so now,
4	latterly not attentive
1	seldom
3	inattentive
2	not at all
2	sick
Total 31	

Source: "A Record of the Members in Society at Allen Street, April, 1825"
(New York, NY: Manuscripts Division, NYPL, Astor, Lenox and
Tilden Foundations, MECR, vol. 149, photocopied).

Chapter 3. Appendix 15
Class Attendance for One Quarter (3 months) in
Stephen Rockwell's Allen Street Church Class

Number of Class Members	Frequency	Percentage of Meetings Attended
1	14/14	100
7	attends constantly	NA
2	very well	NA
1	12/14	85
2	11/14	78
1	10/14	71
1	two thirds	$66^{2/3}$
1	9/14	64
3	8/14	57
5	one half	50
3	5/14	35
1	one third	$33^{1/3}$
1	4/14	28
1	2/14	14
1	1/14	7
1	dismissed for "neglect"	
Total 32		

Source: "A Record of Members in Society at Allen Street, April, 1825"
(New York, NY: Manuscripts Division, NYPL, Astor, Lenox and
Tilden Foundations, MECR, vol. 149, photocopied).

Chapter 3. Appendix 16
"Ration of Attendance the Last Quarter - 12 Weeks," in Cornelius Polhemus's Allen Street Class, 1825

Number of Class Members	Number of Meetings Attended
0	10
0	9
2	8
3	7
2	6
4	5
1	4
3	3
0	2
0	1
3	0
Total 18	

Source: "A Record of the Members in Society at Allen Street, April, 1825" (New York, NY: Manuscripts Division, NYPL, Astor, Lenox, and Tilden Foundations, MECR, vol. 149, photocopied).

Chapter 3. Appendix 17
Thomas McFarland's Class Attendance over a Three
Year Period

Year	Number in class	Number of Class Meetings Attended				
		0-10	10-19	20-29	30-39	40-49
1831	28	5	7	6	7	3
1832	35	6	7	11	8	3
1833	24	0	4	8	11	1

Source: "Forsyth Street Church. Classbook. 1831-1834." (New York,
NY: Manuscripts Division, NYPL, Astor, Lenox and Tilden
Foundations, MECR, vol. 205, photocopied).

Chapter 3.   Appendix 18
Thomas McFarlan's Class Book, 1831

1831	Nan		July ~/ ~/ 31~	8~	Feb 4~	~/	5~/
	Thomas M		l' P		l'	P	P
	R. Kirby.		l'				
	John Brown.	M					
	Henry Johnson.	m	12 6		6		
5	Almeda Cady.	M	l. P P				P
	Robert W. Dean.	m	75 l'				P
	Sihelannah Williamson.	M	l' l' -		l'	P	P
	Margaret Dixon.	N	45 P		l' 12	6	
	Maria Lane.	m	15 P		12		
10	Martha Armstrong.	m ~	P l		l'	P	P
	Catharine Ketchum.	M					
	Hannah Tremper.	M 25			31		
	Jane Bowren	m					P
	Ann Smith.	M	P		l'	P	
15	Zipporah Willis.	m	25				
	Melancthon Palmer.	M	-				
	Maria Dean.	M.					
	Ann Green.	n	P 12		12	P	
	Teressa Gurnee.	M					
20	George Brown.	m	P				

Source: "Forsyth Street Church. Classbook. 1831-1834" (New York, NY: Manuscripts Division, NYPL, Astor, Lenox and Tilden Foundations. MECR vol. 205, photocopied). Reproduced with permission of The New York Public Library.

Chapter 3. Appendix 19

Probationers' Attendance in Thomas McFarlan's Class

Name	1st Month	2nd Month	3rd Month	4th Month	5th Month	6th Month
Sarah Quick	2	3	2	2	2	3
C. Nelson	3	4	2	3	4	1
Jane Welsh	1	1	1	2	2	1
Isaac Vorhees	2	1	2	3	3	2
C. Mead	1	3	1	0	3	1
N. Gorton	4	4	3	4	2	3
Anson Green	2	2	1	1	0	0
Amelia Hoyt	3	3	1	2	1	1
Wm. Martin	4	4	4	3	5	3
M. Marshall	3	5	3	4	2	2
John Brodie	2	4	0	1	2	3
Thom. McCoy	4	3	4	4	4	4
Sarah Brodie	1	2	1	1	1	0
Sarah Tuttle	3	3	2	4	2	2
Silvester Tuttle	3	2	4	4	3	2

Name	Average Monthly Attendance
Sarah Quick	2.3 meetings
C. Nelson	2.8
Jane Welsh	1.3
Isaac Vorhees	2.1
C. Mead	1.5
N. Gorton	3.3
Anson Green	1
Amelia Hoyt	1.8
Wm. Martin	3.8
M. Marshall	3.1
John Brodie	2
Thom. McCoy	3.8
Sarah Brodie	1
Sarah Tuttle	2.6
Silvester Tuttle	3
Total	2.4

Source: "Forsyth Street Church. Classbook. 1831-1834" (New York, NY: Manuscripts Division, NYPL, Astor, Lenox and Tilden Foundations, MECR, vol. 205, photocopied).

Chapter 3. Appendix 20
Outline of Reverend George Coles's Sermon on
Jude 21, "Keep Yourselves in the Love of God"

Source: Reverend George Coles, "Journal" (Madison, NJ: UMCA –
GCAH, "Drew University Methodist Collection." Drew
University), 16 September 1832. Reproduced with permission
of Drew University Library.

Chapter 3.   Appendix 21
Reverend George Coles's Sermon Outline:
"Remarks on Class Meetings"

I. Utility of Class Meetings
    1.   To cherish the smallest seed of grace
    2.   To encourage the weak beginnings of the life of God in the soul
    3.   To promote Christian feeling and brotherly love

II. Evils of Neglecting

    1. A violation of the covenant of admission
    2. Shyness, surmises, suspicion
    3. Coldness, spiritual death
    4. Loss of confidence and affection
    5. Declension in faith and love

Faith is a plant, which must be often watered by prayer
Love is a fire, which can only be kept burning by keeping the brands together -
air is necessary

III. Directions to Class Leaders

    1.   Ascertain and record the spiritual state of each
    2.   Pray for each by name often
    3.   Retire an hour or so before class
    4.   Visit every member occasionally

Source: Reverend George Coles, "Journal" (Madison, NJ: UMCA - GCAH,
Book IV, Poughkeepsie, New York, "Drew University Methodist
Collection," Drew University), 1832. Reproduced with permission of
Drew University Library.

Chapter 3. Appendix 22
Members Expelled for "Neglect of Class," 1824-1827

Number
expelled

```
5

4

3                       *

2      *

1                              *              *

0 _____
      1824          1825          1826          1827
```

Source: "Record of Trials" (New York, NY: John Street United
           Methodist Church).

Chapter 3.   Appendix 23
Church Trial of John Chatterton

The Church
vs.
James Chatterton

On a charge of neglect of Christian Duties

1. In absenting himself from public worship.
2. In neglecting to meet his class.

N. Jarvis witnesseth and saith that the said James has neglected the public worship of God and meeting his class for nearly a twelvemonth and that when called upon would not engage to attend to his Christian duty and where cited to trial refused to attend.

Wm. Howard witnesseth and saith that James Chatterton was in the constant habit of neglecting the ministry of the word and the meeting of class when a member of his class previous to his going to N. Jarvis' class.

After taking the case into consideration (the committee) are of opinion that the said James Chatterton is guilty of the charge contained in the above specifications.

                                    Signed
                                    Isaac Wiltsey
                                    James Demarest   Committee
                                    Wm McLain

A correct copy of the minutes taken at the Trial.

                                    Signed   P. Price

New York March 3, 1825

He is expelled.

                                            P. P. Sandford

Source: "A Record of the Proceedings in the Trials of Members"
                    (Madison, NJ: UMCA - GCAH, "Drew University
                    Methodist Collection," Drew University), 34. Reproduced
                    with permission of Drew University Library.

Chapter 4. Appendix 1
Approved Course of Study for Ministers in the New York Annual Conference

Course	Examiner
1st Year	
The Bible and Its Doctrines	Noah Levings
Wesley's Sermons	P. R. Brown
English Grammar	E. E. Griswold
Fletcher's *Appeal* and *Christian Perfection*	H. Husted
Composition	John C. Lyon
2nd Year	
Bible as to Ordinance or Sacraments	George Peck
Watson's *Life of Wesley*	J. L. Gilder
Bishop Watson's *Apology* and	
Fletcher's *Christian Perfection*	James Young
Methodist *Discipline*	B. Griffen
Geography and Composition	J. Holdich
3rd Year	
Bible as to History and Chronology	Fitch Reed
1st and 2nd Parts of Watson's *Institutes*	W. McK. Bangs
Gregory's *Church History*	H. Bangs
Rhetoric	John M. Pease
Written Essay or Sermon	Daniel Smith
4th Year	
Bible Generally	N. Bangs
3rd and 4th Parts of Watson's *Institutes*	A. M. Osmon
Powell on Apostolical Succession	B. Goodsell
Old Christianity Compared with	
the *Novelties of Popery* by Gideon Ousley	D. I. Wright
Logic	O. V. Amerman
Written Essay or Sermon	C. W. Carpenter

Source: "The Journal and Appointments of the New York Annual Conference Held in the Methodist Episcopal Church in Forsyth Street, New York City, 14-24 May 1845" (Madison, NJ: UMCA - GCAH, Drew University), 19-20. Reproduced with permission of Drew University Library.

Chapter 4.   Appendix 2
Agenda for Leaders' Meeting, John Street Church

<u>Leaders' Meeting</u>
<u>Order of Business (circa 1847-1854)</u>

1. Singing and Prayer
2. Reading of Minutes of Past Meeting
3. Persons Received
       (1) By Letter
       (2) On Probation
4. Dismissed
       (1) By Certificate
       (2) Dropped from Probation
5. Passed for Membership
6. Transfers from Class to Class
7. Sick or Dead
8. Finances
9. Miscellaneous

Source: "John Street Church. Classes. 1842-1854" (New York, NY:
                Manuscripts Division, NYPL, Astor, Lenox and Tilden
                Foundations, MECR, vol. 240, photocopied).

Chapter 4. Appendix 3
Multiple Offices of Class Leaders, Eighteenth Street
Church, 1885

Name	Class Leader	Trustee	Steward	Building Committee
Ernest B. Stavey	x	x		
George H. Tabor	x		x	
Egbert Rinehart	x	x		x
Isaac Bird	x	x		x
Robert O. Jones	x		x	
Richard Terhune	x		x	

Source: Benjamin Force, *The Charter Church of New York Methodism: Eighteenth Street* (New York: Phillips and Hunt, 1885), nonpaginated appendix.

Chapter 4.   Appendix 4
Average Quarterly Class Attendance in Henry
Moore's Allen Street Class

Year	Quarter	# of Class Members	Average Quarterly Attendance	% of Class Members Who Attended
1855-56	11/1 - 1/31	21	6.6	33 1/3
1856	2/7 - 4/24	19	7.2	37
1856	5/1 - 7/31	18	6.5	33 1/3
1856	8/7 - 10/30	18	6.1	33 1/3
1856-57	11/6 - 1/29	15	5.4	37
1857	2/5 - 4/30	14	5	35
1857	5/7 - 7/23	11	5.5	50
1857	10/8 - 12/31	13	5.4	41
1858	1/7 - 4/8	15	6.1	40
1858	4/15 - 7/22	18	5.8	32
1858	7/29 - 10/28	17	6.1	35

Source: "Allen Street Church. Classes. 1855-1859" (New York, NY:
            Manuscripts Division, NYPL, Astor, Lenox and Tilden
            Foundations, MECR, vol. 144, photocopied).

Chapter 4.   Appendix 5
Class Size

Church	Year	10-19 members	20-29 members	30-39 members	40-49 members
Allen Street	1838	5	16	10	8
Allen Street	1845*	7	19	6	2
Forsyth Street	1842-1843	7+	11	8	2
Forsyth Street	1843-1844	3	13	8	1
Forsyth Street	1852	5	6	5	0
John Street	1842**	5	4	6	0
John Street	1843	3	2	6	0
John Street	1844	2	3	4	3
Seventh Street	1837++	5	5	0	0
Seventh Street	1845	6	4	1	1

*	Allen Street also had two classes of under ten members.
+	Forsyth Street also had one class of under ten members.
**	John Street had one class of eight members.
++	Seventh Street had one class of eight members.

Source: "Allen Street Church. Classes. 1838-1845," Forsyth Street Church. Classes. 1842-1854," John Street Church. Classes. 1842-1854," and "Seventh Street Church. Classes. 1837-1864" (New York, NY: Manuscripts Division, NYPL, Astor, Lenox and Tilden Foundations, MECR, vols. 151, 206, 240, and 352, photocopied).

Chapter 4.   Appendix 6
Number of Methodist Episcopal Churches in
Manhattan, 1795-1875

Year	Number of churches	Number of missions	Total membership
1795	2	0	755
1800	4	0	776
1805	4	0	940
1810	5	0	2,200
1815	5	0	2,443
1820	6	0	3,218
1825	6	0	2,623
1830	8	0	3,955
1835	12	0	5,287
1840	13	2	6,722
1845	25	1	9,570
1850	25	0	7,534
1855	31	0	7,083
1860	33	0	9,774
1865	36	0	8,880
1870	38	0	10,598
1875	43	0	10,456

Source: "The Journal and Appointments of the New York Conference,
1840-1845," and "The Journal of the New York East Conference,
1850-1875" (Madison, NJ: UMCA - GCAH, Drew University).
Reproduced with permission of Drew University Library.

Notes

Notes to Preface

1. The phrase "New York City Methodism" actually refers to the Methodist Episcopal Churches in Manhattan only.

2. Roger Finke and Rodney Stark, *The Churching of America, 1776-1990* (New Brunswick, NJ: Rutgers University Press, 1992), 40-46.

3. The class meeting was a weekly gathering of twelve persons and their class leader for reporting on their inward and outward discipleship. John Wesley called it one of the "prudential means of grace" and used it for catechesis and spiritual nurture, especially of new converts.

4. Nathan O. Hatch, "The Puzzle of American Methodism," *Reflections* 88 (1993): 14.

5. See "Secondary Source" bibliography for additional information.

6. Chapters 2, 3, and 4 cover three distinct time periods: 1770 to 1800, 1800 to 1832, and 1832 to 1870, respectively. Along with some contemporary applications, the conclusion briefly examines some of the changes from 1870 to 1890.

Chapter 1: The Class Meeting in Early British Methodism: 1738-80

1. The Evangelical Revival in England spanned the entire eighteenth century and was composed of five main groups. These groups were united in their emphasis on the Reformation doctrine of "justification by faith" but disagreed on certain points in the areas of theology, spirituality, and church structure. These other groups were the Methodists, the Calvinistic Methodists, the Moravians, the half-regular Evangelical clergy, the regular Evangelical clergy. With the exception of the Moravians, who were of German origin, the other four groups had Anglican connections. The half-regular Evangelical clergy were Anglican priests who served parish churches; they supported the Methodist movement in a number of ways such as allowing Methodist itinerant preachers to preach in their pulpits and by attending Wesley's annual conference meetings. In contrast, the regular Evangelical clergy who were also Anglican priests differed from the Methodists in both doctrine and church

order. For a fuller treatment of the similarities and differences of these five groups, see Frank Whaling, ed., *John and Charles Wesley* (New York: Oxford University Press, 1964), 26-42.

2. A society was a grouping of all the Methodists in one town or city (i.e., the Bristol society).

3. The class meeting did not refer to teaching, such as a Bible class. Instead, Wesley used the word *classis* in its original Latin meaning: that of "a little company" or "group." In looking back on the development of the class meeting, Wesley wrote "that it may the more easily be discerned, whether they indeed are working out their own salvation, each society is divided into smaller companies, called classes, according to their respective places of abode," see John Wesley, *The Works of John Wesley*. 3rd ed., vol. 8 (London: Wesleyan Methodist Book Room, 1872; reprint, Grand Rapids, MI: Baker Book House Company), 269.

4. A band meeting consisted of two to five people, all of the same sex, who met weekly to confess their temptations and sins to one another

5. Class manuals were handbooks which provided a job description of the office of class leader as well as exhortation to the leaders to carry out their duties in a pious and energetic manner.

6. David Holsclaw, "The Demise of Disciplined Christian Fellowship: The Methodist Class Meeting in Nineteenth-Century America" (Ph.D. diss., University of California, 1979), 1-48; and David L. Watson, *The Early Methodist Class Meeting* (Nashville: Discipleship Resources, 1985), 67-124.

7. For general histories of John Wesley and early British Methodism, the following should be consulted: Leslie F. Church, *The Early Methodist People* (London: Society for the Promotion of Christian Knowledge, 1948); Robert C. Monk, *John Wesley: His Puritan Heritage* (Nashville: Abingdon Press, 1966); Rupert E. Davies and Gordon Rupp, eds. *A History of Methodism in Great Britain* (London: Epworth Press, 1965); Martin Schmidt, *John Wesley: A Theological Biography* (Nashville: Abingdon Press, 1972); and A. Skevington Wood, *The Inextinguishable Blaze* (Grand Rapids: W. B. Eerdmans Publishing Company, 1960).

8. Latitudinarianism was a new theology which attempted to incorporate the rationalism of the eighteenth century into traditional Christian theology.

9. Anthony Armstrong, *The Church of England, the Methodists, and Society, 1700-1850* (London: University of London Press, 1973), 49-50.

10. Itinerant field preaching referred to the practice of traveling to different places and preaching in market squares and open fields. The Anglican hierarchy generally viewed itinerant preaching as "irregular" since the Church of England did not permit preachers to enter someone else's parish without permission. The same attitude was expressed toward the later Methodist itinerant preachers.

11. Armstrong, *The Church of England, the Methodists, and Society*, 53-54.

12. John Wesley, the founder of Methodism, and his brother, Charles, were both priests of the Church of England. John was born in 1703 and died in 1791. Their father, the Reverend Samuel Wesley was also an Anglican priest as were both their grandfathers. The Wesley brothers grew up in the Epworth

parish rectory. As a young boy, John went to the Charterhouse preparatory school in London, and then to Oxford University where he received his bachelor and master of arts degrees. He was ordained deacon in 1725 and priest in 1727. His younger brother, Charles, also attended Oxford and was ordained a priest. Both brothers experienced deeper religious conversions in May, 1738, and they began preaching an evangelical doctrine of salvation by faith. Additional dates in John Wesley's life and British Methodism can be found in Appendix 1.

13. Armstrong, *The Church of England, the Methodists, and Society*, 60. In 1738, after his return to London from the Georgia colony, Wesley visited the Moravian headquarters in Herrnhut, Germany, and was favorably impressed.

14. Ibid., 91. Armstrong added, however, that the reality may have been that the Established Church was simply not equipped to minister to the large, urban population and that the Anglican clergy actually preferred the comfortable rural setting.

15. Ibid.

16. Jacob Arminius, a moderate Reformed Church theologian of the seventeenth century, had said that God's grace was freely offered to all persons in contrast to the prevailing Calvinistic doctrine of predestination. Calvinistic Methodists, led by the Reverend George Whitefield, believed in predestination. The Wesleyan Methodists were Arminian.

17. Christopher Hill, *From Reformation to Industrial Revolution* (London: Weidenfeld and Nicolson, 1967), 227-28. Hill wrote that "we need not argue that Methodism saved England from revolution to agree that its influence on the outcasts of society was in a profoundly non-revolutionary direction. Wesley, on the other hand, was no enemy of the bourgeois virtues, or of technical innovation."

18. Ibid., 390. This basic theological difference caused a split between many Anglicans and the Methodists. Hill points out on pages 396-97 that even the evangelical movement within Anglicanism adhered to the doctrine of predestination.

19. Ibid. Sykes also stated on page 391 that after Wesley's "Aldersgate experience" in May, 1738, the "Methodist movement became a conscious and deliberate challenge to the rationalistic attitude towards all religious characteristics of the churchmanship of the age."

20. Ibid., 393. Wesley never pressured his lay preachers to become ordained priests or even "readers" since he disliked the parish system.

21. Ibid., 393-94.

22. The Conference was a yearly meeting of Wesley and his traveling preachers which discussed points of theology and other church matters.

23. These tensions became acute in the late eighteenth century but any action was delayed until John Wesley died.

24. Edward. P. Thompson, *The Making of the English Working Class* (New York: Vintage Books, 1963), 40-41. According to Thompson, Wesley believed hard work, even though it was unjust, was an indication that the members were not backsliding since that was always a possibility. In this, Thompson said,

Methodism was similar to the earlier Calvinistic and Puritan teaching on work and the repression of one's feelings.

25. Ibid., 41. Thompson, however, did credit Methodism with providing workers with a small group experience (through the class meetings) and district and national forms of organization. Scholars, such as Robert Southey, believe that the later workers' movement directly borrowed these forms from Methodism. Nevertheless, it was not until the late 1790s and the early 1800s that the two schismatic Methodist groups--the Methodist New Connexion and the Primitive Methodists--became more strongly democratic and supportive of the workers' movement. Thompson noted on page 46 that these two groups took on the characteristics of the French Revolution in their villages. Traditional, orthodox Methodism became even more conservative in the nineteenth century which further alienated many workers.

26. Ibid., 350.

27.Ibid., 53-54.

28. William R. Ward, *The Protestant Evangelical Awakening* (Cambridge: Cambridge University Press, 1992), 340-42.

29. Ibid., 351.

30. Michael Watts, *The Dissenters: From the Reformation to the French Revolution* (Oxford: Oxford University Press, 1978), 406-8.

31. Ibid., 408-9. Watts also examined their specific trades and found that some lay preachers had been employed in the textile industry, tin-mining, building trades, or as bakers. Others had served in the army. Watts disagreed with Alan Gilbert's thesis which stated that the Methodist revival succeeded in the period of the Industrial Revolution because people sought group associations due to changes in the way society had been traditionally organized. By examining the occupations of many of the early lay preachers, Watts was able to show that these Methodist lay preachers had stable employment and family life and did not feel a great need for group associations.

32. Ibid., 410.

33. John Wesley, *The Letters of the Reverend John Wesley, A.M.*, ed. John Telford (London: The Epworth Press, 1960), vol. 4, 266. Wesley's main areas of preaching were London, Bristol, and Newcastle-on-Tyne which included many mines and factories, see Watts, *The Dissenters*, 410.

34. Watts, *The Dissenters*, 411-13. Certain phenomena did occur during Methodist preaching which Wesley attributed to the power of Satan being broken. The phenomena included people falling down, shrieking, appearing to be in agony, fainting, and hysterical laughter.

35. Ibid., 414. Watts noted that many of the early lay preachers listed "fear of death" as the primary factor in their subsequent conversions.

36. Charity schools had been started by the Society for the Promotion of Christian Knowledge in 1699.

37. Watts, *The Dissenters*, 422-24. In Wales, both children and adults attended the charity schools.

38. The Dissenters were groups who had separated from the Anglican Church and had their own chapels and clergy. Two examples of Dissenters were the Baptists and Quakers.

39. Watts, *The Dissenters*, 436-38.

40. A. Skevington Wood, *The Inextinguishable Blaze*, 103-10.

41. Ibid., 166.

42. *The Works of John Wesley*, vol. 8, 251-52.

43. Watson, *The Early Methodist Class Meeting*, 5. Wesley made a distinction between what he called the "instituted means of grace" and the "prudential means of grace." The instituted means of grace were the traditional ways of coming into contact with God; these included searching the Scriptures, fasting, and receiving the sacrament of Holy Communion. The prudential means of grace developed providentially at that particular time of the Methodist revival; these included the society, band, and class meetings, and the love feasts.

44. Holsclaw, "The Demise of Disciplined Christian Fellowship," 1-48.

45. Ibid., 14.

46. *The Works of John Wesley*, vol. 8, *A Plain Account of the People Called Methodists*, 250.

47. David Holsclaw, "The Demise of Disciplined Christian Fellowship," 14.

48. William Dean, "Disciplined Fellowship: The Rise and Decline of Cell Groups in British Methodism" (Ph D. diss., University of Iowa, 1985), 132. These loosely organized societies were later given the name, "The Societies of the People Called Methodists."

49. Thomas Hardy, "Diary," 25 October 1798, p. 31, Methodist Archives and Research Centre, John Ryland University Library, Manchester, England.

50. Wesley bought an abandoned foundry in London and turned it into a Methodist chapel. Later, Wesley purchased a building on City Road which became the City Road Chapel; his three story house also adjoined it.

51. Dean, "Disciplined Fellowship," 141. Prayer meetings were American-style revival meetings which had developed out of the camp meetings held in the early 1800s in Kentucky. Public prayer meetings emphasized fervent evangelical preaching, altar calls, and sustained prayer for "penitents" at the "mourners' bench" or in front of the altar. Prayer meetings also stressed "instantaneous conversions" rather than gradual ones which the "class meetings" tended to produce. For an extended description of the evangelistic function of the prayer meeting in America, see Richard Carwardine, *Transatlantic Revivalism: Popular Evangelicalism in Britain and America, 1790-1865* (Westport, CT: Greenwood Press, 1978).

52. Dr. Anthony Horneck, a German, who had been educated at Oxford University and ordained to the Anglican priesthood, had begun these small parish-based societies in 1678.

53. Anthony Horneck, *Several Sermons upon the Fifth of St. Matthew* (London: Jer. Batley, 1717), vii-x. In February, 1743, John Wesley wrote *The Nature, Design, and General Rules of the United Societies in London, Bristol, and Newcastle-upon-Tyne*. Neither set of rules stressed theological opinions or doctrines, but rather the elements of a dedicated Christian lifestyle, see Wood, *The Inextinguishable Blaze*, 108.

54. Watson, *Early Methodist Class Meeting*, 88-89 and Holsclaw, "Demise of Disciplined Christian Fellowship," 19.

55. Holsclaw, "Demise of Disciplined Christian Fellowship," 19. See also the rules for a weekly meeting for the societies at Poplar and Epworth in Watson, *Early Methodist Class Meeting*, 190, 194.

56. Watson, *Early Methodist Class Meeting*, 72. Wesley's father began this religious society in 1701, two years before John was born. Also, in 1699, he published "A Letter Concerning the Religious Societies" in which he urged the need for pastoral care and spiritual growth, and emphasized that religious societies could help achieve both. In addition, Watson noted, also on page 72, that the elder Wesley "observed that there were precedents for such societies, including those of the Marquis de Renty, and stressed that their purpose was neither to gather new churches out of existing churches, nor to foment schisms or divisions, nor yet to imply that other Christian brethren were heathen, but rather to promote the glory of God in the practice of humility and charity."

57. Ibid., 189. Moreover, only Anglicans were permitted to join Horneck's societies. The Methodist societies had no such restriction, see Holsclaw, "Demise of Disciplined Christian Fellowship," 27.

58. See below for the discussion of the "catechumenate function" of the class meeting.

59. Dean, "Disciplined Fellowship," 145-47. Class tickets were small cards which had the person's name, a Scripture verse, the date, and the minister's signature on it. This card enabled members to get into society meetings, class meetings, and love feasts. It was, however, difficult to enforce this rule. Local societies were often lax on checking to see that each person had a ticket. This later became a problem in the New York Society, too.

60. *The Works of John Wesley*, vol. 5, "Minutes of Several Conversations," 217. Horneck's societies were generally smaller, having about twelve members, and, thus, a ticket system was unnecessary. In contrast, the Methodist societies were groupings of entire towns or cities and could often contain as many as several hundred members. In size, Horneck's religious societies most closely resembled the later Methodist "class meetings."

61. Holsclaw, "Demise of Disciplined Christian Fellowship," 19; Michael Watts, *The Dissenters*, 404.

62. Watson, *Early Methodist Class Meeting*, 191.

63. Ibid., 107.

64. Armstrong, *The Church of England, the Methodists, and Society, 1700-1850*, 51.

65. *The Works of John Wesley*, vol. 8, *The Nature, Design, and General Rules of the United Societies in London, Bristol, Kingswood, & c.*, 270. Stewards were laymen who had a financial rather than a spiritual function, see Dean, "Disciplined Fellowship," 116.

66. Dean, "Disciplined Fellowship," p. 111-15.

67. Watson, *Early Methodist Class Meeting*, 71.

68. Wood, *The Inextinguishable Blaze*, 102-3. After two years in a parish, Wesley had returned to Oxford as a teaching fellow of Lincoln College where he tutored and advised undergraduate students. Charles Wesley, who was still a student himself at Oxford, had gathered together a group of students to study the Scriptures before his older brother's return. John Wesley joined the group

and quickly became its leader. It was at Oxford that the Wesleys met George Whitefield who went on to become one of the greatest preachers of the English revival. It was also at Oxford that this group received the name "Methodists" because of their highly disciplined system of spiritual and social outreach activities.

69. Dean, "Disciplined Fellowship," 123-24. Wesley "borrowed" them from the Moravians whose headquarters he had recently visited in Herrnhut, Germany. In November, 1738, Wesley wrote his own "Rules for the Band Societies." The Fetter Lane society met at the home of James Hutton.

70. Ibid. In February, 1740, however, Wesley and some of his followers separated from the Fetter Lane society because of a theological dispute involving "stillness," in which some of the society members would not say or do anything but simply wait upon God to inspire them.

71. Frederick A. Norwood, *The Story of American Methodism* (Nashville: Abingdon Press, 1974), 34.

72. Watts, *The Dissenters*, 400-1. Watts compared Methodism's attempts to stay loyal to the church with the non-separating Puritans of the early seventeenth century.

73. Ibid., 447.

74. Ibid., 400-6 and 442-43.

75. Wesley, *The Journal of the Reverend John Wesley, A.M.*, ed. Nehemiah Curnock (London: The Epworth Press, 1938), vol. 7, 414.

76. Wood, *The Inextinguishable Blaze*, 174.

77. Ibid., 174-75. In 1795, four years after Wesley's death, the Methodist societies separated from the Church of England to become the Wesleyan Methodist Church.

78. Clifford Towlson, *Methodist and Moravian* (London: Epworth, 1957), 184-85. A number of scholars such as Towlson, David Watson, and Anthony Armstrong all agree that the Moravians directly influenced the Methodist band meeting. Towlson also noted on pages 184-85 that the Moravian system influenced Wesley's bands "especially in the basis of choice, the inner activities, the nomination of leaders, and the disciplining of unsatisfactory members." The Moravians at Herrnhut had divided their members into "choirs" which were smaller groupings of either men or women. Moreover, these "choirs" were eventually subdivided into smaller bands for those who wanted more intimate fellowship. Bands had approximately five members. The bands allowed members to confess their sins and temptations to one another and to strengthen one another's weak areas. Count Zinzendorf had "adopted the idea from the drawing-room meetings of Spener the Pietist, meetings which came to be known as 'churches within the church,' see Towlson, *Methodist and Moravian*, 177. In an address given on 2 July 1747, Count Zinzendorf said the inspiration for the bands had come from Mary's visit to Elizabeth which is mentioned in Luke 1:39-45.

79. Norwood, *Story of American Methodism*, 27.

80. Wesley, *Journal*, vol. 2, 496.

81. Towlson, *Methodist and Moravian*, 189-90.

82. Armstrong, *The Church of England, the Methodists, and Society,* 67. These meetings were also called the "public bands," see Holsclaw, "Demise of Disciplined Christian Fellowship," 32-33.

83. Towlson, *Methodist and Moravian,* 189-90.

84. *The Works of John Wesley,* vol. 8, "Rules of the Band Societies Drawn up December, 1738," 272-73. Each member was required to answer those five questions at every meeting. Moreover, Wesley drew up other questions which were optional. In establishing band meetings, Wesley often referred to James 5:14-16 which joined together confession of sin and healing. In the bands, Wesley wanted each member to speak "in order, freely and plainly, the true state of our souls, with the faults we have committed in thought, word, or deed, and the temptations we have felt, since our last meeting," 272.

85. Wood, *The Inextinguishable Blaze,* 167.

86. Towlson, *Methodist and Moravian,* 209. The love feast, or agape, as it was also called, was part of early Christian worship. It was a service which preceded a meal and included hymns, prayers, Scripture readings, and testimonies; bread and water (taken from a common cup) were shared as a symbol of unity.

87. Wesley, *Journal,* vol. 1, 377. Wesley began love feasts in 1738-1739 in England. See also Towlson, *Moravian and Methodist,* 209-10.

88. Towlson, *Moravian and Methodist,* 214-15. The love feast was held quarterly. Initially, men and women had separate love feasts, but eventually they were mixed. Mixed love feasts were also the norm later in New York City.

89. Armstrong, *The Church of England, the Methodists, and Society, 1700-1850,* 67.

90. *The Works of John Wesley,* vol. 8, *A Plain Account of the People Called Methodists,* 259.

91. The assistant was a lay preacher who was in charge of several circuits. Another name for the assistant was "superintendent of circuits." The later American equivalent to the assistant was the "presiding elder." A circuit was made up of a number of "preaching stations" and was also called "preacher's rounds." The Methodist "connexion" was made up of the total number of circuits. In 1746, the Methodist connexion included seven circuits; in 1791, it had one hundred fourteen. The "quarterly meeting" which began in 1748 brought together all the officers of the all the societies within one circuit for business and worship. The itinerant lay preachers who traveled regularly on the circuits were called "helpers;" itinerant preachers were of three types: lay, ordained, or "half-ordained" (i.e., part-time). Sometimes, traveling preachers "located" and worked in secular employment (i.e., farming, business, or various trades) so they could support their families or because of ill health, see Armstrong, *The Church of England, the Methodists, and Society, 1700-1850,* 67.

92. Wesley, *Letters,* vol. 4, 272-73.

93. Dean, "Disciplined Fellowship," 162-63.

94. Ibid., 164.

95. Ibid., 171.

96. In contrast, one modern scholar credited the French nobleman, Gaston de Renty, with being the prime influence on the Methodist class meeting. For this interpretation, see Henry Bett, "A French Marquis and the Class Meeting," *Wesley Historical Proceedings* 18 (1932), 44-47. Bett noted how strongly de Renty had influenced Wesley by his simplicity, detachment from material possessions and worldly pleasure, communion with God in prayer, and outreach to the poor (Wesley mentioned de Renty several times in his journal). Most importantly, though, Bett asserted on page 44 that de Renty had influenced him through the religious societies de Renty established "at Caen, Toulouse, Paris, and other places (within the Roman Catholic Church, of course) which were almost exact prototypes of the class meeting in Methodism. They were little gatherings of devout people who met weekly, and besides arranging for the relief of the poor, engaged in united prayer, read books of devotion in their assemblies, and discoursed together of their religious experience." Bett further argued on page 45 that Wesley would have known of these seventeenth century societies because his father, Samuel, had referred to them in his "Letter Concerning the Religious Societies." Moreover, Bett noted that "de Renty's societies, were in some respects more closely parallel to the society-classes of Methodism than either the 'Religious Societies' of London (i.e., the Anglican Religious Societies started by Horneck) or the 'Collegia Pietatis' of Pietism in Germany" and, therefore, called de Renty the real "originator of the Methodist class meeting." No other modern scholar has taken that position. It seems likely, however, that class meetings, while similar in some ways to already existing Catholic, Anglican and Moravian structures, were Wesley's original contribution in response to local events.

97. The Bristol society had just built a new "chapel" or "preaching house" called the "New Room."

98. *The Works of John Wesley*, vol. 8, *A Plain Account of the People Called Methodists*, 252. Those who collected the money each week were called "class leaders." These "class collections" remained a part of Methodism well into the nineteenth century. In addition to paying a penny a week, class members also paid a shilling every quarter when they received a new "class ticket." This money helped pay off building debts and assisted those in need. These collections, however, were never enough to keep the societies out of debt. Since many Methodists were also members of the Established Church and paid taxes to support it, Wesley never expected society members to give substantially. Yet, when the Methodist societies became a separate denomination in 1795, fund-raising for salaries and local needs became a major concern. Besides the weekly and quarterly collections, the Annual Conference also made yearly appeals to the classes for various needs such as funds for retired preachers and established a Conference Contingency fund which raised money from the classes for various projects, see Dean, "Disciplined Fellowship," 279-80 and 286.

99. Dean, "Disciplined Fellowship," 175. Moreover, Wesley believed this arrangement would greatly strengthen the pastoral oversight which could be given and wrote that "I called them together all the Leaders of the classes (so we used to term them and their companies), and desired, that each would make

a particular inquiry into the behavior of those whom he saw weekly," in *The Works of John Wesley*, vol. 8, *A Plain Account of the People Called Methodists*, 252-53. Wesley desired that class size be restricted to twelve persons since a small class allowed each member enough time to speak in a one hour meeting. Some classes, however, had up to eighty persons. On the other hand, William Dean believed that the majority of classes rarely went over thirty members. This idea is shown by the 1775 Annual Conference's resolution which said that no class should have more than thirty members. Furthermore, after examining a number of English "class-books," Dean concluded that class size averaged between twelve and twenty and that a class of twenty had an actual attendance of eleven to twelve each week. Also, he noted that large classes were rarely subdivided since class leaders and class members did not want to be separated, in Dean, "Disciplined Fellowship," 275-76, 309.

100. *The Works of John Wesley*, vol. 8, *A Plain Account of the People Called Methodists*, 254. In fact, Wesley felt so strongly about putting new converts into classes that he would not preach in certain areas unless societies and classes could be formed. Exemplifying this is his journal entry of 25 August 1763 in which he said that "the preaching like an apostle, without joining together those that are awakened and training them up in the ways of God, is only begetting children for the murderer. How much preaching has there been for these twenty years all over Pembrokeshire, but no societies, no discipline, no order or connexion; and the consequence is that nine in ten of the once-awakened are now faster asleep," in Wesley, *Journal*, 25 August 1763, vol. 5, 26. In contrast, the Reverend George Whitefield would preach anywhere but neglected to offer his converts some type of disciplined fellowship.

101. Wesley, *Journal*, 25 March 1742, vol. 2, 535. From Bristol and London, the class system soon spread to all the Methodist societies throughout England.

102. Dean, "Disciplined Fellowship," 176.

103. David Watson, "Methodist Spirituality," in *Protestant Spiritual Traditions* ed. Frank C. Senn (New York: Paulist Press, 1986), 212. Unlike the band meetings, which were segregated by sex, the class meetings were often composed of both males and females since the primary consideration in forming a class was geographical proximity.

104. Joseph Barker, "A Methodist Class Meeting, circa 1822," in *Nonconformity in the Nineteenth Century*, ed. David M. Thompson (London: Routledge and K. Paul, 1972), 48. Equally important, he would also give a general exhortation.

105. Ibid., 49.

106. Joseph Nightingale, *A Portraiture of Methodism* (London: For Longman, Hurst, Rees, and Orme, 1807), 181-89.

107. Watson, *Early Methodist Class Meeting*, 115.

108. Towlson, *Moravian and Methodist*, 20.

109. In the 1820s and early 1830s, the "prayer meeting," which had been transplanted from America began to replace the traditional Sunday evening society meeting and quickly became the chief evangelistic tool of Methodism. Prayer meetings of a less revivalistic nature had also existed in Wesley's time.

He approved of them as long as they didn't interfere with band and class meetings.

110. William W. Dean, "The Evangelical Function of the Class Meeting," *Conservative Evangelicals in Methodism Newsletter* 10 (1983) 32-33.

111. "Liverpool Conference of 1820," in *A History of the Methodist Church in Great Britain,* ed. Rupert Davies and Gordon Rupp (London: Epworth Press, 1965), vol. 4, 368.

112. Dean, "Disciplined Fellowship," 301. Moreover, Dean asserted that for the early Methodists, conversion "was an intensely personal matter: at this point in one's religious life, one stood entirely alone before God. If a real change of heart was to occur, the penitent must seek a face to face encounter with God, an encounter to which God was constantly drawing the seeker, through the Holy Spirit. For this reason, Wesley insisted, as some recent studies have pointed out, that preaching services end with a hymn and dismissal, and the people were to return home immediately without any talking, lest impressions are lost through conversation," see Dean, 302.   Gradual conversions were the rule until the 1820s and 1830s when Methodist leaders came to expect instantaneous conversions through the use of American-style revival meetings.

113. Holsclaw, "Demise of Disciplined Christian Fellowship," 10-11. Sometimes the traveling preacher formed an entirely new class; on other occasions, however, the newly awakened persons simply joined existing classes. A three month probation period was required as preparation for baptism and for becoming a full member of the society. During this time, the "seeker" attended the weekly society and class meetings. At the end of the three months, the class leaders of the society, who met regularly in the leaders' meeting, voted to accept or reject the candidate. Moreover, probation could also be extended beyond the normal three months. In New York City, the probationary period was increased to six months and was often extended for those who were "not passed" at the end of their probationary period.

114. A local preacher had a full-time secular occupation such as a business, a farm, or a trade and was licensed by his quarterly conference to preach only in his own town.   Often, local preachers started out as class leaders who eventually felt a "call" to preach.

115. Dean, "Disciplined Fellowship," 208-9. Goodfellow also became the class leader of the class. In contrast, most of the new class meetings in the nineteenth century were started by the traveling preacher.

116. Edward Corderoy, *Father Reeves, The Methodist Class Leader: A Brief Account of Mr. William Reeves, Thirty-four Years a Class Leader in the Wesleyan Methodist Society* (New York: Carlton and Phillips, 1853), 20.

117. Corderoy, *Father Reeves,* 32. Corderoy recalled that during the last hymn of a preaching service, Carvosso's "active eyes would scan the neighboring pews, but especially the free seats, to see whose moistened eye gave evidence that the heart was touched. Many times and oft, the service over, was the good man found planted just in the right place, beside some poor broken-hearted sinner, begging him to come to class."

118. Dean, "Disciplined Fellowship," 303.

119. Watson, *Early Methodist Class Meeting*, 132.

120. Reverend James Wood, *Directions and Cautions Addressed to the Class Leaders* (London: Conference Office, 1803), 8. Similarly, the Reverend Edmund Grindrod wrote to class leaders that "some persons join us whose convictions of sin are very superficial" and that "means should be used to bring them to a deep sense of their sinfulness and guilt; in order to this, frequently set before them the great evil of sin, the strictness and spirituality of God's law, and the awful danger to which they are exposed. Put into their hands, if possible, awakening spirit-stirring tracts," in Reverend Edmund Grindrod, *The Duties, Qualifications, and Encouragements of Class Leaders*, in *Tracts of the Tract Society of the Methodist Episcopal Church*, ed. Abel Stevens (New York: Carlton and Phillips, 1854), Tract 275: 23-24.

121. Watson, *Early Methodist Class Meeting*, 107. A class paper contained three items: the name of each member listed in alphabetical order, a symbol next to the member's name to indicate his spiritual state, and a place to record attendance (usually for one quarter or three months). Class leaders used five letters to mark attendance: "D" for "distant," "S" for sick, "B" for business, "N" for neglect, and "A" for no reason. Three consecutive absences could result in expulsion. Later, a "class book" was used to record attendance.

122. Ibid., 77.

123. Wesley, *Journal*, 5 November 1747, vol. 3, 321. Again, the following year, when Wesley examined the classes at Newcastle, he "found not only an increase of number, but likewise more of the life and power of religion among them than ever I had found before," in Wesley, *Journal*, 13-15 July 1748, vol. 3, 361-62.

124. Ibid., 22 June 1787, 7:294.

125. Holsclaw, "Demise of Disciplined Christian Fellowship," 44. Like the earlier "band ticket," the class ticket included the person's name, a Scripture verse, the date, and the preacher's signature.

126. Ibid.

127. Samuel Bradburn, "Diary," undated entry under March 1813, Methodist Archives and Research Centre, John Rylands University Library, Manchester, England.

128. Dean, "Disciplined Fellowship," 292-93.

129. Wesley, *Journal*, 3 September 1759, vol. 4, 350. Similarly, in 1764, Wesley told the Bristol societies that "if you constantly meet your band, I have no doubt that you will constantly meet your class; indeed, otherwise you are not of our Society. Whoever misses his class thrice together thereby excludes himself, and the preacher that comes next ought to put out his name," in Wesley, "Advice to the Bristol Societies," in *Letters*, vol. 4, 273.

130. Dean, *"Disciplined Fellowship,"* 225-54.

131. *The Works of John Wesley*, vol. 8, *A Plain Account of the People Called Methodists*, 253. This information was invaluable to the traveling preacher since he did not know the individual members as well the class leaders did.

132. Dean, "Disciplined Fellowship," 257-63. By the 1870s, however, leaders' meetings were held on a monthly basis.

133. In the early nineteenth century, the Wesleyan Methodist Church, unlike the other two splinter Methodist denominations (i.e., the Primitive Methodists and the Free Methodists) insisted that only the traveling preachers, and not the class leaders as a body, could discipline class members. Class leaders were initially appointed by Wesley himself; later, the preacher-in-charge (of the circuit) appointed them. Although some Methodists wanted to be able to elect their own class leaders, Wesley firmly rejected that idea. Moreover, class leaders could be removed at any time for ineffectiveness. Class leaders could be either male or female, although a male could never lead a female class. In contrast, the New York Society permitted males to lead female classes.

134. Reverend Edmund Grindrod, *The Duties, Qualifications, and Encouragements of Class Leaders*, in *Tracts of the Tract Society of the Methodist Episcopal Church*, ed. Abel Stevens (New York: Carlton and Phillips, 1854), Tract 275, 23-5.

135. Wesley, "Minutes of Several Conversations," in *Works*, vol. 8, 301.

136. Grindrod, *The Duties, Qualifications, and Encouragements of Class Leaders*, in *Tracts of the Tract Society of the Methodist Episcopal Church*, Tract 275, 16.

137. Charles Perronet, *Class Meetings: Ways and Means of Rendering Them More Animating and Instructive*, in *Tracts of the Tract Society of the Methodist Episcopal Church*, Tract 78, 3.

138. Dean, "Disciplined Fellowship," 261.

139. Wesley, *Journal*, vol. 5, 406.

140. Dean, "Disciplined Fellowship," 242-44.

141. Ward, *Religion and Society*, 144-46.

142. Ibid., 168. The traveling preachers thought that they were the only ones authorized to discipline members.

143. Ibid., 147-48. These Sunday Schools which developed in the early nineteenth century attempted to educate the poor who could neither read nor write. The conservative leadership of the Wesleyan Methodist Church, led by the Reverend Jabez Bunting, saw that as a radical measure and opposed it.

144. Ibid., 148-50.

145. J. Bicknell to Reverend Jabez Bunting, 2 March, 1835, Methodist Church Archives, City Road, London. Each circuit had its own weekly leaders' meeting.

146. Dean, "Disciplined Fellowship," 247.

Chapter 2: The New York Society: 1768-1800

1. Three dates are particularly significant. In 1766, New York City Methodism began when Philip Embury, a Methodist lay preacher from Ireland, preached to a small group in his own home. In 1784, near the end of the Revolutionary War, the American Methodist societies formed the Methodist Episcopal Church. The New York Society, originally a religious society within Trinity Parish on Wall Street, then became the John Street Methodist Episcopal Church. In 1800, New York City Methodism, which had two churches up to

this time, became the "New York Circuit," with six churches and five stationed preachers. For a general history of American Methodism in this period see John Atkinson, *The Beginnings of the Wesleyan Movement in America* (New York: Hunt and Eaton, 1896); Nathan Bangs, *A History of the Methodist Episcopal Church*, 4 vols. (New York: Carlton and Porter, 1860); Emory C. Bucke, ed., *History of American Methodism*, 3 vols. (Nashville: Abingdon Press, 1964); and Frederick A. Norwood, *The Story of American Methodism* (Nashville: Abingdon Press, 1974).

2. "John Street Church. Class Lists, 1785-1796" (New York, NY: Manuscripts Division, The New York Public Library [hereafter NYPL], Astor, Lenox and Tilden Foundations, Methodist Episcopal Church Records [hereafter MECR], vols. 233, 241, photocopied). For the general class meeting situation in England, see Watson, *Early Methodist Class Meeting*, 93-98.

3. Francis Asbury, *The Journals and Letters of Francis Asbury*, vol.1, ed. Elmer T. Clark (Nashville: Abingdon, 1958), 41, 84, and 117; George A. Phoebus, *Beams of Light on Early Methodism in America* (New York: Phillips and Hunt, 1887), 31; Frank Baker, *From Wesley to Asbury* (Durham, NC: Duke University Press, 1976), 196; and Thomas Rankin, "Journal" (Madison, NJ: United Methodist Church Archives - General Commission on Archives and History [hereafter, UMCA - GCAH], Drew University, "Drew University Methodist Collection," typewritten), 4. Reproduced with permission of Drew University Library.

4. Ernst Troeltsch, *The Social Teaching of the Christian Churches* (New York: Harper Torchbooks, 1960), 331-42.

5. "John Street Church" (New York, NY: Manuscripts Division, NYPL, Astor, Lenox and Tilden Foundations, MECR, vol. 241, photocopied).

6. Thomas Rankin, "Journal" (Madison, NJ: UMCA - GCAH, Drew University, "Drew University Methodist Collection," typewritten), 4. Reproduced with permission of Drew University Library. In June, 1773, in Philadelphia, Rankin recorded that he "had an opportunity of conversing with many members of the society in private, and had reason to bless God, that I found some who were newly awakened, and desired to be admitted into the society." At first, Asbury and Rankin divided their time between the Philadelphia and New York Societies, which were the two largest ones in the 1770s.

7. Frederick Norwood, *Church Membership in the Methodist Tradition* (Nashville: Methodist Publishing House, 1958), 34. The "trial" period lasted a minimum of six months and often longer, especially in the first three decades of the nineteenth century. A person was received "on trial" in one of two ways: by the recommendation of another member or by attending three or four class meetings. During this time, the "probationary member" could also attend the private Sunday evening society meeting and the monthly love feast. The Reverend William Jessop, who was stationed at the John Street Methodist Episcopal Church in 1790, has left an example of how this worked. On 5 February 1798, while stationed in Nova Scotia, he went home with a Mr. G. and his wife after a prayer meeting and "conversed with him and his wife concerning religion and explaining to them the rules of the Methodists. When I

had done saying what I had to say; they desired me to set their names down on the class paper, saying they were determined to follow that way as long as the Lord should spare them," in William Jessop, "Journal. 1788" (Madison, NJ: UMCA - GCAH, Drew University, "Drew University Methodist Collection,") 5 February 1788. Reproduced with permission of Drew University Library

8. John S. Simon, *John Wesley and the Methodist Societies* (London: Epworth Press, 1923), 217-18. The steward was to "manage the temporal things of the Society; to receive the weekly contributions of the leaders of the classes; to expend what was needful from time to time; to send relief to the poor; to see that the public buildings were kept in good repair; to keep an exact account of receipts and expenses; to inform the Helpers if the rules of the house, of the schools, of the bands, or of the Society had not been punctually performed; to tell the Helpers, in love, if they thought anything was amiss in their doctrine or life, and if it were not removed, then to send timely notice to the Minister; and finally, to meet his fellow stewards weekly, in order to consult together on 'the preceding heads.'"

9. "John Street Church" (New York, NY: Manuscripts Division, NYPL, Astor, Lenox and Tilden Foundations, MECR, vol. 241, photocopied).

10. Ibid.

11. Methodist Episcopal Church, *The Doctrines and Discipline of the Methodist Episcopal Church in America* [hereafter, *Discipline*](New York: William Ross, 1797), 70. This book was reprinted every year and often revised after each quadrennial General Conference. The 1798 edition was especially important as it contained the annotations of Asbury and Thomas Coke, the two highest ranking Methodist leaders at that time.

12. "John Street Church. List of Exclusions, 1791-1793" (New York, NY: Manuscripts Division, NYPL, Astor, Lenox and Tilden Foundations, MECR, vol. 241, photocopied). Numerous persons, as the various lists indicated, were "excluded" or "laid aside" for "non-attendance," a practice which continued at least into the mid-1820s in New York City Methodism.

13. "Life and Death of Mrs. Prudence Hudson," *Methodist Magazine* 9 (1826): 412.

14. Women outnumbered men in total membership by roughly two to one throughout the 1780s and 1790s.

15. "John Street Church. Class Lists" (New York, NY: Manuscripts Division, NYPL, Astor, Lenox and Tilden Foundations, MECR, vols. 233 and 241, photocopied). Moreover, six other women had two different leaders during 1785 and 1796. There women were, in alphabetical order: Hester Bleecker, Elizabeth Carpenter, Hannah Grant, Mary Lent, Rachel McLean, and Hestor (or Helen) Russell.

16. Wesley, "Minutes of Several Conversations" in *Works*, vol. 8, 301.

17. Francis Asbury, no place indicated, to Reverend Ezekiel Cooper, New York City, no date, Ezekiel Cooper Collection, vol. 18, ms. 12, Garrett Evangelical Seminary, Evanston, Illinois. Reproduced with permission of The United Library, Garrett-Evangelical Theological Seminary, Evanston, Illinois. Judging from his letter, Asbury apparently was hundreds of miles away. Cooper may have been stationed in New York City since Asbury was the one

who made the appointments each year and would have known where to reach him. The letter did not indicate where this abuse had occurred, although it must have been in the east since Asbury felt Cooper could correct the situation. About this new abuse of power Asbury wrote that "we ought to guard against these local presiding elders for three or four years in a town or city that can change or suspend leaders of twenty or thirty years standing, but let it be known for what fault. Then expel them." Asbury also urged Cooper to "state the case of those ejected leaders, many will know whom you mean."

18. Methodist Episcopal Church, *Discipline* (Philadelphia: Henry Tuckniss, 1798), 148.

19. "John Street Church. Class Lists" (New York, NY: Manuscripts Division, NYPL, Astor, Lenox and Tilden Foundations, MECR, vols. 233 and 241, photocopied).

20. Hick was listed as a member of Cornelius Cook's 1785 class and appointed class leader in 1793 and apparently served until 1817.

21. "John Street Church. Class Lists" (New York, NY: Manuscripts Division, NYPL, Astor, Lenox and Tilden Foundations, MECR, vols. 233 and 241, photocopied).

22. 1 Tim. 3:1-13 RSV. The qualifications needed for class leaders were spelled out in later English and American class leader manuals. One popular British manual which was reprinted in America was Reverend Edmund Grindrod, *The Duties, Qualifications, and Encouragements of Class Leaders*, in *Tracts of the Tract Society of the Methodist Episcopal Church*, ed. Abel Strevens (New York: Carlton and Phillips, 1854), tract 275.

23. "John Street Church. List of Exclusions from the Year 1787-1791" (New York, NY: Manuscripts Division, NYPL, Astor, Lenox and Tilden Foundations, MECR, vol. 233, photocopied). William Lupton, a class leader in the New York society in 1785, was one of those excluded in 1787 "for the habitual neglect of family prayer, though he had also treated the minister with great contempt."

24. Much as Paul described the early Christian leaders in 1 Cor. 1: 26-27.

25. "John Street Church. List of Class Leaders for 1793" (New York, NY: Manuscripts Division, NYPL, Astor, Lenox and Tilden Foundations, MECR, vol. 241, photocopied); David Franks, ed., *The New York Directory* (New York: Shepard Kollock, 1786), 45-77; and William Duncan, ed., *The New York Directory and Register for the Year 1793* (New York: T. and J. Swords, 1793), 1-174.

26. An exhorter was a layman who spoke immediately after the sermon. His message, which was called an "exhortation," was not based on a Biblical text (like a Methodist sermon), "but was designed to 'apply' the preacher's sermon to the local situation," in Lester B. Scherer, *Ezekiel Cooper: 1763-1847* (Lake Junaluska, NC: Commission on Archives and History of the United Methodist Church, 1965), 166. The exhortation immediately followed the sermon in a typical preaching service or prayer meeting. Methodist records for the first three decades of the nineteenth century show that it was not uncommon for ordained ministers to also exhort, especially if they felt moved to do so. A local preacher was a layman who could preach only in the local church, as

opposed to a traveling preacher (or ordained elder). Some traveling preachers often "located" when they had to take a secular job in order to support their families. As local preachers, they were no longer considered members of the Annual Conference. This loss of prestige became an issue in the nineteenth century. Both positions, that of exhorter and local preacher, required a license from the Quarterly Conference which had to be renewed annually.

27. "John Street Church. New York Society Church Leaders, 1795" (New York, NY: Manuscripts Division, NYPL, Astor, Lenox and Tilden Foundations, MECR, vol. 241, photocopied).

28. Wesley, *The Nature, Design, and General Rules of the United Societies*, in *Works*, vol. 8, 270. The General Rules of the United Societies called for any member "to inform the Minister of any that are sick, or of any that walk disorderly, and will not be reproved."

29. "John Street Church. List of Exclusions from the Year 1787" (New York, NY: Manuscripts Division, NYPL, Astor, Lenox and Tilden Foundations, MECR, vol. 233, photocopied).

30. Methodist Episcopal Church, *1798 Discipline*, 147.

31. This "mixed" class (i.e., male and female) met on Wednesday evening and was led by William Valleau and William Cooper in 1793 and 1795, respectively. No extant class list exists for 1794. Again, the class may have begun meeting in 1792 and for several years after 1796 as no list exists for 1792 and the next extant list for New York is 1802. Two Mile Stone was, as its name indicates, two miles north of the main population area. In regard to Two Mile Stone, Elmer Clark noted, "Mileage was measured from the Federal Building at the corner of Wall and Nassau Streets. As the Post road moved northward, the two-mile stone was fixed at the 'Forks of the Bowery,' almost at the site of the present Cooper Union Institute. A small rural community had developed at Two Mile Stone, with a Methodist class formed in 1789 by William Valleau, a local preacher, at the home of John Coutant. In 1795 a small house had been occupied on a nearby street," in Asbury, *Journals and Letters*,vol. 2, 673, f.n. 70. This "concession" to a mixed class was due to a geographical concern (i.e., distance) rather than a pastoral one and more clearly reflected Wesley's original plan for forming neighborhood classes.

32. "John Street Church. Class Lists" (New York, NY: Manuscripts Division, NYPL, Astor, Lenox and Tilden Foundations, MECR, vols. 233 and 241, photocopied).

33. Watson, *Early Methodist Class Meeting*, 94.

34. Asbury, *Journals and Letters*, vol. 3, 156, f.n. 8. Joseph Pilmore, who was not as strict as Asbury and Rankin, had appointed Mrs. Thorne. In the early decades of the nineteenth century, it was common for the preachers appointed to the New York Circuit to subdivide their female class and have one of the women lead the second group.

35. Ibid. vol. 3, 153. In his letter to the Baltimore society, dated 1796, Asbury wrote, "Your classical fellowship is very local. It is impressed upon my mind that the want of prayer bands is somewhat supplied in the men's and women's classes."

36. Ibid. Both the class lists themselves and Asbury's journal indicate the existence of classes based on marital status. For instance, on Monday, 25 June 1778, Asbury met "the married sisters in the old church (i.e., John Street)."

37. The rate of increase from 1785 to 1796 is contained in Appendix 9.

38. The Reverend Newell Culver, in a personal memoir, recalled that "in many country classes they were obliged to reserve the privileges of class till the days of the pastor's lecture appointments, once in two weeks in those sections of the circuits where most of the members resided, and then meet after the more public services. In other places they met at noon on the Sabbath, or after the afternoon public services closed," in Reverend Newell Culver, *Methodism Forty Years Ago and Now* (New York: Nelson and Phillips, 1873), 31. LaVere Rudolph has noted that the traveling preachers in the country areas "did not stay very long; he might have twenty to forty classes on his round. After the preaching service the circuit rider would meet the class; he would take the roll from the class leader and call the names one by one, inquiring the spiritual state of each. This was the place to face and resolve differences in family, neighborhood, or class," in LaVere Rudolph, *Francis Asbury* (Nashville: Abingdon Press, 1966), 96.

39. Scherer, *Ezekiel Cooper*, 43.

40. Joseph Pilmore, *Journal*, 74. On 27 January 1771, just three years after classes had been formed in New York, Pilmore recorded that "after preaching I met the Negroes apart and found many of them very happy." He could well have been describing a class meeting since the first extant class list, that of 1785, listed a sole "Negro class" as having twenty-six members. Normally, the "traveling elder," or circuit rider, would meet the various classes during his visits. Similarly, on Sunday, 5 July 1795, Asbury "met the black classes", in Asbury, *Journals and Letters*, vol. 2, 55.

41. Methodist Episcopal Church, *Discipline* (Philadelphia: Charles Cist, 1785), 15. The rule called for "every Preacher, as often as possible meet them (i.e., the Negroes) in class. And let the Assistant always appoint a proper white person as their leader."

42. William Walls, *The African Methodist Episcopal Zion Church* (Charlotte, NC: A. M. E. Zion Publishing House, 1974), 35-38.

43. Ibid., 41-42.

44. Ibid., 23. Regarding this accommodation policy, Walls wrote that "there were spots of Negro membership in white churches, but the fashion of the age was to segregate them."

45. Asbury, *Journals and Letters*, vol. 1, 190 and vol. 2, 355. Throughout his extensive travels, Asbury encountered opposition to his views, especially in the south. In 1776, Asbury recorded that "after preaching at the Point, I met the class, and then met some black people, some of whose unhappy masters forbid their coming for religious instruction. How will the sons of oppression answer for their conduct when the great Proprieter of all shall call them to account?" Four years later in 1780 he noted, "I spoke to some select friends about slavekeeping, but they could not bear it: this I know. God will plead the cause of the oppressed, though it gives offense to say so here. O Lord, banish the infernal spirit of slavery from thy dear Zion." In addition to the opinions

and statements of the leaders, the new church, at the 1784 organizing conference, added "a new and detailed antislavery rule that reflected the legal training of Dr. Coke," in Donald G. Mathews, *Slavery and Methodism* (Princeton, NJ: Princeton University Press, 1965), 10. However, this strong antislavery position of the church was progressively weakened as it met fierce resistance, especially in the southern states.

46. Donald G. Mathews, *Slavery and Methodism*, 96. In the early 1830s, the colonization movement had broad support in certain quarters of the Methodist Episcopal Church, especially in the New York Conference. Mathews noted that "two of the chief officers of the Methodist Young Men's Missionary Society (which was started at John Street), David M. Reese and Gabriel P. Disosway, were ardent colonizationists."

47. Walls, *A. M. E. Zion Church*, 47.

48. "John Street Church. Class Lists" (New York, NY: Manuscripts Division, NYPL, Astor, Lenox and Tilden Foundations, MECR, vol. 233 and 241, photocopied).

49. Ibid.

50. Ibid. Barsary and Kelly were listed first in 1785; Day and Barnet in 1787.

51. Norwood, *Church Membership in the Methodist Tradition*, 89.

52. Wesley, *A Plain Account of the People Called Methodists*, in *Works*, vol. 8, 258. Wesley had written that in order that "their design in meeting might be the more effectually answered, I desired all the men-bands to meet me together every Wednesday evening, and the women on Sunday, that they might receive such particular instructions and exhortations as, from time to time, might appear to be most needful for them."

53. Asbury, *Journals and Letters*, vol. 1, 84 and 117. For example, on 10 July 1773, Asbury wrote, "After preaching this evening I enjoyed a comfortable time in meeting the leaders and the band-society." Again, in June, 1774, he noted that "the next day my soul was also sweetly drawn out in love to God; and found great freedom and happiness in meeting the leaders and the bands." Similarly, on Sunday, 19 September 1773, Rankin recorded that "at the Bands on Saturday evening, I was greatly favoured with the presence of God," and on 26 September 1773, he "found a blessing (as in general I do) in meeting the Band Society on Saturday evening," in Rankin, "Journal" (Madison, NJ: UMCA - GCAH, Drew University, "Drew University Methodist Collection," typewritten), 6. Reproduced with permission of Drew University Library.

54. George A. Phoebus, *Beams of Light on Early Methodism in America* (New York: Phillips and Hunt, 1887), 31. On the evening of Thursday, 21 July 1785, Cooper "met the Band Society, in which we were powerfully blessed." Similarly, on 29 November 1792, Coke, who was in New York for twelve days, wrote that "in meeting the Select Society, I was much satisfied indeed," in Thomas Coke, *Extracts of the Journals of the Reverend Dr. Coke's Five Visits to America* (London: Printed by G. Paramore, 1793), 165-66. The Select Society was another highly committed small group whose members were chosen out of the bands.

168

Notes to Pages 34-36

55. Several band tickets of Mrs. Hannah (Dean) Hick, wife of the class leader, Paul Hick, are shown in Appendix 10.

56. Methodist Episcopal Church, 1798 *Discipline*, 151. Section III. "Of the Band Societies," recognized that class members varied "exceedingly in the state of their minds and the degrees of their experience." In this early period, the class meeting functioned catechetically and evangelistically, seeking to impart basic Christian doctrines and the "new birth" experience to "seekers." Nevertheless, the class meeting could sometimes facilitate this experience. On Sunday, 28 May 1780, during a visit to Sussex County, Virginia, Asbury recorded that "after preaching I met the class; they were stirred up, thirsting for full sanctification," in Asbury, *Journals and Letters*, vol. 2, 354.

57. Ibid., 151-52. In their "Annotations" to the 1798 *Discipline*, Asbury and Coke also highly commended the Select Societies as a setting in which to receive "entire sanctification." The Select Societies, they wrote, "should be composed of believers who enjoy the perfect love of God, or who are earnestly seeking that great blessing. In London, Bristol, in Europe, and in New York these select societies have been very profitable. Each member is at liberty to speak his experience, the preacher giving such advice respecting the grand point their souls are aiming at (i.e., Christian perfection)."

58. "John Street Church. Band Society" (New York, NY: Manuscripts Division, NYPL, Astor, Lenox and Tilden Foundations, MECR, vol. 241, photocopied), undated.

59. Methodist Episcopal Church, *Minutes of the Methodist Conferences Annually Held in America from 1773 to 1794, Inclusive* (Philadelphia: Henry Tuckniss, 1795), 194.

60. Frank Baker, *From Wesley to Asbury* (Durham, NC: Duke University Press, 1976), 196.

61. Asbury, *Journals and Letters*, vol. 1, 118. At the society meeting on 12 June 1774, Asbury "spoke plainly of some who neglected their bands and classes; and informed them that we took people into our societies that we might help them become entire Christians, and if they willfully neglected those meetings, they thereby withdrew themselves from our care and assistance."

62. Methodist Episcopal Church, *1798 Discipline*, 152. Part II, Section III, "Of the Band Societies," referred to the bands as "one of the most profitable means of grace in the whole company of Christian discipline," and added that where bands "have been kept up in their life and power the revival of the work of God has been manifest both in the addition of members to the society, and in the deepening of the life of God in general." The section concluded that, with the proper encouragement of elders, deacons, and preachers, attendance could be improved.

63. Lester B. Scherer, *Ezekiel Cooper*, 91-92. Scherer wrote that the early English missionaries criticized the loose situation in New York "not because Methodists wanted to remain aloof from the rest of human society, but because they felt that certain closed occasions were the necessary means of strengthening them to be God's instruments for redeeming mankind."

64. Methodist Episcopal Church, *1798 Discipline* (New York: William Ross, 1789), 25. The rule stated that "at every other meeting of the society, let no

stranger be admitted. At other times they may; but the same person not above twice or thrice." This membership criteria was known as "fencing in the society."

65. Asbury, *Journals and Letters*, vol. 1, 39.

66. Ibid., vol. 1, 37 Asbury recorded on 2 August 1772 that Wright had been "pretty strict in the society, but ended all with a general love feast; which I think is undoing all he has done." Likewise, when he returned to New York two weeks later, he found "broken classes, and a disordered society, so that my heart was sunk within me," in Asbury, *Journals and Letters*, vol. 1, 39.

67. Ibid., vol. 1, 41, 117. His journal entry for that day gives some idea of the struggle to implement Wesleyan practice: "This (i.e., private society meetings) was doubted by some; but I insisted on it, from our rules and Mr. Wesley's last letter."

68. Rankin, "Journal" (Madison, NJ: UMCA - GCAH, Drew University, "Drew University Methodist Collection," typewritten), 4. Reproduced with permission of Drew University Library. During the first conference which was held in Philadelphia in 1773, Rankin voiced his growing exasperation at the undisciplined state of things. Even though earlier reports had led him to believe that larger societies existed, he recorded that he "was now convinced of the real truth. Some of the above number, I also found afterwards, were not closely united to us. Indeed our discipline was not properly attended to, except at Philadelphia and New York; and even in those places it was upon the decline." Again, on 5 December 1773, during a stay in Philadelphia, Rankin lamented the difficulty he found both there and at New York "by not having our discipline enforced from the beginning! This has given me pain, and it is likely to cause more." The feeling about this was not unanimous, however. Joseph Pilmore, one of Wesley's missionaries, wrote on 17 May 1772 that "contending about opinions and the minute details of discipline" had caused an actual loss of membership, in Joseph Pilmore, *The Journal of Joseph Pilmore* (Philadelphia: Message Publishing Company, 1969), 134.

69. Reverend John Dickens, New York, to Edward Dromgoole, Virginia, 4 July, 1783, Edward Dromgoole Papers, No. 230, Southern Historical Collection, University of North Carolina. Dickens wrote to his friend, Edward Dromgoole, in Virginia, that although the members of the society at John Street desired the extra meetings such as the society, class and band meetings, they were not following Wesley's plan for closed meetings. Dickens, however, resolved to make them adhere to the Wesleyan ideal. Cooper, who had been appointed to John Street in 1794, was told by Asbury to deal with the problem of open love feasts. Cooper then met with the preachers, stewards, and class leaders after the quarterly meeting in order to decide "who should remain in society for another quarter. In that way they were prepared for the 'quarterly visitation,' which might take a week or more. The preachers visited every member and gave out membership tickets for the ensuing quarter. Then the quarterly love feast was held (in effect, the first event of the new quarter), and only those with new tickets were admitted," in Scherer, *Ezekiel Cooper*, 92.

70. Ernst Troeltsch, *The Social Teaching of the Christian Churches* (New York: Harper Torchbooks, 1960), 330-31, 339. The "church-type" was an

institution which worked closely with society and saw its mission as Christianizing civilization. On the contrary, the "sect-type" was a group which radically followed Jesus's teaching and the New Testament lifestyle and usually separated itself from the institutional church. Troeltsch believed that both types made positive contributions. The Church, he wrote, "has its priests and its sacraments; it dominates the world and is therefore also dominated by the world. The sect is lay Christianity, independent of the world, and is therefore inclined towards asceticism and mysticism. Both these tendencies are based upon fundamental impulses of the Gospel. The Gospel contains the idea of an objective possession of salvation in the knowledge and revelation of God, and in developing this idea it becomes the Church. It contains, however, also the idea of an absolute personal religion and of an absolute personal fellowship, and in following out this idea it becomes a sect," 342. In the Middle Ages, sects proliferated because the institutional church was so closely identified with society. Troeltsch saw the sects, both those of the Middle Ages and those which came later, as corrective, rather than deviant, because they restored elements which the institutional church lacked, see 330, 333.

71. Ibid. Troeltsch criticized the sect-type for its reluctance to work with society and for its emphasis on Christ's return and the end of the world since these attitudes prevented them from improving society, see 337.

72. Ibid., 332.

73. Ibid., 342.

74. Ibid., 336.

75. Ibid., 723.

76. Ibid., 721.

77. H. Richard Niebuhr, *The Social Sources of Denominationalism* (New York: World Publishing Company, 1929), 63-64. Niebuhr pointed out that because the Anglican clergy were "settled" in parishes, it was extremely difficult to deploy them where the need was greatest. The Methodist lay preachers, who constantly traveled in circuits, and the resident class leaders provided the pastoral oversight that the Anglican Church lacked.

78. Troeltsch, *The Social Teaching of the Christian Churches*, 721-22.

79. Ibid., 724. According to Niebuhr, British Methodism appealed to the lower classes because "its emotionalism made it at the same time an abomination to the enthusiasm-hating upper classes and the salvation of those for whom religion needed to mean much more than prudential counsel and rationalized belief, if it was to mean anything at all. It furnished that group with a psychologically effective escape from the drudgeries of an unromantic, unaesthetic life," in Niebuhr, *The Social Sources of Denominationalism*, 62.

80. Asbury, *Journals and Letters*, vol. 1, 118-19. On several occasions, Asbury criticized the sermons he heard at those two churches. From 1766 to 1784, the Methodists went to Sunday services at Trinity and St. Paul's after attending the early morning preaching at Wesley Chapel. Trinity was located on lower Broadway; St. Paul's, which was a "chapel" of Trinity Parish, had been built in 1768 and was located near the intersection of John Street and Broadway. At the same time, Asbury found some sermons in the other Protestant churches in Manhattan acceptable, see vol. 1, 23 and 47.

81. Troeltsch, *The Social Teaching of the Christian Churches*, 717.

82. Ibid., 723.

83. Finke, Roger and Rodney Stark, *The Churching of America,1776-1990* (New Brunswick, NJ: Rutgers University Press), 40-46.

84. Max Weber, *On Charisma and Institution Building: Selected Papers* (Chicago: University of Chicago Press, 1968), 54.

85. "John Street Church. State of the Society, 1791" (New York, NY: NYPL, Rare Books and Manuscripts Division, MECR, vol. 241, photocopied). The State of the Society, another "religious society" term, was the name of the membership list of John Street Methodist Episcopal Church.

86. Norwood, *The Story of American Methodism*, 101.

87. From 1800 to 1832, the six Methodist Episcopal Churches in Manhattan were grouped into the "New York Circuit."

Chapter 3:   The New York Circuit: 1800-1832

1. In 1800, the John Street, Duane Street, and Forsyth Street Methodist Episcopal Churches composed the new circuit.

2. The "camp meeting" was an outdoor preaching service which lasted for several days.

3. The "prayer meeting" was an evangelistic meeting composed primarily of preaching and prayer.

4. "Minutes of the New York Conference, 1800-1832" (Madison, NJ: UMCA - GCAH, Drew University). Reproduced with permission of Drew University Library. "Methodist Episcopal Church of New York. Board of Leaders. Minutes. 1811-1823" (New York, NY: Manuscripts Division, NYPL, Astor, Lenox and Tilden Foundations, MECR, vol. 90a, photocopied); "Board of Leaders' Minutes, 1825-1832," MECR, vol. 212; and "Class Book. Forsyth Street Methodist Episcopal Church. 1831-1834," MECR, vol. 205.

5. By the 1820s, the New York Circuit had seven churches: John Street, Duane Street, Greenwich Village, Allen Street, Forsyth Street, Bowery Village, and Willett Street (originally the "Mission House" on Broome Street). The first three churches were on the west side and the last four on the east side. A listing of the important events in New York City Methodism, which includes the founding dates of the individual churches, is contained in Appendix 1. As in the countryside, preaching and class meetings were established first; a church would be built once the class(es) could support one. In 1832, the circuit was subdivided into the New York East and New York West Circuits.

6. In addition to the stationed preachers, a number of other ordained elders assisted with the preaching. These included seminary professors, book agents, and local preachers.

7. Reverend Tobias Spicer, *Autobiography* (Boston: C. H. Peirce and Company, 1851), 70. An actual plan of appointments for the Manhattan Methodist churches can be found in "Appendix T. Printed Plan of Appointments" in Samuel Seaman, *Annals of New York Methodism: 1766-1890* (New York: Hunt and Eaton, 1892), 478-81. Pastoral oversight of a church did not yet mean that they had been appointed to an individual "charge" (i.e., a

local church). During the period of the New York Circuit, one board of Trustees, one Board of Leaders, and one Quarterly Conference conducted the temporal and spiritual affairs of the entire circuit.

8. "Locality" referred to the practice of appointing a preacher to only one church.

9. Asbury, *Journal*, 5 August 1813, vol. 3, 475-85.

10. "Report of the Committee on Safety" (Madison, NJ: UMCA - GCAH, "General Conference Minutebook," 20 May 1816, Drew University), 151. The three member Committee on Safety was formed at the 1816 General Conference and was to "take into consideration that part of the address (i.e., the Bishops' Address to the General Conference) relating to the duty of preachers, to enquire whether our Doctrines have been maintained, Discipline faithfully and impartially enforced, and the stations and circuits duly attended," in "Minutes of the General Conference" (Madison, NJ: UMCA - GCAH, "General Conference Minutebook," 3 May 1816, Drew University), 113.

11. Ibid.

12. Abel Stevens, *Life and Times of Nathan Bangs* (New York: Carlton and Porter, 1863), 203-5. In 1810, Bangs was appointed "preacher-in-charge" of the New York Circuit. For the next fifty years he remained in New York City and had a tremendous influence on the direction Methodism took. Bangs also served as delegate to the New York Conference, editor of the weekly *Christian Advocate and Journal*, and president of the New York Preachers' Meeting. The New York Preachers' Meeting was formed on 22 January 1817 with twenty-seven members; it met on Wednesday evenings at 6:30 p.m. at the Forsyth Street parsonage. According to the minutes of the first meeting, the preachers were to "meet every Wednesday evening for the purpose of conversation and mutual improvement on moral and religious subjects. The chairman or other brother shall propose one or more subjects or questions for the next meeting which the majority must approve." Beginning in 1824, the meeting was moved to Saturday morning at nine a.m. at the parsonage of the preacher-in-charge. In the 1820s and 1830s, the meeting took on a more pastoral tone. The 1824 agenda called for the preachers to "report probationers received during the week, members received on certificate, members removed, deaths, disorderly persons, vacant classes, or the manner in which they have been filled" as well as "propose new leaders and report trials of accused persons," in "New York Preachers' Meeting. Minutes" (New York, NY: Manuscripts Division, NYPL, Astor, Lenox and Tilden Foundations, MECR, vol. 116, photocopied). The Reverend Tobias Spicer wrote that the New York Preachers' Meeting "usually met every week to consult about matters relating to the church. On these occasions there were frequent discussions on doctrines, and manner of preaching, certain rules of discipline, and the proper way of administering them. These meetings and discussions were to me as the school of the prophets," in Spicer, *Autobiography*, 70.

13. Nathan O. Hatch, *The Democratization of American Christianity* (New Haven: Yale University Press, 1989), 202.

14. A conference was the largest Methodist structural unit; it was composed of a number of districts which were, in turn, composed of smaller circuits which contained a number of "preaching stations."

15. "Journal of the New York Annual Conference. 1822" (Madison, NJ: UMCA - GCAH, Drew University, typewritten), 19. Reproduced with permission of Drew University Library. The Discipline specified that "all our Churches be built plain and decent, and with free seats."

16. Ibid., 1828, 126, 135.

17. Ibid., 1830, 8. Heman and Nathan Bangs were brothers. On the denominational level, a group from Philadelphia petitioned the 1832 General Conference to modify its rule on free seats. The petition, in turn, drew a response from the Baltimore City Station which said any modification would be contrary to Methodism's original outreach to the poor. The General Conference rejected the petition but eventually it did pass at a later conference. A number of Methodists who opposed the change left the church and formed the Free Methodist Church.

18. "Journal of the New York Conference. 1818" (Madison, NJ: UMCA - GCAH, Drew University, typewritten), 124. Reproduced with permission of Drew University Library.

19. Fred W. Price, "The Role of the Presiding Elder in the Growth of the Methodist Episcopal Church, 1784-1832" (Ph.D. diss., Drew University, 1987), 300-3.

20. Finke and Stark, *The Churching of America*, 42. The authors define "sect" and "church" as "the end points of a continuum made up of the degree of tension between religious organizations and their socio-cultural environments," 40-41.

21. William Dean, "The Decline of the Class Meeting," in *Action, Reaction and Interaction Report: The Wesley Methodist Historical Society and the British Section of the World Methodist Historical Society Held at Westhill College, Selly Oak, England 5-8 April 1983* (West Sussex, England: World Methodist Historical Society Publications, 1983), 12.

22. William Dean, "The Evangelistic Function of the Class Meeting," *Conservative Evangelicals in Methodism Newsletter* 10 (1983): 34-35. In examining early British Methodist conversion accounts, Dean concluded that "the instances in which a Methodist recorded having been converted in a preaching service are very few indeed, and those such accounts are of very personal and private events in the context of a crowd - no public appeals and massed prayer meetings. Not until the early decades of the nineteenth century do we begin to read of conversions in after-preaching prayer meetings at the communion rail or in the vestry, and it was not until mid-century that conversions became normally associated with the chapel service. Of those Methodists born before 1800 whose conversion accounts I have read, the vast majority record their conversion in the context of a class meeting or the influence of a class leader. The sequence was usually, 'I was convicted of my sin, I went to class meeting, I was converted.'"

23. Spicer, *Autobiography*, 14.

24. Reverend Alonzo Selleck, *Recollections of an Itinerant Life* (New York: Phillips and Hunt, 1886), 34.

25. "Class Meetings," *CAJ*, 23 April 1830. The unnamed writer of this article described the evangelistic approach of the class meeting "as a school for those who are seeking the Lord. Here they are instructed personally, and individually, in the things which belong to their peace. They are exhorted to come to him by faith and prayer. Here they meet, with those who have similar feelings, and also have sought the Lord until they found him as their Savior."

26. Reverend John Bangs, *The Autobiography of Reverend John Bangs* (New York: privately printed, 1846), 35.

27. "Obituary of Mrs. John Bangs," *CAJ*, 12 March 1845.

28. Reverend George Coles, *Heroines of Methodism* (New York: Carlton and Porter, 1857), 252. According to Coles, she "determined to see what a class meeting was. She went, and on that occasion was not able to conceal her feelings. She says, 'I wept aloud, for my heart was ready to break with the anguish I felt.' The third time that she attended the burden of her guilt was removed."

29. Paul K. Conkin, *Cane Ridge: America's Pentecost* (Madison, WI: University of Wisconsin Press, 1990), 83-96. The Cane Ridge camp meeting was actually patterned after the large outdoor communion services held once or twice yearly in the Scottish Presbyterian Church in the eighteenth century. These special services drew up to thirty thousand persons and lasted three to four days. Conversions often occurred and unusual phenomena, such as people falling into a trance and crying out, were also reported, see Conkin, 18-25.

30. Ibid., 62, 86. In September, 1803, the first Methodist camp meeting east of the Alleghenies was held just fifteen miles from Baltimore. In 1806, a camp meeting was held in Tuckahoe (Yonkers), New York.

31. Richard Carwardine, *Transatlantic Revivalism: Popular Evangelicalism in Britain and America, 1790-1865* (Westport, Connecticut: Greenwood Press, 1978), 14. Although the "means" used in the camp meeting divided the Presbyterians, the Methodists had no difficulty adapting them since most of their services such as the love feast and quarterly conference were already revivalistic. In fact, the quarterly conference usually lasted three or four days and concluded with a service of Holy Communion and preaching by the Presiding Elder who was often the best preacher on the District. In addition to the "means," orthodox Presbyterians also believed that too much emphasis was placed on the individual who "made a decision" to accept Christ; Calvinist doctrine stressed God's election of the individual. On the other hand, Methodism had no difficulty; its Arminian theology stressed that an individual had to freely accept God's offer of salvation.

32. Carwardine, *Transatlantic Revivalism*, 333. The Forsyth Street Methodist Episcopal Church used the "call to the altar" as early as 1806.

33. Carwardine, *Transatlantic Revivalism*, 13. Carwardine described the "mourner's bench" as a "pew set aside at the front of the congregation, to which those in a state of concern over their souls could go to be exhorted and prayed for at the close of the sermon, and there be encouraged by the minister and his zealous church members."

34. Reverend James P. Horton, *A Narrative of James P. Horton* (Fishkill, NY: privately printed, 1839), 124.

35. Reverend B. M. Hall, *The Life of Reverend John Clark* (New York: Carlton and Porter, 1856), 30.

36. Reverend Laban Clark, "Sketch of the Rise and Present State of the Methodist Episcopal Church in the City of New York," *CAJ*, 3 March 1827. In his article, Clark described a prayer meeting begun in 1825 at John Street "at the request of a number of pious females, exclusively for their own sex, in one of the class rooms in the basement story of the church."

37. Reverend Heman Bangs, *The Autobiography and Journal of Reverend Heman Bangs* (New York: Tibbals and Son, 1872), 109.

38. From 1810 to 1830, many August camp meetings were held in New Jersey, Long Island, and in the mid-Hudson River Valley area. Class leaders often arranged group transportation from Manhattan to the camp meetings by steamboat.

39. Carwardine, *Transatlantic Revivalism*, 9. Some eastern Presbyterians criticized the new revival style because the converts did not always remain active church members. This, however, was not entirely the converts' fault; the local Presbyterian churches often did not provide a weekly small group setting where the new persons could grow in their faith. While New York City Methodism had the class meeting system, weekly attendance for both probationer and full member was often sporadic.

40. "Methodist Episcopal Church of New York. Class Lists" (New York, NY: Manuscripts Division, NYPL, Astor, Lenox and Tilden Foundations, MECR, vols. 66-67, photocopied).

41. Many new boards and agencies for the entire denomination began in the New York Circuit under the leadership of Nathan Bangs and others; these included the Mission, Tract, Bible, and Sunday School boards. The preachers often directed or served on these boards.

42. Eph 4:11 RSV. "And to some, his gift was that they should be apostles; to some, prophets; to some, evangelists; to some, pastors and teachers; so that the saints together make a unity in the work of service, building up the body of Christ." See also 1 Cor. 12:4-11, Rom. 12:3-8. As in the formative period, some class leaders eventually became exhorters, local preachers, and ordained elders. For instance, the Reverend Elias Vanderlip, who served as a class leader from 1791 to 1802 in the New York Circuit, was later ordained as a traveling elder, see Spicer, *Autobiography*, 13-14. Similarly, John Bangs, who went from class leader, to circuit steward and then exhorter in just several months, was ordained a deacon four years later, in Reverend John Bangs, *Autobiography*, 36-37.

43. "Methodist Episcopal Church of New York. Board of Leaders' Minutes. 1811-1823" (New York, NY: Manuscripts Division, NYPL, Astor, Lenox and Tilden Foundations, MECR, vol. 90a, photocopied). At the 9 February 1814 General Leaders' Meeting, a motion carried which called for the class leaders to be divided into four classes and to meet the preachers every quarter.

44. "List of Class Leaders, 1812 and 1825" (New York, NY: Manuscripts Division, NYPL, Astor, Lenox and Tilden Foundations, MECR, vols. 237 and

66, photocopied); David Longworth, *American Almanac, New York Register and City Directory* (New York: by the author, 1812), 1-354; and Thomas Longworth, *American Almanac, New York Register and New York City Directory* (New York: by the author, 1824-1825), 1-471.

45. Sidney E. Mead, "The Rise of the Evangelical Conception of the Ministry in America (1607-1850)," in *The Ministry in Historical Perspectives*, ed. H. Richard Niebuhr and Daniel D. Williams (New York: Harper and Row Publishers, 1956), 233-34. By the eighteenth century, this was true of all the groups including Baptists and even Quakers.

46. Donald M. Scott, *From Office to Profession* (Philadelphia: University of Pennsylvania Press, 1978), 56-63.

47. Mead, "The Rise of the Evangelical Conception of the Ministry in America," in *The Ministry in Historical Perspectives*, 233.

48. Scott, *From Office to Profession*, 63. By 1827, seventeen seminaries had been founded by the various Protestant denominations.

49. Mead, "The Rise of the Evangelical Conception of the Ministry in America," in *The Ministry in Historical Perspectives*, 242; Scott, *From Office to Profession*, 62.

50. Scott, *From Office to Profession*, 63.

51. "Methodist Episcopal Church of New York. Probationers" (New York, NY: Manuscripts Division, NYPL, Astor, Lenox and Tilden Foundations, MECR, vols. 77-78, photocopied).

52. "Forsyth Street Church. Board of Leaders' Minutes. 1825-1832" (New York, NY: Manuscripts Division, NYPL, Astor, Lenox and Tilden Foundations, MECR, vol. 212, photocopied). While the Board of Leaders did not hesitate to terminate unsatisfactory probationers, class leaders and stationed preachers also showed pastoral concern for those who had fallen away. On 17 June 1830, the New York Preachers' Meeting resolved to "proceed forthwith in conjunction with the Leaders of the several Sections to look up the delinquent Probationers that we may be prepared to report definitely on these cases at the next Leaders' meeting," in "New York Preachers' Meeting. Minutes" (New York, NY: Manuscripts Division, NYPL, Astor, Lenox and Tilden Foundations, MECR, vol. 116, photocopied).

53. As the New York Circuit expanded to seven churches in the 1820s, it became more difficult to hold just one leaders' meeting; consequently, smaller "sectional" meetings and a larger "general" meeting were held. The sectional meetings preceded the general meeting.

54. "Methodist Episcopal Church of New York. Probationers" (New York, NY: Manuscripts Division, NYPL, Astor, Lenox and Tilden Foundations, MECR, vols. 77-78, photocopied). This information was entered on 29 October 1831.

55. "Methodist Episcopal Church of New York. Board of Leaders. Minutes. 1811-1823" (New York, NY: Manuscripts Division, NYPL, Astor, Lenox and Tilden Foundations, MECR, vol. 90a, 11 May 1811, photocopied). The Board of Leaders' meeting appointed two class leaders annually to work with the trustees in each church. The resolution further called for these committees of two class leaders to meet with the Senior Preacher once a quarter to insure

uniformity of worship and to receive instruction on how to regulate worship. These class leader – trustee committees had to form a small choir to lead the singing and post ushers to keep people from interrupting the service. For 1811, the following class leaders were appointed: Philip Arcularius and Stephen Dando (John Street), John Davies and George Taylor (Bowery Village), Abram Hart and Samuel Hopping (Fourth Street), Joseph Graham (Two Mile Stone), Samuel Elsworth and Jessie Coles (Greenwich Village), and Charles Gilman and George Innes (Hudson Street).

56. Ibid., 11 December 1811. The committees rotated to ensure variety. The prayer meetings were held in three "districts" of the New York Circuit. The first district was composed of John Street, the Alms House, Hudson Church, and Greenwich Village Church. The second district included Bowery Village, Valentine's, and Corlear's Hook. The third district included Fourth Street Church, Two Mile Stone, and Manhattan Island. The committees, meeting nights, times, and districts were reviewed every six to twelve months. With some modifications, this basic arrangement continued through the 1820s.

57. Ibid., 14 August 1811, 25 March 1812, and 13 May 1812.

58. "Transcripts of Church Trials for New York Circuit: Thomas Truslow in behalf of the Church versus John Hoare" (Madison, NJ: UMCA - GCAH, Drew University, "Drew University Methodist Collection," 4 October 1824, photocopied), 22. Reproduced with permission of Drew University Library. Truslow charged Hoare with "neglect of duty" and "immoral conduct" (i.e., intemperance and swearing) for which Hoare was expelled. A photocopy of the original trial transcript is contained in Appendix 5.

59. Ibid., 26. Reproduced with permission of Drew University Library. See Appendix 6 for the transcript of this trial and Appendix 7 for that of Parmelia Olmstead.

60. Ibid., 22, 26. Both persons were found guilty and expelled. Trial "committees" usually had three to five members. The defendant's class leader apparently did not serve on the "committee"; he only testified. Other church members, relatives, and friends of the accused could also testify. Church trials in the 1820s were also held for scandal, immoral conduct, fornication, "holding Newtonianism," refusing to pay a debt, profanation of the Sabbath, abuse of family, and marrying an irreligious man or woman, see "Records of Trials, John Street Methodist Episcopal Church, 1824-1827" (New York, NY: John Street United Methodist Church) and "Methodist Episcopal Church of New York. Members. 1811-1817" (New York, NY: Manuscripts Division, NYPL, Astor, Lenox and Tilden Foundations, MECR, vol. 74, photocopied).

61. Clark, "Sketch of the Rise and Present State of the Methodist Episcopal Church in the City of New York," *CAJ*. Apparently classes were also formed before any preaching had even occurred. For instance, Clark noted that the Greenwich Village Methodist Episcopal Church began in 1803 when "the first class was formed consisting of twelve persons; in the year 1806 or 1807 the preachers visited the people in this place and commenced preaching to the villagers in a barn."

62. "Methodist Episcopal Church of New York. Board of Leaders. Minutes. 1811-1823" (New York, NY: Manuscripts Division, NYPL, Astor, Lenox and Tilden Foundations, MECR, vol. 90a, undated, photocopied).

63. "Forsyth Street Church. Board of Leaders. Minutes. 1825-1832" (New York, NY: Manuscripts Division, NYPL, Astor, Lenox and Tilden Foundations, MECR, vol. 212, photocopied).

64. "Methodist Episcopal Church of New York. Board of Leaders. Minutes. 1811-1823" (New York, NY: Manuscripts Division, NYPL, Astor, Lenox and Tilden Foundations, MECR, vol. 90a, 24 June 1812, photocopied). This rule, however, was repealed at the 12 May 1813 General Leaders meeting.

65. The 1823 New York Conference required family prayer for all class leaders and called for the removal of those who didn't. See "Minutes of the New York Conference" (Madison, NJ: UMCA - GCAH, Drew University, *Journal of the New York Annual Conference Held at Malta Balston East Line, NY, 28 May, 1823*, typewritten), 33. Reproduced with permission of Drew University Library.

66. "Methodist Episcopal Church of New York. Class Lists" (New York, NY: Manuscripts Division, NYPL, Astor, Lenox and Tilden Foundations, MECR, vols. 66-67, photocopied) and "John Street Church. Classes" (MECR, vol. 233) and "John Street Church. Probationers" (MECR, vol. 241). The trend toward larger classes actually began in the 1790s, only ten years after the new denomination was formed (see Appendices 10 and 11). The actual class size of nine classes at John Street from 1817 to 1832 is contained in Appendix 12.

67. "Quarterly Conference Minutes, 1804-1824" (New York, NY: John Street United Methodist Church). The 22 October 1821 Quarterly Conference also noted that because of the large classes, the leaders were not able to provide the proper pastoral care but did not make any specific recommendations to reduce class size. In the eighteenth century, at least one British Methodist called for class meetings to also be held on weekdays. The Reverend Charles Perronet, in his "class manual" entitled, *The Advantages of Class Meetings, and the Best Means of Rendering Them Profitable*, noted that Methodists "will attend a prayer meeting, hear two or three sermons, and meet their class on the sabbath day, and probably never come near any place of public worship during the remaining six days of the week. Has not this at least the appearance of hurry and formality? As if they thought it enough to dispatch all their religious concerns on the sabbath. Would it not be better for thousands, who could easily do it, to attend their class meeting on a week day? Such a religious service, in the midst of their secular avocations, would promote their spiritual strength and comfort, and have a powerful tendency to check their ardour in worldly pursuits," in *CAJ*, 4 June 1830.

68. "Methodist Episcopal Church of New York. Board of Leaders. Minutes. 1811-1823" (New York, NY: Manuscripts Division, NYPL, Astor, Lenox and Tilden Foundations, MECR, vol. 90a, 24 June 1812, photocopied).

69. "Methodist Episcopal Church of New York. Class Lists. 1826" (New York, NY: Manuscripts Division, NYPL, Astor, Lenox and Tilden Foundations, MECR, vol. 67, photocopied).

70. "In Memory of Our Mother," 14, in Reverend Heman Bangs, *Autobiography*. At least a few other women led class meetings in the New York Circuit in their class leader's absence. Mrs. Mary Mason related that beginning in 1832 at the Greene Street Methodist Episcopal Church, she led her class when the pastor-class leader was away, in Elizabeth M. North, *Consecrated Talents* (New York: Carlton and Lanahan, 1870), 84.

71. Scherer, *Ezekiel Cooper*, 43. Cooper was appointed to New York City in 1794 and again in 1807-1808. The event alluded to above occurred in Baltimore.

72. "Methodist Episcopal Church of New York. Board of Leaders. Minutes. 1811-1823" (New York, NY: Manuscripts Division, NYPL, Astor, Lenox and Tilden Foundations, MECR, vol. 90a, photocopied) and "Forsyth Street Church. Board of Leaders. Minutes. 1825-1832" (MECR, vol. 212).

73. "New York Preachers' Meeting. Minutes" (New York, NY: Manuscripts Division, NYPL, Astor, Lenox and Tilden Foundations, MECR, vol. 116, photocopied).

74. Evidence for the decline comes from extant "class books," periodicals, journals, and General Conference reports. "Class books" were attendance books in which the class leader recorded the weekly attendance of his class. Originally, a "class paper" had been used. Board of Leaders' Minutes for the 25 March 1812 meeting indicate that the preacher-in-charge collected these "class papers" so that a report on the classes for the entire year could be made.

75. "Allen Street Church. Classbook. 1862-1863" (New York, NY: Manuscripts Division, NYPL, Astor, Lenox and Tilden Foundations, MECR, vol. 149, "A Record of the Members in Society at Allen Street, April 1825," photocopied). Observations on the members of five classes are extant. Those classes were Henry Stiles, William Doughty, Eliphalet Wheeler, Stephen Rockwell, and Cornelius Polhemus. In 1825, Allen Street had a total of eighteen classes. Some of the records of attendance appear to be for one quarter, while others seem to be for the entire year.

76. Ibid., 2. Doughty's observations should be adjusted upward since the following explanation appeared at the bottom of his class list: "By mistake the attendance of the above class is noted too low by about one half."

77. Ibid., 3.

78. Ibid., 4. Nine additional members had no record of attendance; they may have just joined his class as probationers or transferred from another class. Several others on his class list had been crossed out.

79. Ibid., 5. Percentages were based on a total of fourteen meetings for the quarter.

80. "Forsyth Street Church. Class Book. 1831-1834" (New York, NY: Manuscripts Division, NYPL, Astor, Lenox and Tilden Foundations, MECR, vol. 205, photocopied). The three and one half year attendance record of Thomas McFarlan's "mixed class" listed each name followed by "M" (for member) or "Pr" (for probationer). In addition to class attendance, the amount of money given weekly was noted. (see Appendix 18). Also, probationers were listed on a separate page with the date they joined the class and the name of the minister who gave them their "class permit." McFarlan's statistics

indicate that both male and female class attendance had declined. Women had outnumbered men by two to one since 1785 in New York but the decline in class attendance apparently cut across gender lines.

81. Ibid.

82. Coles, "Journal" (Madison, NJ: UMCA - GCAH, Drew University, "Drew University Methodist Collection"), 8 and 24 March 1829, 9 October 1831. Reproduced with permission of Drew University Library. Coles recorded that on Sunday, 8 March 1829, he "preached at Greenwich (Village) in the morning on Class Meeting, Band meetings from James 5:16." Again, on Tuesday, 24 March 1829, he "preached a sermon on class-meetings and then admitted three into full membership and took two on trial." Also, on 9 October 1831, while stationed in Hartford, he preached on class meetings from Malachi 3:6-8 and that "the burden of my discourse was on the nature and utility of Christian community, and the expediency and usefulness of Class Meetings." Likewise, in 1832, after being appointed to the New York Circuit again, he preached a sermon from Jude 21 entitled, "Keep Yourselves in the Love of God," in which he mentioned that class meetings were one of the "means" to that end (see Appendix 20). An extant skeleton of his sermon entitled, "Remarks on Class Meetings," had the following three points: "Why it was important, what happened to those who did not attend, and some general instructions to the class leaders," (see Appendix 21).

83. "New York Preachers' Meeting. Minutes" (New York, NY: Manuscripts Division, NYPL, Astor, Lenox and Tilden Foundations, MECR, vol. 116, 17 July 1828, photocopied). The minutes indicate that the preachers met from one to three classes every week.

84. "On Christian Communion," *Methodist Magazine* 18 (1818): 235. Another "apology" for class meetings appeared in the *Christian Advocate and Journal* on 23 April 1830. In this article, entitled "Class Meetings," the unnamed writer described the Christian life as one in which both minister and laity were equally able to communicate the faith to one another, a view which he claimed was supported by Scripture.

85. Charles Perronet, "The Advantages of Class Meetings, and the Best Means of Rendering Them Profitable," *CAJ*, 4 June 1830. Perronet used the following scriptural references in support of class meetings: 1 Peter 2:3, 7; Acts 2:1; Luke 24:32; and Proverbs 27:17. Class manuals also listed the spiritual qualities needed in a class leader. A number of these were published in England in the eighteenth century. They varied in length from several pages to over twenty. No American class manuals were published until the mid-nineteenth century; however, several English ones were reprinted in full as tracts of the Methodist Episcopal Church Tract Society.

86. Methodist Episcopal Church. *The Doctrines and Discipline of the Methodist Episcopal Church*, 19th ed. (New York: Joshua Soule and Thomas Mason, 1817), 91-92. The *Discipline* stated that "if they do not amend, let him who has the charge of the circuit, exclude them, (in the church) showing that they are laid aside for a breach of our rules of discipline, and not for immoral conduct." It remained unchanged from 1798 through the 1820s. Only seven persons were expelled for "neglect of class" from 1824 to 1827, see "Record of

Trials, John Street Methodist Episcopal Church" (New York, NY: John Street United Methodist Church).

87. Reverend Laban Clark, "Sketch of the Rise and Present State of the Methodist Episcopal Church in the City of New York," *CAJ*.

88. "The Quarterly Examination," *CAJ*, 11 May 1832. The *Discipline* required a regular examination of all class leaders.

89. Reverend George Coles, "Journal" (Madison, NJ: UMCA - GCAH, Drew University, "Drew University Methodist Collection"), 26 October 1829. Reproduced with permission of Drew University Library. The Reverend Daniel Devinne, who was appointed to John Street in 1825 and again in 1834-1835, noted that "soon after the introduction of pews, instrumental music arose; then, in some cases, written sermons and a new style of preaching were noticeable, with a disinclination to Class Meetings," in Reverend Daniel Devinne, *Recollections of Fifty Years in the Ministry* (New York: privately printed, 1883), 69.

90. "Report of the Committee of Safety" (Madison, NJ: UMCA – GCAH, "General Conference Minutebook," 20 May 1816, Drew University), 150. Similarly, at the 1824 General Conference, the Committee on the Itinerancy reported that some deficiencies in Methodist practice were caused by "the great extent of the circuits and scattered state of the population; in some cases to the want of system, but is feared in others the want of that engagedness in the discharge of ministerial duties which becomes us as ministers of the gospel of Christ. There does not appear any remarkable deficiency in the discharge of duty as pastors and teachers, so far as relates to preaching and class Meetings, yet there is a partial inattention to Class meeting, and in most places a total neglect of the bands," in "Report of the Committee on the Itinerancy," (Madison, NJ: UMCA – GCAH, Drew University, "General Conference Minutebook," 28 May 1824), 354-55.

91. Edmund S. Morgan, *Visible Saints* (New York: New York University Press, 1963), 7. In the 1630s, a group of Puritans who emigrated to the Massachusetts Bay Colony believed they were on an "errand into the wilderness." They planned to set up a new political and religious community which they expected the Established Church would adopt. This hope ended when Oliver Cromwell granted religious toleration after the English Civil War. See Perry Miller, *Errand into the Wilderness* (Cambridge: MA The Belknap Press of Harvard University Press, 1964), 14.

92. Ibid., pp. 36-42. To become a member of a Puritan church, one had to agree to the covenant, live righteously, and give a doctrinal understanding of Christianity. Later, some Puritans, including those who settled in Massachusetts, required candidates to relate a conversion experience as well as answer any questions from the church leaders, see page 62.

93. Ibid., 126. The problem of the second generation children became acute for two other reasons: the original members were now dying off and the Puritan churches did not actively evangelize outsiders. Prospective members had to come to the church, see pages 117 and 129.

94. Ibid., 131. According to Morgan, this membership was simply "the continuation of the membership they had had as children: they could not vote in

church affairs, and they could not participate in the Lord's Supper. What they gained were two privileges which had hitherto been denied them in most New England churches: the application of church discipline and baptism for their children. They were 'half-way' members, and the synod's whole solution to the question of their status was dubbed the 'half-way covenant,'" see pages 131-32.

95. Ibid., 136. Morgan believed that the issue of membership for the adult children pointed out that the Puritans were more of a religious community than a church since they "had in fact moved the church so far from the world that it would no longer fit the biological facts of life. Had they been willing to move it a little farther still, by forming monasteries instead of churches, they might have concentrated on their own purity and left to others the task of supplying the church with new members," see page 128.

96. Miller, *Errand into the Wilderness*, 2. Some of these were entitled "New England Pleaded With" and "Eye Salve." These sermons often included lists of afflictions that God was now visiting on the people such as "crop failures, epidemics, grasshoppers, caterpillars, torrid summers, arctic winters, Indian wars, hurricanes, shipwrecks, accidents, and (most grievous of all) unsatisfactory children," see p. 6. Reverend Cotton Mather's *Magnalia Christi Americana* contained "lamentations over the declension of the children, who appear, page after page, in contrast to their mighty progenitors, about as profligate a lot as ever squandered a great inheritance," see Miller, page 15. Miller believed that many of the problems and adaptations occurred because English ideas had been taken out of their native place. America, he felt, offered new opportunities and new land and the people were affected by it, and often for the worse. Miller asserted "that under the guise of this mounting wail of sinfulness, this incessant and never successful cry for repentance, the Puritans launched themselves upon the process of Americanization," see Miller, page 9.

97. Morgan, *Visible Saints*, 142-50. Morgan believed that "by the opening of the eighteenth century, New England Puritans had repudiated in varying degrees the restriction of church membership adopted in the 1630s. Some repudiated gathered churches altogether; some, while retaining church covenants, admitted professing Christians to all privileges of membership without proof of saving faith; and probably almost all admitted them to baptism. Thus, in their different ways, New Englanders tempered their zeal and adjusted their churches to a more worldly purity; and the cycle which began with the gathering of Separatist churches in London and Norwich in the sixteenth century reached its completion."

98. "John Street Church. Board of Stewards and Leaders Minutes. 1859-1868" (New York, NY: John Street United Methodist Church).

99. Ac 6:1-6 RSV.

100. The Presbyterian Church, as a denomination, experienced very small membership increases from 1837 to 1869. In fact, during three of those years, membership actually declined. Moreover, from 1870 to 1890, the number of new Dutch Reformed and Presbyterian congregations in Manhattan slowed markedly; this was also true for the Congregationalists in Brooklyn. For the actual statistics, see *Guide to Vital Statistics in the City of New York. Churches* (New York: Historical Record Survey, Works Projects Administration, 1942),

1-3, 15-20, 24-28, and 35. Actual nineteenth-century membership statistics for the Manhattan Congregational, Presbyterian, and Dutch Reformed churches would yield a much more accurate picture, but the general conditions alluded to above in the text suggest that these churches could easily have felt the denominational liberalization.

101. Patricia U. Bonomi. *Under the Cope of Heaven: Religion, Society, and Politics in Colonial America* (New York: Oxford University Press, 1986), 88-89.

102. Ibid., 90.

103. Ibid., 102-3.

104. Winthrop S. Hudson, *Religion in America: An Historical Account of the Development of American Religious Life*, 4th ed. (New York: Macmillan, 1987), 90. Deism, which had come from England, attempted to end religious division through its five general principles.

105. Ibid., 152. Unitarianism put a "greater emphasis upon the human role in redemption."

106. Ibid., 154-55.

107. Ibid., 116.

108. Ibid., 116-17.

Chapter 4: The Rise of Denominationalism and the Decline of the Class Meeting in New York City Methodism: 1832-1870.

1. A settled pastorate meant that one minister was assigned to only one church, usually for a period of two to three years.

2. Finke and Stark, *The Churching of America*, 145-69; Nathan O. Hatch, *The Democratization of American Christianity* (New Haven: Yale University Press, 1989), 193-95 and 201-6; and David Holsclaw, "Demise of Disciplined Christian Fellowship," 133-53.

3. See the following articles in the *Christian Advocate and Journal* (New York): "Obligation of Members to Attend," 9 July 1845; "Class Meetings," 14 February 1850; "The Scriptural Basis of Class Meetings," 20 March 1851; "Class Meetings as a Condition of Church Membership," 17 March 1853; "Class Meetings: Should We Attend them or Be Excommunicated?" 26 September 1861; and "Class Meeting Controversy," 6 February 1862. See also "New York Preachers' Meeting. Minutes" (New York, NY: Manuscripts Division, NYPL, Astor, Lenox and Tilden Foundations, MECR, vol. 119, 11 October 1868, photocopied).

4. "Journal of the New York Annual Conference for 1839," and "The Journal and Appointments of the New York Annual Conference Held in the Methodist Episcopal Church in Forsyth Street, New York City, May 14-24, 1845" (Madison, NJ: UMCA - GCAH, Drew University, typewritten), 353 (1839) and 13-14, 19-20 (1845). Reproduced with permission of Drew University Library.

5. "New York Examining Committee," *CAJ*, 4 June 1845. An 1841 New York Conference resolution indicated the seriousness of the new course of study: "Resolved, that the candidates to be received into full connection by this

Conference be required to present to the Examining Committee, in writing, the outlines of an original sermon, on any subject, selected by themselves, and that the Examining Committee report to this Conference, the merits of each sermon presented," in "New York Annual Conference Minutes," 28 May 1841, (Madison, NJ: UMCA - GCAH, Drew University), 15. Reproduced with permission of Drew University Library.

6. Local preachers were ordained ministers who, unlike traveling elders, did not itinerate (i.e., receive yearly "appointments" to circuits or stations) but preached in the town or city in which they permanently resided. A local preacher usually had full-time secular employment in order to support his family. During this period, many traveling elders located because of the difficulty in supporting a family on a preacher's salary.

7. "Minutes of the New York Annual Conference Held in the Jane Street Methodist Episcopal Church, May, 1854" (Madison, NJ: UMCA - GCAH, Drew University), 30. Reproduced with permission of Drew University Library.

8. Unlike the required ministerial studies, class leader course of study programs were voluntary.

9. "To Class Leaders," *CAJ*, 25 August 1847. This article was a partial reprint of the Reverend Edmund Grindrod's class leader manual, *Advice to Leaders*, which the Methodist Tract Society published as tract number 275 in the early 1850s. Grindrod was a British Methodist minister. John Wesley, *The Nature, Design, and General Rules of the United Societies in London, Bristol, Kingswood, &c.*, in *Works*, 3rd ed. (London: Wesleyan Methodist Book Room, 1872; reprint, Grand Rapids, MI: Baker Book House), 269-71 and John Wesley, *An Earnest Appeal to Men of Reason and Religion*, in *Works*, 1-45.

10. Reverend Charles Keys, *The Class Leader's Manual, or an Essay of the Duties, Difficulties, Qualifications, Motives, and Encouragements of Class Leaders* (New York: Lane and Scott, 1851), 165-67. In the late nineteenth century, the General Conference finally instituted a recommended course of study for class leaders.

11. "New York Preachers' Meeting. Minutes" (New York, NY: Manuscripts Division, NYPL, Astor, Lenox and Tilden Foundations, MECR, vol. 118, 14 June 1858, photocopied).

12. Ibid., 18 January 1869.

13. Finke and Stark, *The Churching of America*, 35-36, 77; Andrew L. Drummond, *The Story of American Protestantism* (Edinburgh: Oliver and Boyd, 1949), 127-29, 213. In the eighteenth century most of the other Protestant clergy had at least a college education. Congregational ministers received their education at Harvard and Yale. In contrast, most of the clergy of the other Protestant denominations were educated in Europe and then came to America. This changed, however, in the nineteenth century as many of the Protestant denominations founded their own colleges and universities in the United States; nevertheless, Methodists were slow to follow. At the same time, these denominations also began to establish theological seminaries for the first time. For instance, Congregationalists established Andover Theological Seminary in 1808. Next, the Dutch Reformed Church founded a seminary in

New Brunswick, New Jersey, in 1810. Then, in 1812, the Presbyterians founded the College of New Jersey (later known as Princeton). Five years later, in 1817, the Protestant Episcopal Church opened General Theological Seminary in New York City. Next, Harvard and Yale established separate "divinity schools" within their universities in 1819 and 1822, respectively. A few years later, the Lutherans opened Gettysburg Seminary in Pennsylvania (1826). Finally, in 1836, the Presbyterians founded another seminary, Union Theological Seminary, in Manhattan. In addition, the Baptists established several seminaries in this period with almost all of them being in the north. In contrast, the Methodists founded Wesleyan University in 1831 in Middletown, Connecticut, and one of their first seminaries, Garrett Biblical Institute, in 1855. Finke and Stark noted that the first Methodist seminary was established in 1847. Also, Finke and Stark reported that, in 1831, Congregational seminaries had 254 students enrolled, Presbyterians 257, Episcopalians 47, and Baptists 107. Moreover, in 1859, the Congregationalists had 275 seminarians enrolled, Presbyterians 632, Episcopalians 130, Baptists 210, and the Methodists only 51.

14. "Journal of the New York Annual Conference. 1834" (Madison, NJ: UMCA - GCAH, Drew University, typewritten. Reproduced with permission of Drew University Library.), 126.

15. "Journal of the New York Annual Conference. 1838" (Madison, NJ: UMCA - GCAH, Drew University, typewritten), 271. Reproduced with permission of Drew University Library.

16. Ibid., 1858, 16. Reproduced with permission of Drew University Library. This new emphasis on education at all levels is clear from the 1858 New York Conference "Report on Education," which stated that "the intimate relation which subsists between the intellectual and the moral development of human society renders it important that the Church should lend her sanction and support to the cause of education. Experience has shown that thorough mental culture and solid learning are most efficient auxiliaries of true religion, and indispensable to the highest usefulness of the Christian ministry. We look, therefore, with a lively interest upon the several institutions of learning to which we, as a conference, sustain special relations, and rejoice in their continued prosperity."

17. Benjamin Q. Force, *Charter Church of New York Methodism* (New York: Phillips and Hunt, 1885), 45. At the beginning of this period, pew rentals were still strongly discouraged. For instance, at the New York West Circuit's Quarterly Conference of 12 June 1833, a committee was appointed to see that churches were built without rented pews, but that rule was generally disregarded over the next thirty years. Another "loosening" of traditional Methodism, which Force noted on page 38, occurred when the prohibition against mixed seating was dropped. Late in 1837, the Board of Trustees for the New York East and the New York West Circuits gave permission for the churches to seat their members together, if they wished to do so.

18. Ibid., 48-49. Another example of dissatisfaction with the pew rental policy came from the diary of Mrs. Mary Mason, a member of Greene Street Methodist Episcopal Church, who wrote in her diary on 29 July 1855 that she

"went to a pewed Methodist Episcopal Church. Congregation small - so small that if every individual occupied a pew there would be many pews to spare. I made an attempt to enter three, but they were bolted. I shrunk back to the paupers' seat abashed. The preacher in prayer said, 'This is the house of God.' I thought, 'If it is I am shut out, '" in North, *Consecrated Talents*, 210.

19. "Journal of the New York Annual Conference. 1834" (Madison, NJ: UMCA - GCAH, Drew University, typewritten), 139. Reproduced with permission of Drew University Library.

20. "Minutes of Local Preachers' Association" (New York, NY: NYPL, Rare Books and Manuscripts Division, MECR, 26 March 1842, vol. 88, photocopied). Terry also felt that the new "choirs" were partially replacing the congregational singing which, in his opinion, went against traditional Methodism.

21. Force, *Charter Church*, 44, 48, 53-54. The organ would have been installed sooner except for the problem of paying for it.

22. Reverend J. B. Finley, "Rules for Leading Class," *CAJ*, 19 November 1845. Reverend Finley noted how many Methodist sermons had become dry and devoid of evangelistic fervor in the 1830s and 1840s. Many ministers, he noted, now read a text "which had been skeletonized for him by someone, and drone on one hour; and then come out with a little pathos in another; and all on some queer, dry, metaphysical speculation, built on some hypothesis that neither he nor anyone else understands. No one is enlightened, no hungry soul is fed with either the milk or meat of the Gospel; no sinner is awakened by the thunders of God's word."

23. North, *Consecrated Talents*, 209. This occurred in June, 1855. The unnamed preacher may have been her pastor, Reverend Hermance, who had been appointed the year before.

24. Ibid., 211.

25. "Sermons, Written and Unwritten," *CAJ*, 27 March 1851.

26. "Journal of the New York Annual Conference. 1855" (Madison, NJ: UMCA - GCAH, Drew University, typewritten), 34. Reproduced with permission of Drew University Library.

27. "New York West Circuit. Quarterly Conference Minutes. 1832-1838" (New York, NY: Manuscripts Division, NYPL, Astor, Lenox and Tilden Foundations, MECR, vol. 101, photocopied).

28. Quick, *Charter Church*, 38. The division of the New York West Circuit into separate churches began early in 1837, when the Bedford Street Church asked the Trustees of the Methodist Episcopal Church in New York to be allowed to become an independent church. At the following meeting, other New York West Circuit churches made similar requests. A committee of the Trustees, made up of one trustee from each church, favored the division. The chief difficulty was dividing up the sixty-four thousand dollar debt among the several churches. The actual division into individual stations occurred on 16 November 1838, when four New York West Circuit churches (i.e., John Street, Bedford Street, Duane Street, and Greene Street) became separate appointments. This division was apparently done without the direct involvement of the presiding elder or the bishop. "Unauthorized" subdividing

of circuits into individual stations had been occurring since the 1820s and several General Conferences had criticized the practice as undermining the itinerant plan.

29. "Itinerant Arrangements - Stations and Circuits," *CAJ*, 27 October 1841.

30. A helper was a traveling or itinerant lay preacher.

31. John Wesley, "Minutes of Several Conversations," in *Works*, vol. 8, 309.

32. Wesley, *Letters*, vol. 1, 286. Wesley himself was appointed to only one parish; he assisted his father in two country parishes for two years upon graduation from Oxford. He believed that his ordination and his position as Fellow of Lincoln College, Oxford, permitted him to preach anywhere in the British Isles. Wesley believed that God had raised up Methodism to "spread Scriptural holiness over the land." From the start, the movement was evangelistic.

33. Wesley, *Works*, vol. 8, 310.

34. Ibid.

35. Russell E. Richey, "Itineracy in Early Methodism," in *Send Me? The Itineracy in Crisis*, ed. Donald E. Messer (Nashville: Abingdon Press, 1991), 37.

36. J. Manning Potts, ed. *The Journal and Letters of Francis Asbury* (Nashville: Abingdon Press, 1958), vol. 3, 491-92.

37. Richey, *"Itineracy in Early Methodism,"* 29.

38. Methodist Episcopal Church, *The Methodist Discipline of 1798: including the Annotations of Thomas Coke and Francis Asbury* (Philadelphia: Henry Tuckniss, 1798; reprint, Rutland, VT: Academy Books, 1979), 42.

39. *The Methodist Magazine*, 25 (1843): 278.

40. Richey, *"Itineracy in Early Methodism,"* 27-28. Despite this high regard for Wesleyan itineracy, the system actually flourished more in the south and west than in the north and east. Richey noted on page 26 that "early American Methodism was primarily a movement of the Chesapeake, middle colonies, and upper south, not of the north. In those contexts, itineracy was a way of life necessitated by widespread settlements, very few settled clergy, religious and linguistic diversity, and parishes or areas of religious responsibility defined in square miles, not by village squares."

41. Ibid., 28, 32-33.

42. Potts, *Journal and Letters of Francis Asbury*, 9 July 1805, vol. 2, 474.

43. In 1812, on a national level, local preachers outnumbered full-time traveling elders two thousand to seven hundred. In 1854, the total number of local preachers had grown to eight thousand five hundred. See Norwood, *Story of American Methodism*, 134.

44. Richey, "Itineracy in Early Methodism," 36-37. Not everyone, however, criticized the transformation to a settled ministry, especially in the urban areas. The Reverend Nathan Bangs believed that, especially in the northern and eastern sections of the country, stationed preachers were a healthy development since having one pastor assigned to one church helped "meet the expense of sustaining the worship of God, and also to secure permanent congregations; and the preachers could more fully and effectually discharge all the duties of pastors, in overseeing the temporal and spiritual affairs of the Church, such as

visiting from house to house, attending upon the sick, burying the dead, meeting the classes, and regulating sabbath school, tract, and missionary societies," in Nathan Bangs, *A History of the Methodist Episcopal Church,* (New York: Carlton and Porter, 1860), vol. 3, 304.

45. The Board of Stewards dealt with the financial concerns of the local Methodist Episcopal Church. They received the class collections from the class leaders and paid the minister.

46. The Board of Leaders was comprised of all the class leaders in the local Methodist Episcopal Church. They met monthly with the minister to vote on probationers who were seeking to become full members of the church and to report any members who were not living according to Christian norms of behavior. In addition, the Board of Leaders created new committees as needed.

47. "Board of Leaders Minutes. Forsyth Street Methodist Episcopal Church" (New York, NY: Manuscripts Division, NYPL, Astor, Lenox and Tilden Foundations, MECR, vol. 213, 4 March 1844, photocopied).

48. Ibid., 6 January 1845.

49. Ibid., 3 April 1848. Apparently the Forsyth Street leaders' meeting preferred the circuit plan because it provided a variety of preachers, not just the same one. Also, they probably felt that the circuit plan prevented the problem of an ineffective preacher ruining a local church over a long period of time.

50. "Circuits in the City of New York: To the Members of the Methodist Episcopal Church in the City of New York," *CAJ,* 1 March 1848. In 1848, New York City had twenty-five "stations." In calling for a return to the circuit system, the writer also said that "the mischief which has in some degree paralyzed the Methodists, has been the abandonment of the essence of an itinerant ministry, both in the country and city, by the destruction of circuits, and the multiplication of stations. The remedy is to retrace our steps, go back to the point where we diverged from the straight line of Methodism and seek out and follow the old paths."

51. Ibid.

52. "Petition to the 1848 General Conference Held in Pittsburgh" (Madison, NJ: UMCA - GCAH, "General Conference Minutebook," 1 May 1848, Drew University). A number of New York City Methodists, including several class leaders such as John Affleck and Samuel Throckmorton, signed the petition.

53. "Itinerant Arrangements - Stations and Circuits," *CAJ,* 27 October 1841. This "calling" process, so similar to the one in the Congregational Church, continued throughout the nineteenth century in New York City Methodism. More affluent churches, like the Eighteenth Street Church, "called" preachers from as far as Philadelphia. One such example occurred in spring, 1881, when "the Quarterly Conference decided to invite Reverend James M. King, D. D., to accept the pastorate of the Eighteenth Street Church from April, 1882. The preliminaries were arranged, and the appointing powers being pleased to agree with the wishes of the people, Dr. King began his active work of three years among the people of the old church," in Quick, *Charter Church,* 72.

54. The cabinet consisted of the bishop and his presiding elders who were responsible for the various "districts" of the conference. The bishop usually relied on the advice of his presiding elders in making the appointments.

55. "New York Methodism," *CAJ*, 12 March 1863.

56. "Journal of the New York Annual Conference. 1836" (Madison, NJ: UMCA - GCAH, Drew University, typewritten), 200.   Reproduced with permission of Drew University Library.

57. "The General Conference of 1848," *CAJ*, 19 April 1848.

58. Ibid. "The General Conference of 1848" article further stated "that the free exercise of it is as much required in the Church now as at any former period of our history; and, indeed, we think we could show that there are causes demanding it which did not formerly exist.   But that a resumption of the practice should have its full beneficial effect, transfers should be made to the least desirable as well as to the most desirable appointments - to the poorest circuits, as well as to the richest stations."

59. Ibid.

60. Reverend George Coles, "Journal" (Madison, NJ: UMCA - GCAH, Drew University, "Drew University Methodist Collection"), 13.November 1832 Reproduced with permission of Drew University Library. Reverend Coles can be considered an accurate observer of changes in New York City Methodism as he spent nearly fifty years serving churches or working as an editorial assistant for the *Christian Advocate and Journal* in Manhattan.

61. Ibid., 10 January 1833.

62. "New York Preachers' Meeting. Minutes. 1815-1872" (New York, NY: Manuscripts Division, NYPL, Astor, Lenox and Tilden Foundations, MECR, vols. 115-20, photocopied).   The following excerpt from the journal of Reverend George Coles reveals just how formal things had become. He wrote that "having a matter of business to propose to the preachers I attended their meeting this morning, where my ideas of perfect order were far from being realized. Among the brethren there is, if I mistake not, an unjustifiable tenacity for having every question taken up, discussed, and disposed of in, what is called, a parliamentary manner, and yet there is a great want of deference to the chairman and to each other," in Reverend George Coles, "Journal" (Madison, NJ: UMCA - GCAH, Drew University, "Drew University Methodist Collection"), 26 November 1842.   Reproduced with permission of Drew University Library.

63. To be sure, one of the other big changes in Methodism, required ministerial studies, probably also had some effect on the class leaders. As more expectations were being placed on the Methodist clergy, similar higher expectations were being placed on the class leaders in terms of their education and knowledge (both secular and theological). Moreover, some class leader manuals in this period advised class leaders to leave their places of secular employment early so they could make more home visitations. Conversely, the other significant change in New York City Methodism - the trend toward more formal Sunday worship - most likely affected them less since their role was one of pastoral oversight instead of preaching and the administration of the sacraments.

64. Holsclaw, "Demise of Disciplined Christian Fellowship," 175. Stationed preachers, even before the Manhattan Methodist churches became "independent" had always had the weekly pastoral oversight of one or two

classes; these were titled "Preacher's Class" on the class lists. Again, in urban areas like New York City, the shift away from total lay leadership had been already happening since 1800, the year that the "New York Circuit" was formed. Since 1800, from four to six preachers were appointed to this circuit on a yearly basis. Therefore, in a limited way, they had already begun to take on more "parish-based" activities.

65. Ibid., 106. These new priorities were clearly evident in Dr. Bangs's resolution at the 1833 New York Annual Conference in which he proposed "for the purpose of more effectually advancing the interests of the Bible, Missionary, Sunday School and Tract Societies, together with their auxiliaries; to adopt as far as possible such concerted measures as shall best promote the great objects of benevolence; and to this end that the anniversaries in each district be so arranged as to be holden in successive order and that deputations be appointed beforehand in the districts to attend and address those anniversaries; and furthermore, whenever practicable that delegations be sent from the parent societies to co-operate and address these auxiliaries, that the greatest possible extension, influence, and usefulness may be given to these institutions," in "Journal of the New York Annual Conference for the Session of 1832" (Madison, NJ: UMCA - GCAH, Drew University, typewritten.) Reproduced with permission of Drew University Library. Moreover, British Methodism in the early nineteenth century experienced the same shift in pastoral priorities. William R. Ward has stated that "as the Wesleyan community grew larger and more complex ministerial authority had been extended to the Sunday Schools, to appointments under the Missionary Society, and to enlarging the scope of Missionary District meeting. The growth point of the preachers' labors was organization rather than pastoral care," in Ward, *Religion and Society*, 239.

66. "Pastoral Address: To the Members of the Methodist Episcopal Church within the Bounds of the New Jersey Conference," *CAJ*, 5 August 1858. The Pastoral Address was the annual report of the bishop at the yearly conference meeting.

67. "New York West Circuit. Quarterly Conference Minutes. 1832-1838" (New York, NY: Manuscripts Division, NYPL, Astor, Lenox and Tilden Foundations, MECR, vol. 101, 25 March 1833, photocopied)

68. "Board of Leaders' Minutes. Forsyth Street Methodist Episcopal Church" (New York, NY: Manuscripts Division, NYPL, Astor, Lenox and Tilden Foundations, MECR, vol. 213, 5 January 1846, photocopied).

69. "Forsyth Street Church. Board of Leaders. Minutes. 1825-1832 and 1837-1855" (New York, NY: Manuscripts Division, NYPL, Astor, Lenox and Tilden Foundations, MECR, vols. 213-14, photocopied); "John Street Church. Board of Stewards and Leaders. Minutes. 1859-1868" (MECR, vol. 244, photocopied); "Seventh Street Church. Board of Stewards and Leaders. Minutes. 1846-1872" (MECR, vol. 357, photocopied); and "Willett Street Church. Board of Leaders. Minutes. 1850-1864" (MECR, vol. 388, photocopied). The "Order of Business" for a leaders' meeting is contained in Appendix 2.

70. Quick, *Charter Church*, 23. Three out of five of the original building committee members were also class leaders.

71. "Forsyth Street Classes, 1852-1856" (New York, NY: Manuscripts Division, NYPL, Astor, Lenox and Tilden Foundations, MECR, vol. 210, photocopied).

72. Quick, *Charter Church*, 59. Hunt died on 18 May 1874. See Appendix 3 for a list of class leaders in the Eighteenth Street Church who had multiple church responsibilities in 1885.

73. Keys, *Class Leader's Manual*, 128-31.

74. "Board of Leaders Minutes. Forsyth Street Methodist Church" (New York, NY: Manuscripts Division, NYPL, Astor, Lenox and Tilden Foundations, MECR, vol. 213, 2 July 1838, photocopied).

75. Ibid., 3 May 1841.

76. Ibid., 6 April 1846.

77. Ibid., February, 1849. The Board of Leaders did appoint a temperance committee at the meeting.

78. Eventually, the General Conferences of both Methodist denominations (north and south) dropped required weekly classes. The stationed clergy's role in this seems passive. Along with some of the class leaders, they did not visit or seek to expel members who neglected their class.

79. In his denominational study, David Holsclaw listed five principal reasons for the decline of the class meeting. First, increased wealth and interest in entertainments caused a drop in attendance. Second, the success of the itineracy (i.e., gaining many new members) caused class meetings to decline since quality was sacrificed to quantity. For example, classes were allowed to become too large and close supervision was thereby lost. Third, as American Methodism became more popular and accepted, the need for the close support of the class meeting diminished. Fourth, Methodist families could now inculcate Christian values in the home instead of relying on the class meeting. Fifth and last, the development of voluntary associations drew the people's time and efforts away from the class. See Holsclaw, "Demise of Disciplined Christian Fellowship," 198, 201-5. In addition, Christine L. Heyrman agrees with Holsclaw's fourth reason. In *Southern Cross*, she asserted that, in the 1830s, southern evangelical Christians, including the Methodists, had popularized the "cult of domesticity" which viewed the home as a "little church." Moreover, as Methodist class meeting attendance declined in the south, Methodist parents instructed their children in the faith at home, see Christine L. Heyrman, *Southern Cross* ((New York: Alfred A. Knopf, 1997), 158-59.

80. Class books contained weekly attendance figures.

81. Class books were normally arranged in quarters (i.e., each page contained a three month period).

82. "Seventh Street Class Book. 1833-1837" (New York, NY Manuscripts Division, NYPL, Astor, Lenox and Tilden Foundations, MECR, vol. 143, photocopied). This attendance was for the period from 22 January 1833 to 1 August 1837. Over this four year period, this class had three class leaders:

James Floy became class leader on 6 May 1832 and Thomas McFarlan replaced him on 6 October 1835.

83. "Eighteenth Street Church Class Book. 1850-1854" (New York, NY: NYPL, Manuscripts Division, NYPL, Astor, Lenox and Tilden Foundations, MECR, vol. 191, photocopied). The actual drop went from 20 percent, then to 16, then to 11, and finally to 8.

84. "Allen Street Church Class Book. 1855" (New York, NY: Manuscripts Division, NYPL, Astor, Lenox and Tilden Foundations, MECR, vol. 143, photocopied). His class had a membership of from fifteen to twenty-two, depending on the quarter.

85. Ibid., vol. 144. These figures were recorded in the period from 1 November 1855 to 19 January 1860. A more complete breakdown is contained in Appendix 4.

86. Ibid., vol. 146.

87. Ibid., vol. 145. Average attendance from 10 November 1859 to 3 May 1860, however, was slightly higher: 7 out of 50 attended, or approximately 14 percent.

88. Ibid., vol. 147.

89. Ibid. McIntosh's class attendance covered the period from 1 July 1862 to 13 January 1863.

90. "Class Book of Richard Newton. Lexington Avenue Methodist Episcopal Church. 1871-1873" (New York, NY: Manuscripts Division, NYPL, Astor, Lenox and Tilden Foundations, MECR, vol. 253, photocopied).

91. "Report of the New York District" (Madison, NJ: UMCA - GCAH, Drew University, "Minutes of the New York East Annual Conference Held at Simpson Methodist Episcopal Church, Brooklyn, April 8-15, 1874 [New York: N. Tibbals and Company, 1874], 6. Reproduced with permission of Drew University Library.

92. "Report of the Brooklyn District" (Madison, NJ: UMCA - GCAH, Drew University, "Minutes of the New York East Annual Conference Held in Summerfield Methodist Episcopal Church, Brooklyn, New York, March 31 - April 6, 1880 [New York: Phillips and Hunt, 1880], 7. Reproduced with permission of Drew University Library.

93. Since most of the following information (in the form of class leader manuals, periodical articles, and books) was published in Manhattan and included personal testimonies from Manhattan class leaders, editorials from Methodist preachers located in Manhattan, and authors who served in the New York Conference, it seems reasonable to assume that the reasons given for the decline could be applied locally, as well as denominationally.

94. Reverend J. B. Finley, "Rules for Leading Class," *CAJ*, 19 November 1845. Long prayers at public worship and prayer meetings had also become a serious problem. See also the following articles in the *CAJ*: "Class Meetings, Number II - How Conducted to Be Useful," 2 July 1845; "Class Meetings," 12 April 1839; and "Class Meetings - Needed Reform in Them," 18 February 1858.

95. Ibid. Finley criticized those class leaders who had allowed their class meetings to become like "love-feasts," where general testimonies were allowed.

In the class meeting, each member was supposed to briefly describe his or her spiritual progress both in inward and outward discipleship.

96. "Class Meetings - A Suggestion," *CAJ*, 27 January 1853.

97. "John Street Methodist Episcopal Church. Classes. 1842-1854" (New York, NY: Manuscripts Division, NYPL, Astor, Lenox and Tilden Foundations, MECR, vol. 240, photocopied).

98. "Forsyth Street Methodist Episcopal Church. Classes. 1842-1854" (New York, NY: Manuscripts Division, NYPL, Astor, Lenox and Tilden Foundations, MECR, vol. 206, photocopied). In 1852, however, Forsyth Street Church had seven classes in the 10-19 range and only nine in the 20 to 29 category.

99. "Allen Street Methodist Episcopal Church. Classes. 1838-1845" (New York, NY: Manuscripts Division, NYPL, Astor, Lenox and Tilden Foundations, MECR, vol. 151, photocopied).

100. "Seventh Street Methodist Episcopal Church. Classes. 1837-1864" (New York, NY: Manuscripts Division, NYPL, Astor, Lenox and Tilden Foundations, MECR, vol. 352, photocopied).

101. "Class Meeting - Needed Reform in Them," *CAJ*, 18 February 1858.

102. "Rules for Leading Class," *CAJ*, 19 November 1845.

103. Of course, some class meetings were effective and spiritually uplifting. Reverend Coles recorded numerous instances of meeting classes in which he often noted the attendance and a short comment on how the meeting went. The following three comments are taken from a four month period during which he was located in Manhattan: "class at three o'clock - there were twenty present and it was a very profitable time" (Tuesday, 20 November 1832); "the class was small but we had a soul refreshing time" (Thursday, 6 December 1832); and "at eleven I met my class - seven present - a solemn and refreshing time. In the evening I met a class at Sister Wigton's consisting of four women - they all seemed to enjoy the meeting very much, particular Sister Wigton who has been a long time sick" (Thursday, 21 February 1833), in Reverend George Coles, "Journal" (Madison, NJ: UMCA - GCAH, Drew University, "Drew University Methodist Collection"). Reproduced with permission of Drew University Library. Also, Mrs. Mary Mason, who spent many years in several Manhattan churches wrote on 7 August 1835 that she "attended class this afternoon, and although but few were there, we had a refreshing season." Again, on 1 April 1836 she wrote that "I had my spiritual strength much renewed, by attending my inestimable weekly privilege (class-meeting) this afternoon." See North, *Consecrated Talents*, 120, 128.

104. "The Duty of a Class Leader," *CAJ*, 23 December 1840.

105. "Class Meetings," *CAJ*, 25 November 1840. The following questions were also recommended: "Do you love all your brothers and sisters? Do you never speak evil of their imperfections behind their backs? Do you never feel that you have sinned by indulging in your appetites? by going into worldly company? by taking on politics? Have you never been afraid that you have not told the truth? Does not the world share too much in your affections?"

106. "Formality in Class Meetings," *CAJ*, 19 January 1854.

107. Ibid.

108. "I Don't Like Class Meeting," *CAJ*, 24 November 1853.

109. "Class Meetings - Prevailing Defects," *CAJ*, 21 January 1858.

110. Reverend Noah Levings, "Backsliders," *CAJ*, 5 March 1846.

111. "Formality in Class Meeting," *CAJ*, 19 January 1854.

112. "Responsibilities of Class Leaders," *CAJ*, 3 January 1850.

113. "To Class Leaders," *CAJ*, 25 August 1847. In addition, this article recommended that leaders also read a good commentary and "other standard works in divinity, particularly Wesley's and Fletcher's works, Watson's *Theological Institutes*, the writings of Dr. Adam Clarke, and others."

114. "Class Meetings, Number II - How Conducted To Be Useful," *CAJ*, 3 January 1850.

115. "Responsibilities of Class Leaders," *CAJ*, 3 January 1850.

116. "Interchange of Leaders," *CAJ*, 28 June 1843. On the other hand, the Reverend Charles Keys recommended that only the best class leaders should meet other classes, see Keys, *Class Leader's Manual*, 217.

117. Ibid. Of course, in many rural areas, it was not possible to rotate leaders since some areas only had one class.

118. Ibid.

119. Keys, *Class Leader's Manual*, 215-17. Keys gave two reasons for replacing a leader: advanced age and a "backslidden" state.

120. "The Class Leader," *CAJ*, 4 December 1851.

121. Ibid. Apparently, the question of who should appoint new class leaders had become an issue in Methodism. Traditionally, the preacher-in-charge had appointed new class leaders; now some class members wanted to pick their own leader. The article, "Who Shall Appoint Them?" pointed out that class members might select someone who lacked true piety and who might hesitate to speak frankly to each member since he "owed" his election to those same members. Also, popularly elected class leaders could cause splits between rival groups in the same class. Granted, popular elections worked in politics, but it would most likely be detrimental to the church. Morever, an elected class leader would feel awkward knowing that a number of the class members had not voted for him. The article suggested the following procedure: "If in making the appointment, he (i.e., the preacher) consult the most judicious among the members respecting the appointment of the leader, all agreeing to submit to his arrangements, the above named difficulties are all avoided. Especially as the rule provides that when it is found that the leader is not the most suitable person, the preacher shall remove him and appoint another in his place," in "Who Shall Appoint Them?" *CAJ*, 4 June 1845.

122. "Class Meetings: Existing Evils - Remedy Proposed," *CAJ*, 2 March 1854. The writer, identified only as "H. K.," was a female who had observed that British classes led by female leaders had been yielding positive results.

123. Keys, *Class Leader's Manual*, 60.

124. "Class Leaders - Their Duties," *CAJ*, 20 August 1845.

125. "Do You Visit Your Delinquent Class Members?" *CAJ*, 8 March 1843.

126. The fifth question in the section on class meetings in the Discipline said, "What shall we do with those members of our Church who wilfully and repeatedly neglect to meet their class?" In the first sixty years of New York

City Methodism, members who repeatedly neglected class were put on trial and usually expelled.

127. "Old-Fashioned Methodism," *CAJ*, 27 October 1841.

128. Ibid.

129. A Member of the Philadelphia Conference, "Class Delinquency," *CAJ*, 28 March 1834. According to the writer, this decision, although initially difficult to implement, had been successful. The writer, who had been stationed in Philadelphia at one time, also wanted the enforcement of the attendance rule to be an official policy of the entire Philadelphia area conference. Yet, when a fellow minister brought up the subject on the conference floor, the conference took no action on it.

130. Ibid. The writer theorized that some of these non-attenders were either rich members, or the spouses of the preachers, class leaders, and stewards. He felt that by not disciplining them, it would be impossible to discipline anyone else.

131. Finley, "Rules for Leading Class," *CAJ*, 19 November 1845.

132. "Duty of Class Leaders," *CAJ*, 3 October 1845. The writer, identified only as "W. R. M.," also urged that class leaders should only accept small classes from the minister so that they could carry out visitation; a large class would make it impossible. Moreover, class members should only join classes in their neighborhood so that they could attend more easily. In the 1860s and 1870s, members who lived uptown but were members of downtown churches, like John Street, had difficulty getting to their class meetings.

133. Ibid.

134. Ibid. This anonymous writer viewed class leader visitation with utter seriousness. In concluding his article, he lamented, "O how many souls now lost, for ever lost, would have been saved if on the first neglect, the first spell of lukewarmness, the leader had visited and performed his duty in the fear of God. How many, now dead weights on the church, would be warmed to life, and become useful members if their leaders would thus visit them."

135. "Class Leaders II - Their Duties," *CAJ*, 11 June 1845.

136. "Do You Visit Your Delinquent Class Members," *CAJ*, 15 February 1843.

137. Ibid. Upon his return to class, the member testified that "I had transgressed; I was led to reflect; I went to hear the Reverend John N. Maffit preach and on the invitation being given, went to the altar, and did so the following night, when the Lord gave me the blessing, and ever since I have enjoyed peace and comfort."

138. "Class Leaders II - Their Duties," *CAJ*, 11 June 1845.

139. These associations were local and national groups (often interdenominational) which were formed in the early nineteenth century to advance particular causes such as the Sunday School movement or missionary outreach. Many of these had begun in New York City, including some which were formed at John Street.

140. Holsclaw, "Demise of Disciplined Christian Fellowship," 205.

141. Ibid.

142. "Board of Leaders' Minutes. Forsyth Street Methodist Church. 1837-1856" (New York, NY: Manuscripts, NYPL, Astor, Lenox and Tilden Foundations, MECR, vol. 213, photocopied).

143. Ibid., 7 November 1842 and 6 February 1843.

144. In 1844, the Methodist Episcopal Church split into two separate groups over the issue of slavery. These new churches were known as the Methodist Episcopal Church and the Methodist Episcopal Church, South. The Methodist Episcopal Church, South, abolished the rule on required class meetings at its 1868 General Conference. The two churches reunited again in 1939 as The Methodist Church.

145. Still, some supporters of required class meetings occasionally tried to justify the rule by using specific biblical texts such as an 1862 *Pittsburgh Advocate* article (reprinted in the New York *CAJ*) which used Matthew 10:32-33, "Whosoever, therefore, shall confess me before men, him will I confess also before my father which is in heaven. But, whosoever shall deny me before men, him will I also deny before my father which is in heaven." The editorial mentioned how in these verses Christ described the lives of Christians before his Father; therefore, Methodist Christians should describe their lives in Christ with others, in "Class Meeting Controversy," *CAJ*, 6 February 1862. This editorial also stated that "the class meeting simply represents and systematizes Christian conversations, or the relation of religious experience. Is a rehearsal of our life experiences not right? Is it not Scriptural? The Psalmist did not think it wrong to cry out: 'Come and hear, all ye that fear God, and I will declare what he hath done for my soul.'" Other specific verses used to support class meetings were John 20:26 where "Jesus came to his disciples when the door was shut," and Mark 4:34 which states that Jesus preached publicly to the people, and "when he was alone he expounded all things to his disciples," in "Class Meetings and Love Feasts," *CAJ*, 4 December 1842.

146. "Class Meetings as a Condition of Church Membership," *CAJ*, 17 March 1853.

147. John 21:15 RSV.

148. Keys, *Class Leader's Manual*, 25-26, 31-33, 41-42.

149. "The Scriptural Basis of Class Meetings," *CAJ*, 20 March 1851.

150. Ibid.

151. "New York Preachers' Meeting. Minutes" (New York, NY: Manuscripts Division, NYPL, Astor, Lenox and Tilden Foundations, MECR, vol. 119, 11 October 1868, photocopied). The ten speakers were G. W. Woodruff, D. O. Ferris, S. Foster, S. D. Brown, W. P. Corbit, J. E. Searles, W. S. Harris, J. P. Durbin, H. Bangs, and E. G. Andrews. The minutes show that the question was also discussed on 26 October, 2 November, and 16 November, 1868.

152. Ibid.

153. Reverend Hiram Mattison, "Class Meetings: Should We Attend Them or Be Excommunicated?" *CAJ*, 26 September 1861.

154. Charles Adams, "Class Meeting," *CAJ*, 24 October 1861. In his article, Adams noted "that the Christian sober sense of our ministry has come to shrink almost universally from the enforcement of the class meeting rule. It is

presumed that not one in a hundred of the excellent men composing the Methodist pastorship would hazard the experiment of coercion on pain of exclusion."

155. Ibid. Seven year later, in 1868, the New York Preachers' Meeting formally discussed the question, "Is attendance on class meeting a condition of membership in the Methodist Episcopal Church?" The question was also discussed on 28 September, 5 October, and 12 October, 1868. The discussion was apparently heated as two "camps" emerged from within the group. The minutes of 28 September 1868 recorded that "it was moved to take up the question for discussion. W. H. Boole moved to lay that motion on the table. Lost. The question for discussion, 'Is attendance on class meeting a condition of membership in the Methodist Episcopal Church' was then taken up and spoken to at some length by Bros. Crawford, Pease, and Buckley. Bros. Bangs, Pierce, Woodruff, and Foss also made some remarks on the subject. W. H. Boole offered the following: 'Resolved, that it is the sense of this meeting that attendance on class is not constitutionally a condition of membership in the Methodist Episcopal Church.' On motion, the resolution was laid on the table," in "New York Preachers' Meeting Minutes" (New York, NY: Manuscripts Division, NYPL, Astor, Lenox and Tilden Foundations, MECR, vol. 119, 28 September 1868, photocopied). On 5 October 1868 the following amendment was made: "Is it practicable to enforce the rule of discipline which requires attendance at the class meeting?" That, too, was "laid on the table." Apparently, none of the motions or amendments were passed which probably indicates that a deep split among the preachers existed.

156. "Class Meetings as a Condition of Church Membership," *CAJ*, 17 March 1853. Hence, required class meetings were viewed as "a voluntary social contract, which, when not fulfilled implies a renunciation of the compact, which, it is admitted, everyone has a right to make, whenever he repents his engagements; but he cannot dissolve the compact and still retain the privileges which grow out of it."

157. "Obligations of Members to Attend," *CAJ*, 9 July 1845. See also N. Vansant, "Class Meetings," *CAJ*, 17 October 1861.

158. "Class Meetings," *CAJ*, 14 February 1850.

159. Reverend Hiram Mattison, "Class Meetings: Should We Attend Them or Be Excommunicated?" *CAJ*, 26 September 1861.

160. Charles Adams, "Class Meetings," *CAJ*, 24 October 1861.

161. "Class Meetings," *CAJ*, 9 June 1837. The editorial said that "we were about to call these the soul of Methodism, for indeed were these to be given up, the Wesleyan polity would soon die: and, we may add, as a part of the same truth, that in proportion as these are attended or neglected, all other things being equal, in the same proportion will the power of religion increase or decrease."

162. "Class Meeting Controversy," *CAJ*, 6 February 1863. See also, "Class Meeting," *CAJ*, 25 November 1840 and N. Vansant, "Class Meetings," *CAJ*, 17 October 1861. Opponents of required class meetings believed that the relaxation of the rule would cause more people to join the church. In his 1861 article, Vansant believed that by keeping required class meetings "we should

avoid our chief element of weakness, namely, our too rapid numerical increase. What are numbers without loyalty? 'A house divided against itself cannot stand.'"

163. "The Journal and Appointments of the New York Conference. 1840-1845" and "The Journal of the New York East Conference. 1850-1875" (Madison, NJ: UMCA - GCAH, Drew University). Reproduced with permission of Drew University Library. New York City (i.e., Manhattan) Methodism increased steadily during its first one hundred years in both membership and in the number of churches. In 1795, John Street and Forsyth Street had a combined total of 755 members; in 1875, forty-three churches had 10,456 members. From 1830 to 1870, the years in which class meeting attendance most seriously declined, membership increased from 3,955 (in 1830) to 10,598 (in 1870). Also, the number of churches during that same period grew from eight (in 1830) to 38 (in 1870). The number of Manhattan Methodist Episcopal Churches and total membership from 1795 to 1875 in five year intervals can be found in Appendix 6.

Conclusion: The Class Meeting and the Churches Today

1. Finke and Stark, *The Churching of America*, 150-53. The authors have pointed out that the usual outcome of a "sect to church" transformation is the eventual formation of a new sect which seeks to return to the original vision and spirituality of its founder. Indeed, this outcome of a new "sect" has occurred both within Methodism in the nineteenth century and, more recently, across denominational lines since the 1970s.

2. That was one of the arguments advanced against dropping the mandatory class meeting rule (i.e., that Wesley had only intended it for members of a religious society and not for an entire church).

3. Mt 13:24-43 RSV.

4. Finke and Stark, *The Churching of America*, 42. Similarly, they noted on page 148 that "the same underlying processes that transformed the Puritan sect into the Congregational Church subsequently transformed the upstart Methodists into the Methodist Episcopal Church. When successful sects are transformed into churches, that is, when their tension with the surrounding culture is greatly reduced, they soon cease to grow and eventually begin to decline."

5. Ibid., 238. Similarly, Dean Kelly, in *Why Conservative Churches Are Growing* (New York: Harper and Row, 1977) constructed a model of what a truly vital religious group should contain. Like Finke and Stark, he included, on page 58, the following characteristics under the heading "Commitment" - "Willingness to sacrifice status, possessions, safety, life itself, for the cause of the faithful, a total response to a total demand; group solidarity, and total identification of individual's goals with group's." Kelly then tested his model against four historical religious groups: the Anabaptists, the Wesleyan Revival, the Mormons, and the Jehovah Witnesses, see Chapter V, "Traits of a 'Strong' Religion," pp. 58-77. Finke and Stark stated on page 238 that religious

organizations were stronger to the degree that they imposed "significant costs in terms of sacrifice and even stigma upon their members."

6. Dean Kelly, *Why Conservative Churches Are Growing*, 1. The following mainline Protestant denominations all decreased in membership during the 1960s: Presbyterian, Episcopal, Methodist, Lutheran, and the United Church of Christ (formerly the Congregational Church). In 1997, the United Methodist Church had the greatest decrease of all denominations listed in the yearly statistics of the National Churches of Christ. In that year, the United Methodist Church lost 45,463 members for a percentage change of -.53, see Kenneth E. Bedell, ed., *Yearbook of American and Canadian Churches. 1997* (Nashville: Abingdon Press, 1997), 2-3.

7. For statistical information on membership in Methodism see the following: Finke and Stark, *The Churching of America*, 25, 55; Edwin S. Gaustad, *Historical Atlas of Religion in America* (New York: Harper and Row, 1962), 79; Dean Kelly, *Why Conservative Churches Are Growing*, 5; and Richard Wilke, *And Are We Yet Alive* (Nashville: Abingdon Press, 1986), 161.

8. Finke and Stark, *The Churching of America*, 145. The Methodist Episcopal Church consistently declined in the south from 1850 to 1890 with its greatest decline from 1890 to 1906. The Baptists who retained traditional doctrinal standards eventually became the largest Protestant denomination (actually the Southern Baptists; the northern Baptists also experienced a liberalizing trend in the nineteenth century and went into decline). A comparison of Methodist decline and Baptist growth in the South (1850-1926) is contained in Finke and Stark, *The Churching of America*, 147.

9. The four main boards were the Sunday School, Tract, Missionary, and Bible Societies. Other more specialized boards also existed at the local level, especially in Manhattan. For instance, the Juvenile Missionary Society had originated at the John Street Church.

10. "Presiding Elders in Council," *CAJ*, 17 January 1884.

11. A number of Presiding Elders' Conventions were held in the 1880s at various regional locations (including several in Manhattan) to assist the presiding elders with their spiritual, administrative, and financial responsibilities.

12. "Presiding Elders Convention," *CAJ*, 21 August 1884. This regional meeting was held in Des Moines, Iowa.

13. "The Presiding Elders Convention," *CAJ*, 11 December 1884. The topics in quotation marks in the text are titles of the actual papers given at the conference. Many were later printed in full in the Christian Advocate and Journal, thus giving the meetings an even wider circulation. Obviously, this was an important concern at the time. A year later, at another presiding elder convention held at the Washington Square (Manhattan) Methodist Episcopal Church, the following papers were given: "What are wise and unwise methods of finance?" and "What is the relation of the presiding elders to the million-dollar line in the collection for missions." At these presiding elder conventions, papers were limited to thirty minutes and discussion of the paper to five minutes. Normally, ten or more papers were read during a three day convention.

14. Ibid.

15. Holsclaw, "The Demise of Disciplined Christian Fellowship," 176.

16. Complaints were also being voiced that quarterly conferences, once the evangelistic and fellowship highlight of the church year, had become tedious because the meetings had deteriorated into repetitive question-and-answer sessions.

17. Finke and Stark, *The Churching of America*, 153-54. From 1804 to 1864, the maximum pastoral stay allowed was two years.

18. Ibid., 72-73. Finke and Stark described the earlier Methodist local congregation as "congregational" (i.e., one in which the adult members had the day-to-day spiritual and temporal care of the local church). In contrast, by the beginning of the nineteenth century, the Congregational Church was no longer "congregational" since the educated, settled pastor had control. The Methodists, however, attracted people from 1800 to 1850 because a democratically-run church could meet more of the special needs of the people and utilize high numbers of the laity in ministry.

19. Ibid., 154-55.

20. Ibid., 155. In that year, the average Methodist salary was $784.00, the average Baptist salary was $536.00, and the average salary for "all" ministers was $663.00. Finke and Stark noted that Methodist preaching had been successful in the earlier period because, unlike the Congregational, Presbyterian, and Episcopal clergy, the Methodist preachers were not formally educated. This lack of formal education put them on the same level as the people to whom they preached. Moreover, higher educational requirements for the other Protestant clergy actually led to a clergy shortage since only a small number of clergy had been able to acquire that kind of college-level training. Conversely, the Methodists did not have that problem since more itinerant preachers were continually emerging out of the class system. Obviously, these Methodist lay preachers were paid lower salaries, but their lifestyles and career aspirations were vastly different from the other clergy in this period. For a fuller treatment, see Finke and Stark, pages 75-81.

21. Ibid., 155-59. Finke and Stark asserted on page 158 that these German-trained Methodist seminary professors challenged "American Methodism's traditional notions of sin, conversion, and perfection. These challenges were quickly passed on to students at the seminaries and the 'course of study' also underwent numerous revisions to accommodate the new insights."

22. Ibid., 42, 153.

23. "Old School Methodism" referred to those who favored the traditional Wesleyan doctrines and practices. In contrast, "New School Methodism" accepted newer practices such as pew rentals, bureaucratization, liberal doctrines, and accommodation to the world.

24. Finke and Stark, *The Churching of America*, pp. 150-52.

25. The largest of these newer churches are called "mega-churches." Mega-churches are defined as churches which average two thousand persons per week at all of their weekend services. At this time, approximately four hundred of these churches exist in the United States. According to Gustav Niebuhr, mega-churches are seen as "one of the most influential forces on the religious

landscape" and that "by their ability to draw people by the thousands, mega-churches were 'setting the agenda for every religious community in the country.' They are doing so in part because they are growing when membership in most of the nation's fifteen largest Christian churches is stagnant, according to the National Council of Churches figures," in *New York Times* (New York), 16 April 1995. Donald E. Miller, who researched what he has called the "new paradigm churches" (this chapter will use Miller's designation when referring to these newer churches which are both large and small), has asserted that they are growing for several reasons. First, they fill a need for human community which so many people are lacking today. Second, parents are drawn to these churches as a help in raising their children; the environment is safe, children's and youth activities abound, and parents like the wholesome approach. Third, these "new paradigm churches" provide help for people with specific problems, especially through the small group experience. Last of all, these churches offer hope through their message, see Donald E. Miller, *Reinventing American Protestantism*, (Berkeley: University of California Press, 1997), 184-85. Miller views these "new paradigm churches" principally through the lens of three "movements" which are Calvary Chapel (founded 1965), Vineyard Christian Fellowship (founded 1974), and Hope Chapel (founded 1971). Hope Chapel is associated with the Foursquare Gospel Church.

26. Andrew M. Greeley, *Religious Change in America* (Cambridge, MA: Harvard University Press, 1989), 34-35. The survey compared the denomination in which a person was raised to the one in which the person is currently a member. The complete survey results can be found in Greeley, *Religious Change in America*, 36.

27. Ibid., 36-37. Father Greeley sees this exodus as critical for the four largest mainline denominations (which includes the United Methodist Church) because "they are losing the (apparently) more devout of the recent cohorts to other denominations. As this happens, the level of religious practice in the mainline may begin to decline, and the defection of those with stronger religious propensities from future cohorts may diminish their proportion of the American population even more." Greeley's findings provide further proof for Finke and Stark's thesis that new sects form once the original sect becomes too "church-like."

28. Charles Trueheart, "The Next Church," *Atlantic Monthly*, August 1996, 42. Towards the end of his insightful article, while discussing the "names" of these churches, the "sect to church to new schism" process can be seen. Trueheart notes that "though many congregations in the Next Church (his term for the newer, mostly unaffiliated churches) retain nominal membership in mainline or evangelical denominations, and some are thriving as parts of a greater ecclesiastical whole, what they are concealing in the names they have chosen is at the heart of the great convulsion in American church life: the challenge to denominations." Furthermore, he pointed out on pages 56 and 57 that the "unaffiliated churches have led the way in acting individually, creatively, aggressively, competitively, intentionally to build huge communities of people whose lives orbit the church seven days a week." A sampling of these church names include Willow Creek Community Church, the Fellowship

of Las Colinas, Saddleback Valley Community Church, Mariner's Church, Wooddale Church (Baptist), and Calvary Chapel. Moreover, Calvary Chapel has already spawned another seven hundred more "Calvary Churches" around the country.

29.   Ibid., 40.   Trueheart believes that "these busy and tight-knit congregations of thousands, inside and outside traditional Protestant denominations, have become sanctuaries from the world ('islands in the stream,' to use a phrase often heard in these parts), and as such they are proving themselves to be breeding grounds for personal renewal and human connectedness."

30.   Ibid.

31.   Ibid., 41. For example, at the beginning of one of the Sunday morning services at the Mariner's Church in California, "a tall and smartly dressed woman shared a little about her Bible study experience, and the help she got from the Bible in accepting her husband instead of trying to change him." Similarly, Methodist love feasts consisted largely of personal testimonies, hymns, and prayers.

32.   Albert C. Outler, "The Place of Wesley in the Christian Tradition," in *The Place of Wesley in the Christian Tradition*, ed. Kenneth E. Rowe (Metuchen, NJ: Scarecrow Press, 1976), 15.

33.   Ibid., 15. Outler further asserted on page 16 that "it was Wesley - heir to the Protestant agony but rooted in an older richer tradition of Scripture and tradition - who recognized more clearly than any other theologian of his time that the old Reformation polarities had ceased to define the Christian future."

34.   Ibid., 29-30.   According to Outler, "Latin Christianity has been dominated by forensic images, metaphors from the law courts (Roman and medieval); Greek Christianity has been fascinated by visions of ontological 'participation in God' - *metousia theou*. One stresses the Cross; the other points to the Cross but also past it, to the glory beyond." Moreover, Outler believed Wesley had "grasped this vital unity firmly, and this is what gives him his distinctive 'place' - then and now. For classical Protestantism - to put no finer point on it - has been dominated by the forensic-pardon theme...in conscious contrast to all forgiveness - participation themes. Roman Catholicism has maintained the participation theme but has linked it with theories of sacramental action and a sacerdotal control of the means of grace that marks it off from the patristic traditions of Irenaeus, Gregory of Nyssa, Maximos the Confessor, et al."

35.   Ibid., 15. Outler noted that "*mutatis mutandis*, the live issue at the heart of the tumultuous controversies in the Roman Catholic Church - in Jansenism and in the *De Auxiliis* battle - was not a speculative issue but the question as to what it means to become a Christian."

36.   Ibid., 15-16. For instance, the Roman Catholic Church's 1974 Synod of Bishops discussed the question of "The Evangelization of the Modern World" and called for an evangelization which was both a proclamation of the Good News and a deeper call to holiness in the local Christian community. Recent Protestant ecumenical assemblies at Bangkok, Lausanne, and Jerusalem have also examined evangelism and Christian nurture.

37. Pope Paul VI, *On Evangelization in the Modern World* (Boston: St. Paul Books and Media, 1975), sect. 14, 8. This papal encyclical was drawn from the discussions held at the 1974 Synod of Bishops meeting in Rome on the subject of evangelization. The pope also said that "evangelizing is in fact the grace and vocation proper to the church, her deepest identity. She exists in order to evangelize, that is to say, in order to preach and teach, to be the channel of the gift of grace, to reconcile sinners with God," p. 8. Significantly, the pope wrote in section 22, page 19, that a verbal proclamation is necessary since the witness of one's life and behaviour "always remains insufficient, because even the finest witness will prove ineffective in the long run if it is not explained, justified - what Peter called always having 'your answer ready for people who ask you the reason for the hope you all have' - and made explicit by a clear and unequivocal proclamation of the Lord Jesus."

38. Pope John Paul II, *Mission of the Redeemer* (Boston: St. Paul Books and Media, 1990), sect. 3, 12. Over the past twenty years, Pope John Paul has called for both a "new evangelization" directed toward those who have never heard the Gospel before and a "re-evangelization" for those who have heard it but have drifted away.

39. Avery Dulles, "The New Evangelization: What Does It Mean?" (Detroit, MI: 1994), 9. Similarly, at the "John Paul II and the New Evangelization Conference," in describing what the recent popes have called the "new evangelism," Fr. Avery Dulles has said that it "is currently not seen simply as a first announcement of the Christian message but rather as a comprehensive process of 'Christianization.' The proclamation of the basic Christian message is an indispensable first step, but it is only the beginning of a lifelong process."

40. Richard Wilke, *And Are We Yet Alive*, 66. Bishop Richard Wilke, a United Methodist bishop (now retired) of the Arkansas area, pastored this church beginning in 1974. In the period from 1961 to 1974, membership in that church went from 3,875 to 2,300 and actual worship attendance dropped from 1,000 to 500. This decline was all the more alarming since the city of Wichita was actually experiencing a period of sustained growth. For a complete account of this church's revitalization, see Chapter IV, "Up from the Ashes," 65-83.

41. Ibid., 69. Wilke believes that a welcoming community can be contagious and can draw the unchurched in. He notes on page 70 that "following the anti-institutionalism of the sixties and taking seriously the suspicion of sophisticated urban America, people want to know religion is real before they are ready to believe. Some don't know enough about Jesus to accept him."

42. Adult Sunday School classes somewhat approximate the early Methodist class meeting. These adult classes usually meet on Sunday morning before or after church (as the class meetings often did) and, depending on the topic and type of study, the class members often spend much of the hour relating personal experiences with their classmates.

43. Wilke, *And Are We Yet Alive*, 71-73.

44. Ibid., 74. Early New York City Methodism also had class meetings for married women which usually met at 11:00 a.m. or 3:00 p.m.

45. Ibid., 77-78.

46. Ibid., 79. In addition, Wilke stated on pages 79 and 80 that "centripetal witnessing means to invite people into the fellowship and to help them grow toward the center or axis, which is in Christ himself; we are talking about inverted evangelism, witnessing turned inside out. Instead of inviting people to accept Christ, then join the church, then become a part of the body life of the church, the strategy is 180 degrees in the opposite direction. Bring people into the corporate life; that is, toward the center. Let them experience the joy, the music, the Scriptures, the prayers, the love of the people." See also Daniel T. Benedict, *Come to the Waters: Baptism and Ministry of Welcoming Seekers and Making Disciples.* (Nashville: Discipleship Resources, 1989) and George G. Hunter, *The Celtic Way of Evangelism.* (Nashville: Abingdon Press, 2000).

47. Ibid., 80.

48. Miller, *Reinventing American Protestantism*, 137. Miller also adds that these small groups provide a type of extended family network which offers emotional and, at times, economic support. This is especially important to those who experienced divorce as children and never had a close family relationship.

49. Trueheart, "The Next Church," 40.

50. Ibid., 54-55. These small groups are usually limited to ten or less. Trueheart also noted that "some 10,500 of the more than 15,000 worshipers at Willow Creek, and comparable proportions at other churches, belong to small groups."

51. Miller, *Reinventing American Protestantism*, 42. In some new paradigm churches, a "lay shepherd" oversees approximately six small groups.

52. Ibid., 137. These new paradigm churches seem to be avoiding the difficulty of many nineteenth century Manhattan class meetings: class sizes of forty, fifty, and even higher. They seem to have the "will" to mandate it, perhaps because they are in their "first fervor." As Methodism entered its second generation in New York City, it seemed to lack the resolve which was needed to keep class meeting size to twelve persons, the size Wesley had originally mandated.

53. Ibid., 54. The format of a small group meeting varies in the new paradigm churches. One group which Miller observed began with twenty minutes of singing, followed by forty minutes of Bible study in which members made application of the Biblical text to their lives and to the church. After the Bible study, the members divided into groups of three to pray for one another. The entire small group meeting lasted two and a half hours. The account of this meeting is found on pages 134-36.

54. Trueheart, "The Next Church," p. 54-55.

55. Miller, *Reinventing American Protestantism*, 150. Accountability, however, does not seem to include "exclusion" of a member who is habitually absent from the small group meeting or who refuses to amend his or her ways. Errant members apparently respond to the gentle admonition conveyed in the loving atmosphere of the small group.

56. Ron Stodgill, "God of Our Fathers," *Time*, 6 October 1997, 37. The "second promise" which men are asked to make states that "a Promise Keeper is committed to pursuing vital relationships with a few other men,

understanding that he needs brothers to help him keep his promises." Also, Miller notes on page 116 that while nearly all of the new paradigm pastors are male, women are allowed to lead all-women's group and "teach."

57. Miller, *Reinventing American Protestantism*, 42.

58. Wilke, *And Are We Yet Alive*, 76. "I. C. U." stands for "Intensive Care Unit".

59. Ibid., 93.

60. Ibid., 93-94.

61. United Methodist Church, *Discipline* (Nashville: United Methodist Publishing House, 1992), para. 128, 129. The *Discipline* said, in part, that "the pastor in cooperation with the Administrative Council or the Council on Ministries may arrange the membership in groups - with a leader for each group - designed to involve the membership of the church in its ministry to the community. These groups shall be of such size, usually not larger than eight or ten families, as to be convenient and effective for service."

62. United Methodist Church, *Guidelines for Leading Your Congregation: Class Leader* (Nashville: Abingdon Press, 1996), 18.

63. Ibid., 8. The *Guidelines* clearly state the "pastoral" role of the class leader, which is "to develop active Christian discipleship as you encourage, nudge, guide, and watch over in love a small subgrouping of your congregation."

64. Ibid., 8-9, 15, and 18.

65. Ibid., 9. In addition, the United Methodist Church has developed the "General Rule of Discipleship" which is meant to closely parallel Wesley's rules for the Methodist societies. A diagram of this rule is contained in *Guidelines for Leading Your Congregation: Class Leader*, 10.

66. United Methodist Church, *Discipline*, para. 168-69, 269 and para. 128, 229.

67. An extensive bibliography could easily be compiled consisting of recent books, dissertations (twelve dissertations on the class meeting have been done from 1982 to 1992), and articles. A wealth of primary sources for both the English and American class meeting could also be consulted. These include class manuals, tracts on the class meeting, periodical articles, biographies, autobiographies, class lists, class attendance books, and minutes of leaders' meetings. See the Secondary Source bibliography for a complete listing of the recent dissertations and articles.

68. The three sub-levels within an Annual Conference are the district, cluster, and local church. A cluster might contain ten to fifteen churches. A district is usually made up of three or more clusters.

Bibliography: Primary Sources

PUBLISHED WORKS

A. BOOKS

Absence from Class: A Dialogue. In *Tracts of the Tract Society of the Methodist Episcopal Church,* ed. Abel Stevens, no. 369. New York: Carlton and Phillips, 1854.

Advice to the Members of the Methodist Episcopal Church; Being a Revision of Reverend R. Newstead's Advices to One Who Meets in Class. In *Tracts of the Tract Society of Methodist Episcopal Church,* ed. Abel Stevens, no. 349. New York: Carlton and Phillips, 1854.

Asbury, Francis. *The Journals and Letters of Francis Asbury.* 3 vols. Ed. By Elmer T. Clark. Nashville: Abingdon Press, 1958.

Atkinson, John. *The Class Leader: His Work and How to Do It.* New York: Phillips and Hunt, 1882.

Bainbridge, T. H. and I. E. Page, eds. *Thoughts for Class Leaders: First Series.* London: C. H. Kelly, 1895.

Bangs, Heman. *The Autobiography and Journal of Reverend Heman Bangs.* New York: Tibbals and Son, 1872.

Bangs, John. *Autobiography of Reverend John Bangs.* New York: privately printed, 1846.

Browning, William G. *Grace Magnified.* Poughkeepsie, NY: privately printed, 1887.

Calendar of the Ezekiel Cooper Collection of Early American Methodist Manuscripts. Chicago: The Illinois Historical Records Survey Project, Division of Professional and Service Projects, Work Projects Administration, 1941.

Carter, Thomas. *French Mission Life.* New York: Carlton and Porter, 1857.

Cartwright, Peter. *Autobiography of Peter Cartwright.* Nashville: Abingdon Press, 1956.

Carvosso, William. *A Memoir of Mr. William Carvosso, Sixty Years a Class Leader.* New York: Lane and Tippett, 1846.

Christophers, Samuel W. _Class-Meetings in Relation to the Design and Success of Methodism._ London: Wesleyan Conference Office, 1873.

A Class Book: Containing Directions to Class Leaders, Ruled Forms for Leaders' Weekly Accounts, and the Rules of the Methodist Societies. London: Thomas Cordeux, 1820.

Class Meetings: Ways and Means of Rendering Them More Animating and Instructive. In *Tracts of the Tract Society of the Methodist Episcopal Church,* ed. Abel Stevens, no. 78. New York: Carlton and Phillips, 1854.

Coke, Thomas and Francis Asbury. *Doctrines and Discipline of the Methodist Episcopal Church in America, with Explanatory Notes.* Philadelphia: Henry Tuckniss,1798. Reprint, Rutland: Academy Books, 1979.

Coke, Thomas. *Extracts of the Journals of the Reverend Dr. Coke's Five Visits to America.* London: G. Paramore, 1793.

Coles, George. *Incidents of My Later Years.* New York: Carlton and Phillips, 1855.

_____. *My Youthful Days.* New York: Lane and Scott, 1852.

Culver, Newell. *Methodism Forty Years Ago and Now.* New York: Nelson and Phillips, 1873.

DeVinne, Daniel. *Recollections of Fifty Years in the Ministry.* New York: privately printed, 1883.

Do You Attend Your Class? In *Tracts of the Tract Society of the Methodist Episcopal Church,* ed. Abel Stevens, no. 356. New York: Carlton and Phillips, 1854.

Episcopal Address to Class-Leaders and Course of Reading for Them. New York: Hunt and Eaton, 1890.

Fish, Henry. *The Class-Leader's Manual: Being Letters Addressed to a Class Leader, on All Matters Relating to his Office.* London: J. Mason, 1849.

Fisher, William S. *New York City Methodist Marriages: 1785-1893.* Camden, Maine: Picton Press, 1994.

Fitzgerald, Oscar P. *Bible Night: McKendree Class-Meeting Talks.* Nashville: Southern Methodist Publishing House, 1887.

_____. *The Class-Meeting: In Twenty Short Chapters.* Nashville: Southern Methodist Publishing House, 1880.

Goodell, Charles L. *The Drillmaster of Methodism: Principles and Methods for the Class Leader and Pastor.* New York: Eaton and Mains, 1902.

Grindrod, Reverend Edmund. *The Duties, Qualifications, and Encouragements of Class Leaders; Being the Substance of Five Addresses Delivered to several Persons Appointed to that Office in the Wesleyan Methodist Society in Hull*. London: privately printed, 1831.

Haller, J. George. *The Redemption of the Prayer Meeting*. Cincinnati: Jennings and Graham, 1911.

Historical Records Survey. *Guide to Vital Statistics in the City of New York, Borough of Manhattan. Churches*. New York: Work Projects Administration, 1942.

Horneck, Anthony. *Several Sermons upon the Fifth of St. Matthew; Being Part of Christ's Sermon on the Mount*. London: Jer. Batley, 1717.

Horton, Reverend James. *A Narrative of James P. Horton*. Fishkill, NY: privately printed, 1839.

Howe, John M., ed. *Memoir of Mrs. Mary Howe of the City of New York*. New York: G. Lane and P. P. Sandford, 1843.

Hughes, Thomas. *The Condition of Membership in the Christian Church: Viewed in Connection with the Class Meeting System in the Methodist Body*. London: Hodder and Stoughton, 1868.

Hunt, Jacob. *Appointment of Class Leaders: Delivered before the Class Leaders' Convention on Northern New York Conference, June, 1882*. Utica, NY: privately printed, 1882.

Hutchins, James H. *The Narrow Way: Experience Illustrated: Reminiscences, Sub-pastoral Work*. Utica, New York: T. J. Griffiths, 1891.

Jackson, Thomas, ed. *The Lives of Early Methodist Preachers, Chiefly Written by Themselves*. 6 vols. London: Wesley Conference Office, 1876.

Janes, Edmund S. *Address to Class-Leaders*. New York: Carlton and Lanahan, 1868.

Jobson, Frederick J. *A Mother's Portrait: Being a Memorial of Filial Affection, with Sketches of Wesleyan Life and of Religious Sources in Letters to a Younger Sister*. Nashville: E. Stevenson and F. A. Owen, 1857.

Keys, Charles C. *The Class-Leader's Manual, or, an Essay on the Duties, Difficulties, Qualifications, Motives, and Encouragements of Class Leaders*. New York: Lane and Scott, 1851.

Law, William. *A Serious Call to a Devout and Holy Life*. London: William Innys, 1729.

Lee, Jesse. *A Short History of the Methodists*. Baltimore: Magill and Clime, 1810.

Longden, Henry. *The Life of Henry Longden: Minister of the Gospel, Compiled from the Memoirs, Diary, Letters, and other Authentic Documents*. New York: Thomas Mason and Lane, 1837.

Merwin, Samuel. *The Substance of a Sermon Preached on Opening the Methodist Church in John Street, in the City of New York*. New York: John C. Totten, 1818.

Methodist Episcopal Church. *Catalog of Books and Tracts*. New York: Lane and Scott, 1851.

_____. *A Form of Discipline for the Ministers, Preachers, and Members of the Methodist Episcopal Church in America*. New York: William Ross, 1789.

_____. *The Nature, Design, and General Rules of the United Societies of the Methodist Episcopal Church in America*. New York: William Ross, 1788.

_____. *A Short Scriptural Catechism*. New York: Daniel Hitt and Thomas Ware, 1813.

Miley, Reverend John. *Treatise on Class Meeting*. Cincinnati: Swormstedt and Power, 1851.

Minutes of the Methodist Conferences, from the first, held in London, by the late Rev. John Wesley, A. M., in the Year 1744. London: Wesleyan Conference Office, 1812.

Newstead, Robert. *Advices to One Who Meets in Class*. New York: G. Lane and P. P. Sandford, 1843.

Nightingale, Joseph. *A Portraiture of Methodism: Being an Impartial View of the Rise, Progress, Doctrines, Discipline, and Manners of the Wesleyan Methodists*. London: Longman, Hurst, Rees, and Orme, 1807.

Pearse, Mark G. *The Earnest Evangelist and Successful Class Leader: Memoir of William Thompson*. London: Wesleyan Conference Office, 1811.

Phoebus, William. *Memoirs of the Reverend Richard Whatcoat*. New York: J. Allen, 1828.

Pilmore, Joseph. *The Journal of Joseph Pilmore*, ed. by Frederick Maser. Philadelphia: Message Publishing Company, 1969.

Presbyterian Reunion: A Memorial Volume, 1837-1871. New York: Lent and Company, 1870.

Prize Essays on the Class Meeting: Its Value to the Church, and Suggestions for Increasing Its Efficiency and Attractiveness...with Supplement, containing further Suggestions, Topics, Bible Readings, etc. London: T. Woolman, 1889.

Punshon, William M. *Tabor, or, The Class Meeting: A Plea and an Appeal*. Carlisle: I.F. Whitridge, 1848.

Rimius, Henry. *A Candid Narrative of the Rise and Progress of the Herrnhuters, Commonly Called Moravians, or, Unitas Fratrum; with a Short Account of their Doctrines, Drawn from Their Own Writings*. London: privately printed, 1753.

Robinson, George C. *Seed Thoughts: A Handbook of Doctrine and Devotion Designed for Class Leaders.* New York: Carlton and Porter, 1863.

Rogers, Hester Ann. *A Short Account of the Experience of Mrs. Hester Ann Rogers,* ed. Thomas Coke. New York: Ezekiel Cooper and John Wilson, 1806.

Rosser, Leonidas. *Class Meetings: Embracing their Origin, Nature, Obligation, and Benefits. Also, the Duties of Preachers and Leaders, and Appeal to Private Members: and Their Temporal Advantages.* Richmond: by the author, 1855.

Sandford, Peter P. *Memoirs of Mr. Wesley's Missionaries in America.* New York: G. Lane and Peter P. Sandford, 1843.

Scarlett, Reverend John. *The Life and Experience of a Converted Infidel.* New York: Carlton and Phillips, 1854.

Scougal, Henry. *The Life of God in the Soul of Man.* London: privately printed, 1726.

Selleck, Alonzo. *Recollections of an Itinerant Life.* New York: Phillips and Hunt, 1886.

Simon, John S. *A Manual of Instruction and Advice for Class Leaders.* London: Charles H. Kelly, 1893.

Spener, Philip Jakob. *Pia Desideria,* trans. and ed. Theodore G. Tappert. Philadelphia: Fortress Press, 1964.

Spicer, Reverend Tobias. *Autobiography.* Boston: C. H. Pierce and Company, 1851.

Sutcliffe, Joseph. *The Mutual Communion of Saints: Shewing the Necessity and Advantages of the Weekly Meetings for a Communication of Experience.* Trowbridge: Abraham Small, 1794.

United Methodist Church. *Discipline.* Nashville: United Methodist Publishing House, 1992.

————. *Guidelines for Leading Your Congregation: Class Leader.* Nashville: Abingdon Press, 1996.

Weber, Herman C. *Presbyterian Statistics through One Hundred Years, 1826-1926: Tabulated, Visualized, and Interpreted.* Philadelphia: The General Council, Presbyterian Church in the U.S.A., 1927.

Weekly Class Collections. In *Tracts of the Tract Society of the Methodist Episcopal Church,* ed. Abel Stevens, no. 350. New York: Carlton and Phillips, 1854.

Wesley, John, ed. *A Christian Library.* 50 vols. Bristol: W. Pine, 1749-1755.

————. *John Wesley,* ed. Albert C. Outler. New York: Oxford University Press, 1964.

_____. *The Journal of The Rev. John Wesley, A.M.   Standard edition.* 8 vols. Edited by Nehemiah Curnock. London: Robert Culley, 1909.

_____. *The Letters of The Rev. John Wesley, A.M.   Standard edition.* 8 vols. Edited by John Telford. London: Epworth Press, 1931.

_____. *The Nature, Design, and General Rules of the United Societies in London, Bristol, King-wood, and Newcastle upon Tyne.* Newcastle upon Tyne: John Gooding, 1743.

_____. *A Plain Account of the People Called Methodists.* In *The Works of John Wesley,* vol. 9. Nashville: Abingdon Press, 1989.

_____.   *The Works of John Wesley.* 14 vols. London: Wesleyan Conference Office, 1872. Reprint, Grand Rapids, MI: Baker Book House, 1979.

Whaling, Frank, ed. *John and Charles Wesley: Selected Writings and Hymns.* New York: Paulist Press, 1981.

Wood, James. *A Class Book: Containing Directions to Class Leaders.* London: Thomas Cordeux, 1820.

_____. *Directions and Cautions Addressed to Class Leaders.* London: Wesleyan Conference-Office, 1804.

Wright, Samuel. *The Story of My Life: the Experience of Samuel Wright, for Forty Years a Class leader in the Methodist Episcopal Church.* New York: by the author, 1891.

B. ARTICLES

"From Mrs. K. to her Class."*Methodist Magazine* 25 (1802): 83-85.
"Life and Death of Mrs. Prudence Hudson." *Methodist Magazine* 9 (1826): 412.
"On Christian Communion." *Methodist Magazine* 18 (1818): 235.

C. NEWSPAPERS

Christian Advocate and Journal (New York)
1 February 1827   "New York District"
3 March 1827   "Sketch of the Rise and Present State of the Methodist Episcopal Church in the City of New York"
      "The Love Feast"
9 November 1827   "Class Meetings"
4 January 1828   "Class Meetings"

25 January 1828   "A Class Leader"
                           "Class Meetings Formed into Tract Societies"

8 February 1828   "Pastoral Care: Letter to the Preacher's Class"

14 March 1828   "The Circuit Preacher: No. VI. Class Meetings"

14 August 1829   "Weekly Class Collections: An Appeal"

23 April 1830   "Class Meetings"

4 June 1830   "Advantages of Class Meetings, and the Best
                           Means of Rendering Them Profitable"

11 November 1831   "Class Collections"

11 May 1832   "The Quarterly Examination"

28 September 1832   "The Class Leader"

24 January 1834   "My Neglected Class Meeting"

28 March 1834   "Class Delinquency"

13 March 1835   "Class Meetings"

2 June 1837   "Class Meetings: Primitive Usages, Rules,
                           Discipline"

9 June 1837   "Class Meetings"

28 July 1837   "Class Meetings"

9 March 1838   "To Class Leaders"

1 June 1838   "Class Meetings"

14 September 1838   "The Faithful Class Leader"

4 January 1839   "Evils of a Lax Administration of Discipline"

12 April 1839   "Class Meetings"

24 May 1839   "Class Examination"

9 August 1839   "Utility of Class Meetings"

8 November 1839   "Carvosso's Memoirs"

31 January 1840   "Of the Right Method of Meeting Classes and
                           Bands, in the Methodist Societies"

25 November 1840   "Class Meetings"

23 December 1840   "The Duty of a Class Leader"

27 October 1841   "Itinerant Arrangements - Stations and Circuits"
                           "Old-Fashioned Methodism"

4 December 1842   "Class Meetings and Love Feasts"

8 March 1843   "Do You Visit Your Delinquent Class
                           Members?"

28 June 1843   "Interchange of Leaders"

12 March 1845   "Obituary of Mrs. John Bangs"

4 June 1845   "New York Examining Committee"
                           "Who Shall Appoint Them?"

11 June 1845   "Class Leaders No. II - Their Duties"

2 July 1845   "Class Meetings, No. II - How Conducted To be
                           Useful"

9 July 1845   "Obligation of Members to Attend"

20 August 1845	"Class Leaders - Their Duties"
3 October 1845	"Duty of Class Leaders"
19 November 1845	"Rules for Leading Class"
5 March 1846	"Backsliders"
25 August 1847	"To Class Leaders"
1 March 1848	"Circuits in the City of New York: To the Members of the Methodist Episcopal Church in the City of New York"
19 April 1848	"General Conference of 1848"
3 January 1850	"Responsibilities of Class Leaders"
14 February 1850	"Class Meetings"
20 March 1851	"The Scriptural Basis of Class Meetings"
27 March 1851	"Sermons, Written and Unwritten"
4 December 1851	"The Class Leader"
7 January 1853	"Class Meetings - A Suggestion"
24 November 1853	"I Don't Like Class Meeting"
17 March 1853	"Class Meetings as a Condition of Church Membership"
19 January 1854	"Formality in Class Meetings"
2 March 1854	"Class Meetings: Existing Evils - Remedy Proposed"
21 January 1858	"Class Meetings - Prevailing Defects"
18 February 1858	"Class Meetings - Needed Reform in Them"
5 August 1858	"Pastoral Address: To the Members of the Methodist Episcopal Church within the bounds of the New Jersey Conference"
26 September 1861	"Class Meetings: Should We Attend Them or Be Excommunicated?"
17 October 1861	"Class Meetings"
24 October 1861	"Class Meetings"
6 February 1862	"Class Meeting Controversy"
12 March 1863	"New York Methodism"
17 January 1884	"Presiding Elders in Council"
21 August 1884	"Presiding Elders Convention"
11 December 1884	"Presiding Elders Convention"

D. CITY DIRECTORIES

Duncan, William, ed. *The New York Directory and Register, for the Year 1793*. New York: T. and J. Swords, 1793.
Franks, David, ed. *The New York Directory*. New York: Shepard Kollock, 1786.

Longworth, Thomas, ed. *American Almanac, New York Register and City Directory.* New York: by the author, 1812, 1824, and 1825.

E. REPORTS AND PROCEEDINGS

Methodist Episcopal Church. *Minutes of the Methodist Conferences Annually Held in America from 1773 to 1794, Inclusive.* Philadelphia: Henry Tuckniss, 1795.
New York Conference. *Journal of the New York Annual Conference.* New York: Methodist Book Concern, 1821-1839.
New York Conference. *Journal of the New York Conference.* Madison, NJ: UMCA - GCAH, Drew University, 1840-1845, 1854-1855, and 1858.
New York East Conference. *Journal of the New York East Conference.* Madison, NJ: UMCA - GCAH, Drew University. 1850-1875.
New York East Conference. "Report of the New York District." In *New York East Conference Journal.* Madison, NJ: UMCA - GCAH, Drew University, 1874.
New York East Conference. "Report of the Brooklyn District." In *New York East Conference Journal.* Madison, NJ: UMCA - GCAH, Drew University, 1880.

F. ENCYCLICALS

Pope Paul VI. *On Evangelization in the Modern World.* Boston: St. Paul Books and Media, 1975.
Pope John Paul II. *Mission of the Redeemer.* Boston: St. Paul Books and Media, 1990.

G. UNPUBLISHED WORKS

1. MANUSCRIPTS

Bradburn, Samuel. "Diary." Methodist Archives and Research Centre, John Rylands University Library, Manchester, England.
Coles, Reverend George. "Journal." UMCA - GCAH, "Drew University Methodist Collection," Drew University, Madison, NJ.
Hardy, Thomas. "Diary." Methodist Archives and Research Centre, John Rylands University Library, Manchester, England.

Jessop, Reverend William. "Journal." UMCA - GCAH, "Drew
    University Methodist Collection," Drew University, Madison, NJ.
Rankin, Reverend Thomas. "Journal." Typewritten. UMCA - GCAH,
    "Drew University Methodist Collection," Drew University,
    Madison, NJ.
Smith, Reverend Daniel. "Draft of an Address on the History of
    Bowery Church from 1836-1847." UMCA - GCAH, "Drew
    University Methodist Collection," Drew University, Madison, NJ.

2. LETTERS

Asbury, Francis, no location, to Ezekiel Cooper, New York City,
    undated, Ezekiel Cooper Collection, vol. 18, ms. 12, Garrett
    Evangelical Seminary, Evanston, Illinois.
Bicknell, J., no location, to Jacob Bunting, no location, 2 March, 1835,
    Methodist Church Archives, City Road, London.
Dickins, John, New York, to Edward Dromgoole, Virginia, 4 July
    1783. Southern Historical Collection, Edward Dromgoole Papers,
    no. 230, University of North Carolina.
McCoombs, Lawrence, Philadelphia, to Ezekiel Cooper, Philadelphia,
    25 February, 1807. UMCA - GCAH, "Drew University Methodist
    Collection," Drew University, Madison, NJ.

3. CLASSBOOKS

Reed, Reverend John. "Classbook. 1840." UMCA - GCAH, "Drew
    University Methodist Collection," Drew University, Madison, NJ.

4. REPORTS AND PROCEEDINGS

Methodist Episcopal Church. *General Conference Minutebook. 1800-
    1828.* UMCA - GCAH, Drew University, Madison, NJ.
Journal of the New York Annual Conference. 1800-1839. Typewritten.
    UMCA - GCAH, Drew University, Madison, NJ.
"Petition to the General Conference Held in Pittsburgh, May, 1848." In
    General Conference Minutebook. UMCA - GCAH, Drew
    University, Madison, NJ.
"Record of the Proceedings in the Trials of Members of the New York
    Circuit." New York: John Street United Methodist Church, 1824-
    1827.

"Report of Committee on Safety to the General Conference Held in Baltimore, May, 1816." In *General Conference Minutebook.* UMCA - GCAH, Drew University, Madison, NJ.

"Report of Committee on the Band Rules to the General Conference Held in Baltimore, 1824." In *General Conference Minutebook.* UMCA – GCAH, Drew University, Madison, NJ.

"Report of Committee on the Itinerancy to the General Conference Held in Baltimore, May, 1824." In *General Conference Minutebook.* UMCA - GCAH, Drew University, Madison, NJ.

"Transcripts of Church Trials for New York Circuit." UMCA - GCAH, Drew University, Madison, NJ.

5.   METHODIST EPISCOPAL CHURCH RECORDS.

The following photocopied records are from the Manuscripts Division, The New York Public Library, Astor, Lenox and Tilden Foundations.

"Methodist Episcopal Church of New York." vols. 66-68, 71, 77-82, 88, 90-90a, 92-93

"Methodist Episcopal Church of New York. West Circuit." vols. 100-1

"New York Preachers Meeting." vols. 115-22e

"Allen Street Methodist Episcopal Church." vols. 141-52, 155

"Forsyth Street Methodist Episcopal Church." vols. 203-6, 208-10, 212-14, 221-22

"Greene Street Methodist Episcopal Church." vols. 228-29

"John Street Methodist Episcopal Church." vols. 233-34, 236-48

"Lexington Avenue Methodist Episcopal Church." vol. 253

"Second Street Methodist Episcopal Church." vols. 287, 289, 296, 316-17

"Seventh Street Methodist Episcopal Church." vols. 347, 349-52

"Willett Street Methodist Episcopal Church." vols. 380-81, 388

6. LECTURES

Dulles, Avery. "The New Evangelization: What Does It Mean?" Detroit, MI: John Paul II and the New Evangelization Conference, May, 1994. Draft manuscript.

Bibliography: Secondary Sources

A. BOOKS

Ahlstrom, Sydney E. *A Religious History of the American People.* Garden City, New York: Image Books, 1975.

Armstrong, Anthony. *The Church of England, the Methodists and Society, 1700-1850.* London: University of London Press, 1973.

Atkinson, John. *The Beginnings of the Wesleyan Movement in America.* New York: Hunt and Eaton, 1896.

Baird, Robert. *Religion in America.* New York: Harper and Brothers, 1844.

Baker, Frank. *From Wesley to Asbury.* Durham, North Carolina: Duke University Press, 1976.

_____. *Methodism and the Love Feast.* London: Epworth Press, 1957.

Baker, Osmon C. *A Guide Book to the Administration of the Discipline of the Methodist Episcopal Church.* New York: Phillips and Hunt, 1884.

Banks, John. *The Church in Your Home.* London: Epworth Press, 1964.

Bangs, Nathan. *A History of the Methodist Episcopal Church.* 4 vols. New York: Carlton and Porter, 1860.

Banks, Louis A. *A Year's Prayer-Meeting Talks.* New York: Funk and Wagnall's Company, 1899.

Bate, John. *The Class Leader's Assistant.* London: Hamilton, Adams, and Company, 1865.

_____. *Objections to the Methodist Class Meeting Answered: A Book for Hearers and Members.* London: Hamilton, Adams, and Company, 1866.

_____. *The Usual Objections to Methodist Class Meetings, Considered and Answered.* London: R. M. Abbott, 1849.

Bedell, Kenneth E. *Yearbook of American and Canadian Churches. 1977.* Nashville: Abingdon Press, 1997.

Bilhartz, Terry D. *Urban Religion and the Second Great Awakening.* Rutherford, New Jersey: Fairleigh Dickinson University Press, 1986.

Blackwell, John. *The Methodist Class Leader, or the Duties, Qualifications, Difficulties, and Encouragements of a Class Leader Considered.* London: T. Blanshard, 1818.

Blake, Thomas. *The Class-Meeting.* New York: Hunt and Eaton, 1896.

Bonomi, Patricia U. *Under the Cope of Heaven: Religion, Society, and Politics in Colonial America.* New York: Oxford University Press, 1986.

Bowmer, John C. *Pastor and People: A Study of Church and Ministry in Wesley Methodism from the Death of John Wesley (1791) to the Death of Jabez Bunting (1858).* London: Epworth Press, 1975.

Bradley, Sidney B. *The Life of Bishop Richard Whatcoat.* Louisville: Pentecostal Publishing Company, 1936.

Bright, Samuel. *The Class Leader as a Shepherd.* New York: Hunt and Eaton, 1892.

Bouyer, Louis A. *History of Christian Spirituality.* Vol. 3, *Orthodox Spirituality and Protestant and Anglican Spirituality.* London: Burns and Oates, 1969.

Bucke, Emory C., ed. *History of American Methodism.* 3 Vols. Nashville: Abingdon Press, 1964.

Bush, Joseph. *The Class-Meeting: Hints for Members, Showing How They may Impair Usefulness.* London: Wesley-Conference Office, 1866.

Butler, David. *Methodists and Papists.* London: Darton, Longman, and Todd, 1995.

Caldecott, William S. *Good Works.* London: Elliott-Stock, 1875.

Cameron, Richard M. *Methodism and Society in Historical Perspective.* Nashville: Abingdon Press, 1961.

Carwardine,Richard. *Transatlantic Revivalism:Popular Evangelicalism in Britain and America, 1790-1865.* Westport, CT: Greenwood Press, 1978.

Chamings, William H. *The Class Meeting as a Form of Christian Fellowship.* London: Wesley-Conference Office, 1890.

Chiles, Robert E. *Theological Transition in American Methodism, 1790-1935.* New York: Abingdon Press, 1965.

Church, Leslie F. *The Early Methodist People.* London: Society for the Promotion of Christian Knowledge, 1948.

_____. *More about the Early Methodist People.* London: Epworth Press, 1949.

Clark, Elmer T. *An Album of Methodist History.* New York: Abingdon-Cokebury Press, 1952.

The Class-Leader, His Work and How to Do It: with Illustrations of Principles, Needs, Methods, and Results. New York: Nelson and Phillips, 1824.

The Class-Leader at Work. London: C. H. Kelly, 1905.

The Class-Leader's Companion. London: Robert Culley, 1908.

The Class-Leader's Companion. London: C. H. Kelly, 1911.

The Class-Leader's Companion. London: C. H. Kelly, 1913.

Cole, Richard L. *Love-Feasts: A History of the Christian Agape.* London: C. H. Kelly, 1916.

Coles, George. *Heroines of Methodism.* New York: Carlton and Porter, 1857.

Conkin, Paul K. *Cane Ridge: America's Pentecost.* Madison, WI: University of Wisconsin Press, 1990.

Corderoy, Edward. *Father Reeves, the Methodist Class-Leader.* London: Hamilton Adams, 1853.

Cragg, Gerald R. *The Church and the Age of Reason, 1648-1789.* Baltimore: Penguin Books, 1960.

_____. *Reason and Authority in the Eighteenth Century.* Cambridge: Cambridge University Press, 1964.

Crowther, Jonathan. *A True and Complete Portraiture of Methodism.* New York: James Eastburn, 1813.

Currie, Robert. *Methodism Divided: A Study in the Sociology of Ecumenicalism.* London: Faber and Faber, 1968.

Davies, Rupert E. and Gordon Rupp, eds. *A History of the Methodist Church in Great Britain.* 4 vols. London: Epworth Press, 1965.

Dolliver, Robert H. *The Story of Old John Street Methodist Episcopal Church: 1766-1936.* New York: John Felsberg, 1936.

Drummond, Andrew L. *The Story of American Protestantism.* Edinburgh: Oliver and Boyd, 1949.

Duffy, Eamon. "Wesley and the Counter-Reformation." In *Revival and Religion since 1700,* ed. Jane Garnett and Colin Matthew, 1-19. London: The Hambledon Press, 1993.

Dupre, Louis and Don E. Saliers. *Christian Spirituality: Post Reformation and Modern.* New York: Crossroad, 1989.

Ellis, James E. *Ventures in Fellowship: Suggestions for Class-Leaders.* London: Epworth Press, 1943.

Emerick, Samuel, ed. *Spiritual Renewal for Methodism: A Discussion of the Early Methodist Class Meeting and the Values Inherent in Personal Groups Today.* Nashville: Methodist Evangelistic Materials, 1958.

Ernst, Robert. *Immigrant Life in New York City, 1825-1863.* New York: Octagon Books, 1979.

Ferguson, Charles W. *Methodists and the Making of America: Organizing to Beat the Devil.* Austin, Texas: Eakin Press, 1983.

Fettretch, James. *Class-leader's Companion.* New York: S. Hamilton, 1869.

Finke, Roger and Rodney Stark. *The Churching of America, 1776-1990: Winners and Losers in Our Religious Economy.* New Brunswick, NJ: Rutgers University Press, 1992.

Force, Benjamin Q. *The Charter Church of New York Methodism: Eighteenth Street.* New York: Phillips and Hunt, 1885.

Foster, Rev. John O. *Life and Labors of Mrs. Maggie Newton Van Cott.* Cincinnati: Hitchcock and Walden, 1872.

Fry, Benjamin St. James. *The Life of Rev. Richard Whatcoat.* New York: Carlton and Phillips, 1855.

Gaustad, Edwin S. *Historical Atlas of Religion in America.* New York: Harper and Row, 1962.

Gorrie, P. Douglass. *Episcopal Methodism as It Was and Is.* Auburn: Derby and Miller, 1852.

Goss, C. C. *Statistical History of the First Century of American Methodism.* New York: Carlton and Porter, 1866.

Gravely, Will B. "African Methodisms and the Rise of Black Denominationalism." In *Perspectives in American Methodism,* ed. Russell E. Richey, Kenneth E. Rowe, and Jean Miller Schmidt. Nashville: Kingswood Books, 1993.

Greeley, Andrew M. *The Denominational Society.* Glenview, Illinois: Scott, Foresman, and Company, 1972.

_____. *Religious Change in America.* Cambridge, MA: Harvard University Press, 1989.

Halevy, Elie. *A History of the English People in the Nineteenth Century. Vol. 1, England in 1815.* Trans. and ed. E. I. Watkin and D. A. Barker. New York: Barnes & Noble, 1961.

Hall, Reverend B. M. *The Life of Rev. John Clark.* New York: Carlton and Porter, 1856.

Hambrick-Stowe, Charles E. *The Practice of Piety.* Williamsburg, VA: University of North Carolina Press, 1982.

Hamilton, J. Taylor and Kenneth G. Hamilton. *History of the Moravian Church.* Bethlehem, PA: Interprovincial Board of Christian Education, Moravian Church in America, 1967.

Hatch, Nathan O. *The Democratization of American Christianity.* New Haven: Yale University Press, 1989.

Hedding, Elijah. *A Discourse on the Administration of the Discipline.* New York: Lane and Tippett, 1847.

Heyrman, Christine L. *Southern Cross.* New York: Alfred A. Knopf, 1997.

Hill, Christopher. *Change and Continuity in Seventeenth Century England.* Cambridge, MA: Harvard University Press, 1975.

_____. *From Reformation to Industrial Revolution.* London: Weidenfeld and Nicolson, 1967.

Hodges, George W. *Early Negro Church Life in New York.* New York: privately printed, 1945.

_____. *Touchstones of Methodism.* New York: Compact-Reflector Press, 1947.

Holland, John. *Memoirs of the Life and Ministry of the Rev. John Summerfield.* New York: American Tract Society, 1850.

Hood, James H. *One Hundred Years of the African Methodist Episcopal Zion Church.* New York: A.M.E. Zion Book Concern, 1895.

Hudson, Winthrop S. *Religion in America: An Historical Account of the Development of American Religious Life,* 4th ed. New York: Macmillan, 1987.

Hutchinson, William R., ed. *Between the Times: The Travail of the Protestant Establishment in America, 1900-1960.* Cambridge: Cambridge University Press, 1989.

Kelly, Dean. *Why Conservative Churches Are Growing.* New York: Harper and Row, 1977.

Kirkpatrick, Dow, ed. *The Doctrine of the Church.* New York: Abingdon Press, 1960.

Lednum, John. *A History of the Rise of Methodism in America.* Philadelphia: by the author, 1859.

Lee, Umphrey. *The Historical Backgrounds of Early Methodist Enthusiasm.* New York: Columbia University Press, 1931.

Mathews, Donald G. *Slavery and Methodism.* Princeton: Princeton University Press, 1965.

McLoughlin, William G. *Revivals, Awakenings, and Reform.* Chicago: University of Chicago Press, 1978.

Miller, Donald E. *Reinventing American Protestantism.* Berkeley, CA: University of California, 1997.

Miller, Perry. *Errand into the Wilderness.* Cambridge, MA: The Belknap Press of Harvard University Press, 1964.

Monk, Robert C. *John Wesley: His Puritan Heritage.* Nashville: Abingdon Press, 1966.

Moore, John J. *History of the A. M. E. Zion Church in America.* York, PA: Teachers' Journal Office, 1884.

Morgan, Edmund S. *Visible Saints.* New York: New York University Press, 1963.

Niebuhr, H. Richard. *The Social Sources of Denominationalism.* New York: The World Publishing Company, 1957.

Niebuhr, H. Richard and Daniel D. Williams, eds. *The Ministry in Historical Perspective.* New York: Harper and Row, 1956.

Nightingale, Joseph. *A Portraiture of Methodism.* London: for Longman, Hurst, Rees, and Orme, 1807.

North, Elizabeth M. *Consecrated Talents, or, The Life of Mrs. Mary W. Mason.* New York: Carlton & Lanahan, 1870.

Norwood, Frederick A. *Church Membership in the Methodist Tradition*. Nashville: Methodist Publishing House, 1958.

_____. ed. *The Methodist Discipline of 1798: Including the Annotations of Thomas Coke and Francis Asbury*. Rutland, VT: Academy Books, 1979.

_____. *The Story of American Methodism*. Nashville: Abingdon Press, 1974.

Nuttall, Gregory. *Visible Saints: The Congregational Way 1640-1660*. Oxford: Basil Blackwell, 1957.

Oden, Thomas C. *The Intensive Group Experience: The New Pietism*. Philadelphia: Westminster Press, 1972.

Orcibal, Jean. "The Theological Originality of John Wesley and Continental Spirituality." In *A History of the Methodist Church in Great Britain*, ed. Rupert Davies and Gordon Rupp, vol. 1, London: Epworth Press, 1965.

Outler, Albert C. "The Place of Wesley in the Christian Tradition." In *The Place of Wesley in the Christian Tradition*, ed. Kenneth E. Rowe, Metuchen, NJ: The Scarecrow Press, Inc., 1976.

Peters, John L. *Christian Perfection and American Methodism*. Nashville: Abingdon Press, 1956.

Phoebus, George A., ed. *Beams of Light on Early Methodism in America*. New York: Phillips and Hunt, 1887.

_____. *Memoirs of the Rev. Richard Whatcoat*. New York: J. Allen, 1828.

Piette, Maximin. *John Wesley in the Evolution of Protestantism*. New York: Sheed and Ward, 1937.

Pilkington, James P. *The Methodist Publishing House*. 2 vols. Nashville: Abingdon Press, 1968.

Pointer, Richard W. *Protestant Pluralism and the New York Experience: A Study of Eighteenth-Century Religious Diversity*. Bloomington: Indiana University Press, 1988.

Richey, Russell E., ed. *Denominationalism*. Nashville: Abingdon, 1977.

_____. "Itinerancy in Early Methodism." In *Send Me? The Itinerancy in Crisis*, ed. Donald E. Messer. Nashville: Abingdon Press, 1991.

Ridgaway, Henry B. *The Life of Edmund S. Janes*. New York: Phillips and Hunt, 1882.

Rosenwaike, Ira. *Population History of New York City*. Syracuse, NY: Syracuse University Press, 1972.

Rudolph, LaVere C. *Francis Asbury*. Nashville: Abingdon Press, 1966.

Scherer, Lester B. *Ezekiel Cooper, 1763-1847: An Early American Methodist Leader.* Lake Junaluska, NC: Commission on Archives and History of the United Methodist Church, 1965.

Schmidt, Martin. *John Wesley: A Theological Biography.* 3 vols. Trans. Norman P. Goldhawk. Nashville: Abingdon Press, 1972.

Schneider, Louis. *Religion, Culture, and Society.* New York: Wiley, 1964.

Scott, Donald M. *From Office to Profession: The New England Ministry , 1750-1850.* Philadelphia: University of Pennsylvania Press, 1978.

Seaman, Samuel A. *Annals of New York Methodism.* New York: Hunt and Eaton, 1892.

Sherman, David. *History of the Revisions of the Discipline of the Methodist Episcopal Church.* New York: Nelson and Phillips, 1874.

A Short Historical Account of the Early Society of Methodists, Established in the City of New York in the Year 1763. New York: W. and P. C. Smith, 1824.

Silber, William B. *A History of St. James Methodist Episcopal Church.* New York: Phillips and Hunt, 1882.

Simon, John S. *John Wesley and the Religious Societies.* London: Epworth Press, 1921.

Smith, Timothy L. *Revivalism and Social Reform.* New York: Harper and Row, 1965.

Smith, W. C. *Annals of Deceased Preachers of the New York and New York East Conferences.* New York: Carlton and Lanahan, 1870.

Smith-Rosenberg, Carroll. *Religion and the Rise of the American City: the New York City Mission Movement, 1812-1870.* Ithaca, NY: Cornell University Press, 1971.

Snyder, Howard A. *The Radical Wesley and Patterns for Church Renewal.* Downers Grove, IL: InterVarsity Press, 1980.

Spann, Edward K. *The New Metropolis: New York City, 1840-1857.* New York: Columbia University Press, 1981.

Stevens, Abel. *History of the Methodist Episcopal Church in the United States of America.* 4 vols. New York: Carlton and Porter, 1867.

_____. *Life and Times of Nathan Bangs.* New York: Carlton and Porter, 1863.

Streeter, Lewis R. *Past and Present of the John Street Methodist Church, 1760-1913.* New York: privately printed, 1913.

Sykes, Norman. *Church and State in England in the XVIIIth Century.* Hamden, CT: Archon Books, 1962.

_____. *The English Religious Tradition.* London: SCM Press, 1953.

Thompson, David M., ed. *Nonconformity in the Nineteenth Century*. London: Routledge and K. Paul, 1972.

Thompson, Edward P. *The Making of the English Working Class*. Harmondsworth: Penguin, 1968.

Towlson, Clifford W. *Moravian and Methodist*. London: Epworth Press, 1957.

Troeltsch, Ernst. *The Social Teaching of the Christian Churches*. 2 Vols. New York: The Macmillan Company, 1931.

Tyerman, Luke. *The Life and Times of the Rev. Samuel Wesley, M. A., Rector of Epworth*. London: Simpkin, Marshall and Company, 1866.

Upham, Francis. *The Story of Old John Street Methodist Episcopal Church*. New York: privately printed, 1932.

Wakefield, Gordon S. *Puritan Devotion*. London: Epworth Press, 1957.

_____. *The Spiritual Life in the Methodist Tradition 1791-1945*. London: Epworth Press, 1966.

Wakeley, Joseph B. *Lost Chapters Recovered from the Early History of American Methodism*. New York: by the author, 1858.

Walls, William J. *The African Methodist Episcopal Zion Church*. Charlotte, NC: African Methodist Episcopal Zion Publishing House, 1974.

Walsh, John. "The Origins of the Evangelical Revival." In *Essays in Modern English Church History*, ed. Gareth V. Bennett, 132-62. New York: Oxford University Press, 1966.

Ward, William R. *Early Victorian Methodism: The Correspondence of Jabez Bunting 1830-1858*. Oxford: Oxford University Press, 1976.

_____. *Faith and Faction*. London: Epworth Press, 1993.

_____. *The Protestant Evangelical Awakening*. Cambridge: Cambridge University Press, 1992.

_____. *Religion and Society in England, 1790-1850*. London: Batsford, 1972.

Watson, David L. *The Early Methodist Class Meeting: Its Origins and Significance*. Nashville: Discipleship Resources, 1985.

_____. "Methodist Spirituality." In *Protestant Spiritual Traditions*, ed. Frank C. Senn, 217-73. New York: Paulist Press, 1986.

Watts, Michael R. *The Dissenters*. Oxford: Clarendon Press, 1978.

Weber, Max. *Max Weber on Charisma and Institution Building; Selected Papers*. Chicago: University of Chicago Press, 1968.

Whaling, Frank, ed. *John and Charles Wesley*. New York: Oxford University Press, 1964.

Wilentz, Sean. *Chants Democratic: New York City and the Rise of the American Working Class, 1788-1850.* New York: Oxford University Press, 1984.

Wilke, Richard. *And Are We Yet Alive.* Nashville: Abingdon Press, 1986.

Willett, William M. *A New Life of Summerfield.* Philadelphia: J. B. Lippincott and Company, 1857.

Wilson, Bryan R. "Analysis of Sect Development." In *Patterns of Sectarianism,* ed. Bryan R. Wilson, 24-25. London: Heinemann, 1967.

Wilson, George W. *Methodist Theology vs. Methodist Theologians.* Cincinnati: Jennings and Pye, 1904.

Wise, Daniel. *A Saintly and Successful Worker, or, Sixty years a Class-Leader.* New York: Phillips and Hunt, 1879.

Wood, Arthur Skevington. *The Burning Heart.* Grand Rapids, MI: W. B. Eerdmans Publishing Company, 1967.

_____. *The Inextinguishable Blaze: Spiritual Renewal and Advance in the Eighteenth Century.* Grand Rapids, MI: W. B. Eerdmans Publishing Company, 1960.

Woodward, Josiah. *An Account of the Rise and Progress of the Religious Societies in the City of London, etc.* London: J. Downing, 1724.

Wuthnow, Robert. *The Restructuring of American Religion: Society and Faith since World War II.* Princeton, NJ: Princeton University Press, 1988.

B. ARTICLES

Abbey, Richard. "Ecclesiastical Penalties in reference to Class Meetings." *Methodist Quarterly Review* 7 (1853): 417-28.

Bett, Henry. "A French Marquis and the Class Meeting." *Wesley Historical Proceedings* 18 (1932): 43-45.

Carwardine, Richard. "The Second Great Awakening in the Urban Centers: An Examination of Methodism and the 'New Measures.'" *Journal of American History* 59 (1972-73): 327-41.

"Class Meetings." *Methodist Quarterly Review* 12 (1858): 507-35.

Davies, James A. "Small Groups: Are They Really so New?" *Christian Education Journal* 5 (1984): 43-52.

Dean, William W. "The Decline of the Class Meeting." *World Methodist Historical Society (April 1983)*

_____. "The Evangelistic Function of the Class Meeting." *Conservative Evangelicals in Methodism Newsletter* 10 (1983): 32-37.

_____. "The Methodist Class Meeting: The Significance of Its Decline." *Proceedings of the Wesley Historical Society* 53 (1981): 41-48.

Droholm, Richard R. "Evangelizing Community and Social Transformation." *Foundations* 20 (1977): 352-61.

Lim, Isaac. "Wesley Preaching and the Small Group Ministry: Principles and Practices." *Asia Journal of Theology* 3 (1989): 509-23.

Lubach, James L. and Thomas L. Shanklin. "Arbitrations and Trials of Members in the Methodist Episcopal Church, 1776-1860." *Methodist History* 9 (1971): 30-49.

Outler, Albert C. "Pastoral Care in the Wesleyan Spirit." *Perkins Journal* 25 (1971): 4-11.

Pike, David. "The Religious Societies in the Church of England (1678-1723) and Their Influence on Early Methodism." *Proceedings of the Wesley Historical Society* 35 (1965): 15-20, 32-38.

Rack, Henry. "The Decline of the Class-Meeting and the Problems of Church Membership in Nineteenth-Century Wesleyanism." *Proceedings of the Wesley Historical Society* 39 (1973-74): 12-21.

Sasnett, William J. "Theory of Methodist Class Meetings." *Methodist Quarterly Review* 5 (1851): 265-84.

Schwenk, James L. "The Class Meeting in the United Evangelical Church, 1894-1922." *Evangelical Journal* 12 (1994): 21-28.

Stodgill, Ron. "God of Our Fathers." *Time* (1997)

Trueheart, Charles. "The Next Church." *Atlantic Monthly* (August 1996): 37-58.

Vincent, John H. "The Class Meeting in Methodism." *Methodist Review* 83 (1901): 681-93.

Wakefield, Gordon S. "The Function and History of Religious Societies." *London Quarterly and Holborn Review* 188 (1963): 104-10.

C. THESES AND DISSERTATIONS

Andrews, Dee. "Religion and the Revolution: The Rise of the Methodists in the Middle Atlantic, 1760-1800." Ph.D. diss., University of Pennsylvania, 1986.

Adkins, Gregory L. "Facilitating the Nurture of New Church Members." Ph.D. diss., Candler School of Theology at Emory University, 1987.

Cook, Charles W. "The Disciplined Small Group in the Local Church." Ph.D. diss., Perkins School of Theology, 1982.

Dean, William W. "Disciplined Fellowship: The Rise and Decline of Cell Groups in British Methodism." Ph.D. diss., University of Iowa, 1985.

Dickey, Richard J. "Group Spiritual Companioning: Toward a Contemporary Wesleyan Paradigm." Ph.D. diss., Andover Newton Theological School, 1992.

Green, Stuart C. "The Development of a Contemporary Model of Outreach and Nurture Based on the Wesley Class Meeting and for Use in a New Congregation." Ph.D. diss., Candler School of Theology at Emory University, 1988.

Hahm, Young Hwan. "The Training of Korean Class Leaders for Shared Ministry Contributing to Congregational Growth and Maturity." Ph.D. diss., Garrett-Evangelical Theological Seminary, 1994.

Heitzenrater, Richard P. "John Wesley and the Oxford Methodists, 1725-1735." Ph.D. diss., Duke University, 1972.

Henderson, David M. "John Wesley's Instructional Groups." Ph.D. diss., Indiana University, 1980.

Holsclaw, David F. "The Demise of Disciplined Christian Fellowship: The Methodist Class Meeting in Nineteenth-Century America." Ph.D. diss., University of California, 1979.

Horton, John E. "A Critical Analysis of John Wesley's Class Meeting." D.Min. thesis, San Francisco Theological Seminary, 1986.

Mackenzie, Peter D. "The Methodist Class Meeting: A Historical Study." Ph.D. diss., University of St. Andrews, Scotland, 1969.

McMurray, Scott A. "Allowing the Means of Grace to Restore Vitality in the Contemporary Church." Ph.D. diss., McCormick Theological Seminary, 1991.

Mohler, Hallock N. "The Methodist Class Meeting: Origin, Nature, Purpose and Relevance." Ph.D. diss., Colgate Rochester, 1982.

Perry, Roger D. "Responsible Evangelism through Disciple-Making." Ph.D. diss., Garrett-Evangelical Theological Seminary, 1993.

Pettit, Marilyn H. "Women, Sunday Schools, and Politics: Early National New York City, 1797-1827." Ph.D. diss., New York University, 1991.

Price, Fred W. "The Role of the Presiding Elder in the Growth of the Methodist Episcopal Church, 1784-1832." Ph.D. diss., Drew University, 1987.

Reed, Clara M. "A Model for Revival in the Local Church Derived from the Work of Finney and Wesley." Ph.D. diss., Perkins School of Theology, 1992.

Roberts, Rodney E. "The Value of the Early Methodist Class Meeting for the United Methodist Church Today: An Experiment." Ph.D. diss., Perkins School of Theology, 1982.

Robey, James A. "The Role of the Pastor in Spiritual Formation Using a Wesleyan Class Meeting Approach." Ph.D. diss., Candler School of Theology at Emory University, 1984.

Stauffer, Virgil L. "How 'Groups with Purpose' Stimulate Spiritual Formation in a Local Church." Ph.D. diss., Asbury Theological Seminary, 1988.

Thompson, John R. "A Methodist Model for Lay Ministry." Ph.D. diss., Pittsburgh Theological Seminary, 1984.

Tingle, Larry O. "The Wesley Class Meeting: Its History and Adaptability for the Twentieth-Century Church." Ph.D. diss., Wesley Theological Seminary, 1984.

Index

Adult Sunday School 101
Anglican religious societies
  17-20
Asbury, Francis 35, 36, 40,
  44, 74
Assimilation 101

Band meeting 11-13, 34-35
Bangs, Rev. Nathan 45, 74, 89
Board of Leaders, *see* leader's
  meeting

Camp meeting 48
Carvosso, William 16
Catechesis 101, 102
Catechumenate 94, 99
Church trials 30, 54, 59
Class books 58, 77, 92
Class collection 19
Class leader
  additional duties of 53, 75-
  77
  changing of 28
  course of study 66-67
  dialogue with members 80-
  82
  female 31, 33
  higher expectations of 20-21
  length of service as 29
  occupations of 29, 51-52
  relationship with members
  27-28, 50-51
  role of 19-23, 50-55
  rotation of 82-83
  tensions with hierarchy 21-
  23

visitation of members 19,
  83-86
Class manual 20, 59
Class meeting
  attendance at 57-60, 77-80
  criticism of 87-90
  decline of 77-87
  description of 15
  disciplinary function 30
  evangelistic function 15-17,
  26-27, 47-48
  gender separation in 30-32
  leadership development 28-
  30, 51-52
  length of 79-80
  origin of 14
  racial segregation of 32-33
  reintroduction of 105-6
  requirement of membership
  87-90
  sermons on 58-59
  size of 33, 55-57, 62, 79-80
  see also Anglican religious
  societies
class paper 17
Cooper, Reverend Ezekiel 57
Coles, Reverend George 58,
  73-74 *see also* class
  meeting: sermons on

Exhorters 28, 75

General Conference
  Committee on the Itinerancy
  72
  Committee on Safety 44-45,
  60

Biographical Sketch

Philip F. Hardt, son of Frederick and Mary Hardt, was born on March 21, 1951, in West Haven, Connecticut. He graduated from West Haven High School in 1969 and Southern Connecticut State college in 1974 with a Bachelor of Science degree in English-Secondary Education. After teaching in the upper elementary grades for several years, he entered Yale Divinity School in 1982. He received the Master of Divinity degree in 1986 and was ordained deacon and elder in the New York Annual Conference of the United Methodist Church in 1986 and 1988, respectively. From 1986-1988, he served as Assistant Pastor at Trinity United Methodist in Windsor, Connecticut. Then, from 1988 to 1990, he served as pastor of East Pearl Street United Methodist Church in New Haven, Connecticut while working on a master of Sacred Theology degree at Yale which he received in 1992.

He then entered Fordham University in 1990, and earned his doctoral degree in Historical Theology in 1998 under the mentorship of Fr. Mark Massa, S.J. At the same time, he also assisted at the Fordham United Methodist Church in the Bronx, New York, and, during the time of researching and writing the dissertation, he attended the John Street Church United Methodist in lower Manhattan. From July, 1994, to June, 1995, during a one year leave of absence, he pastored the Vail's Gate United Methodist Church in Vail's Gate, New York.. Since 1995 he has served as an adjunct professor at Mount Saint Mary College, New Brunswick Theological Seminary, Mercy College and Fordham College of Liberal Studies. He and his wife Vineeta live in Riverdale, New York.